PRAISE FOR RICHARD SHELTON

"Shelton has a generous sense of humor, a clear vision of the world, and, ultimately, wonderful stories to tell."
—*New York Times Book Review*

"Shelton writes with skill and candor about society's exiles and their hidden talents, which he was able to bring out in his workshops."
—*Library Journal*

"Humor, poignancy, humaneness, word magic."
—*Journal of the West*

"A poet of elegance and precision."
—*Harvard Review*

"Shelton's literary touch is sure, and he seemingly achieves his effects—nostalgic, witty, inspirational—with little effort."
—*Kirkus Reviews*

"He's a magician, hypnotizing his audience. A gift for observation, and golden sense of humor."
—*Booklist*

"Shelton knows the lore and life of southern Arizona, and his diction, both precise and evocative, reflects his poetic skills."
—*Publishers Weekly*

"Shelton's work is wonderfully and terrifyingly real."
—*Iowa Review*

D0474060

Nobody Rich or Famous

NOBODY RICH
OR FAMOUS

A Family Memoir

RICHARD SHELTON

THE UNIVERSITY OF
ARIZONA PRESS

TUCSON

The University of Arizona Press
www.uapress.arizona.edu

Printed in the United States of America
21   20   19   18   17   16   6   5   4   3   2   1

ISBN-13: 978-0-8165-3400-5 (cloth)
ISBN-13: 978-0-8165-3399-2 (paper)

Cover design by Leigh McDonald
Cover photo: *The Snake River in Mid Winter* by Jess Johnson

"August" and excerpt from "November" from *The Tattooed Desert*, by Richard Shelton, © 1971. Reprinted by permission of the University of Pittsburgh Press.

Library of Congress Cataloging-in-Publication Data
Names: Shelton, Richard, 1933– author.
Title: Nobody rich or famous : a family memoir / Richard Shelton.
Description: Tucson : The University of Arizona Press, 2016.
Identifiers: LCCN 2016007478 | ISBN 9780816534005 (cloth : alk. paper) | ISBN 9780816533992 (pbk. : alk. paper)
Subjects: LCSH: Shelton, Richard, 1933—Family. | Shelton, Richard, 1933—Anecdotes. | Shelton, Richard, 1933—Homes and haunts—Idaho—Boise River Valley. | Boise River Valley (Idaho)—Description and travel. | LCGFT: Biographies. | Autobiographies. | Anecdotes.
Classification: LCC PS3569.H39367 Z46 2016 | DDC 811/.54—dc23 LC record available at http://lccn.loc.gov/2016007478

♾ This paper meets the requirements of ANSI/NISO Z39.48-1992 (Permanence of Paper).

In memory of Lois

CONTENTS

Part IV. Charlotte's Journals

Part V. Hazel's Journals

Part VI. Beautiful

Nobody Rich or Famous

PROLOGUE

This is the story of a family and how it got that way. Looking back through a long span of time, I can see us as characters in a drama most of us did not understand the nature of. We often showed up on stage dressed in the wrong costumes and without having learned our lines. We stumbled and ad-libbed. We entered and exited at the wrong times, and some of us didn't seem to know what we were doing during our time on stage. I am the last living member of that cast, chasing the ghosts of our earlier performances and finding that even most of the third-rate houses we performed in have been torn down long ago.

We worked hard and our successes were few and temporary, but we never played tragedies. We were good for sentimental comedies, pathos, and melodrama. Above all, we bounced back. Even when the reviews were terrible, we kept the show going in our clumsy way because we had to make a living, although a minimal one.

Once, a few years before his death, I asked my older brother—my only brother—if he ever told his children the stories about things that happened when we were growing up. "No," he said, "I never tell anyone what it was like when we were growing up. They wouldn't believe me."

I didn't agree with him then, and I don't now. When compared with the childhoods of millions of other children born into poverty and its attendant sorrows, our childhoods were not so unusual, and we were better off than many are today. It wasn't high drama. Yet there are elements of our story that might illuminate the lives of many in our culture—those Americans who hover precariously between the middle and lower classes with no safety net beneath them, buffeted by the whims of politics, good times or bad times. Those who somehow absorb it all while fending off bill collectors and landlords, needing charity but too proud to accept it, acquainted with grief and bus drivers, and striving always toward that ultimately elusive goal of comfortable respectability.

Today, as the chasm between the *haves* and the *have-nots* widens each year in America and more families slip into poverty, I remember how it was with us. Again I feel the cold of a drafty old ramshackle rented house, the home of the working poor. How many consider themselves lucky to have that house today, and how many have lost even that?

I could not have written this account without the help of three women in my family, all of whom are now gone. They were my great-grandmother, Josephine Cummings Adams; my grandmother, Charlotte Adams Beech; and my mother, Hazel Josephine Shelton— mother, daughter, and granddaughter. All three of these women kept a journal or journals, and their cumulative record keeping covers many years. I have used these journals as a kind of script for the drama that they sometimes openly refer to but more often mask. When my mother died, all the journals came into my possession. They have proven to be invaluable, and I have tried to treat them with the respect they deserve.

PART I

HAZEL AND RED

SIX BOISE SCENES

July 1920

Two very pretty girls are hesitating at the edge of State Street in Boise, Idaho. The street has been recently paved, but it is soft in spots and muddy from a late afternoon rain. Traffic is heavy. In a few blocks State Street will become Highway 44, once part of the Oregon Trail that leads across the Boise Valley toward the border between Idaho and Oregon. Both girls are eighteen, and they have been best friends for four years, since they started high school together in Pendleton, Oregon. Neither of them quite finished high school.

One is a dark, sultry-looking Italian girl, with bobbed hair and magnificent, enormous black eyes. The other one is pert and pretty rather than beautiful, with a decidedly turned-up nose, hazel eyes, and a riot of chestnut curls only partly controlled by a fashionable green headband that covers much of her forehead. She has the best figure of the two, a figure so stunning it will cause her to be whistled at by rude men on the street for more than the next twenty years. Her waist is so small and her . . . well, never mind. She will someday be my mother.

The girls are currently working as waitresses in a large boarding house one block up State Street, and they live in the same boarding house. They came to Boise together a little more than a year ago and quickly obtained jobs as dancers in the chorus of a Boise theater that presented musical revues and vaudeville acts. They had no previous experience dancing on the stage, but the training went with the job, and although the pay was low, they decided to take it.

Neither of them had secretarial skills, and the alternative was clerking in a five-and-dime. Girls who clerked in five-and-dimes usually got "patted down" by the managers as they left the stores every night, just to make sure they weren't stealing any of the merchandise. Many of the managers—always men—got very enthusiastic when performing this part of their duties. So the two girls had decided to take their chances on the stage. They'd thought it would be exotic and exciting, although not entirely respectable, but it wasn't. It was neither exotic nor exciting, and it was much too respectable.

They rehearsed for long hours during the day and performed six nights a week. Their feet hurt all the time, and the shoes provided with their costumes seldom fit. All the girls in the chorus had to live in the same grim building, and they were closely chaperoned by an elderly battle-ax whom they spent much of their time making fun of behind her back. They were not allowed to have dates unless the date was willing to come to the parlor on Sunday afternoons and talk to the lady of his choice under the owl-eyes of the battle-ax. The girls called the building they lived in "the nunnery."

The costumes they danced in were very conservative, they thought, as compared to the glamorous and revealing costumes of chorus girls in Chicago and New York. In Boise they wore mostly loose bloomers that reached to the knees and tops that were anything but interesting. And their dance routines were boring and dumb. Mostly walking around in circles, carrying artificial flowers and wearing a frozen smile and baggy bloomers. Sometimes a turn and kick. Not much else. And the smile—always the smile.

So when their first year's contract was up, the two girls quit and took jobs in a boarding house as waitresses while they looked for something better. Now they are trying to get across State Street on their day off to go downtown to a picture show. They need a sizeable break in the traffic because their skirts are tight around the ankles and they can't go very fast. At last they see a break and decide they can make it, at least halfway across to where the tracks of the interurban trolley run down the center of the street. If a trolley should come while they are stranded on the tracks—well, it will just have to stop, that's all.

They start out, hanging on to one another, and make it to the trolley tracks without any problems. After some traffic goes by, they start out again. Suddenly a motorcycle with two young men on it bears down on them at great speed. They scream and hurry on to get out of its way, hoisting their skirts as far as they dare. The motorcycle maneuvers around them, barely missing them, makes a U-turn, jumps the trolley tracks, and comes back. The girls have now made it to the edge of the street, breathless and shaken. The motorcycle pulls up beside them, and over the noise of its idling motor, both young men begin to talk at once.

"Gosh Jehoshaphat, ladies, I'm sorry. I didn't mean to scare you like that," the driver says. "I couldn't see you until I got around that truck, and then it was almost too late."

He is larger than the young man riding behind him, blond and rawboned. He looks like a farm boy wearing a city cap, which is exactly what he is.

"You almost killed us!" the Italian-looking girl says, opening her huge black eyes wider in anger.

The passenger on the motorcycle thumps the driver on the head and says, "I'm sure glad he didn't hit you, ladies. He's blind, you know. Can't see a thing. Can't see a couple of beautiful gals when he's almost runnin' over 'em." He's talking to both girls, but he's looking at the one with the chestnut curls and incredible body.

"I wouldn't talk if I was you," the driver says. "Ask him why we're both on the same motorcycle—just ask him." The girls seem to be getting over their fright.

"Aw, shut up," says the passenger. He is well built and slender, with delicate small hands and feet. He has bright red hair lying in tight waves across his head and a cigarette he's rolled himself behind his ear. His eyes, laughing now, are the bluest eyes either of the girls has ever seen.

"He drove his motorcycle through a cow," the driver says. "Right through it! Talk about blind . . ."

The girls giggle in disbelief.

"No, really. Right through a cow."

"Did it . . . did it . . . kill the cow?" the dark-haired girl asks faintly.

"Did it kill the cow!" the driver says. "Why, it strung that cow about a half a mile down the road."

The girls look horrified.

"Well," the young redhead on the back of the motorcycle says defensively, "there's a lot of stuff inside a cow. Guts and stuff. Excuse me, ladies."

The girls are on the verge of laughing, but the one with chestnut curls says, "But didn't it hurt you?"

"Aw, naw," says the cow-killer, blushing bright red. "It just banged me up a little and broke my collarbone, but it sure was messy. I think the doctor broke my collarbone trying to get me cleaned up."

Encouraged by the girls' laughter, he plunges into one of the stories of which he will later prove to have an endless supply. "Did you hear about the time two guys were riding one motorcycle, like us, and it was real cold, so the driver put his coat on backwards to keep the wind out?"

The girls look dubious but shake their heads. All those chestnut curls shaking at once.

"Well," he continues, "they are going like hell—I mean like heck—down the road, and they run into a tree. Terrible mess. People come running from the farms around there to help them. Finally the ambulance gets there. The ambulance driver jumps out and says, 'Are they dead?' 'Well,' says one of the farmers, 'One of them was dead when we got here, and by the time we got the other one's head turned around, he was dead too.'"

The girls laugh. They are charmed by this young redhead with the funny stories.

"I'm Leonard," he says, "Leonard Shelton, but everybody calls me Red. You can call me anything you want, just so you call me. This here is Herbert the Sherbert. We call him Sherbert because his brains are like mush. But he's OK for a blind driver."

"I'm Angie," the dark-haired girl says, "and this is Josie, only that's her middle name. Her first name is Hazel. Lately she wants everybody to call her Hazel because Josie was her grandmother's name and she thinks it's old-fashioned. She's nuts."

Ten months later the handsome young storyteller and the girl with chestnut curls and an incredible figure will be married in a tiny house on the wrong side of the tracks in Boise. It is the rented home of one of the groom's older brothers, who already has a growing family. The bride's father, George Washington Ashlock, whom no one ever mentions in the presence of the bride's mother, will be absent, as he has been for nearly ten years. The bride's handsome mother, Charlotte Lunette (Adams) Ashlock, will be there, with her two youngest sons: William (called Wig), age fifteen, and Robert (called Bob), twelve.

The groom's mother, Martha (Pryor) Shelton, has been dead for seven months, but his father, Charles Elmer Shelton, will be at the wedding, thin and drooping like his moustache, which almost hides his weak chin. He is leaning on a handsome cane he made himself, a cane I now possess. He will move in with the newlyweds during their first year of housekeeping and spend the remaining time he has—two and a half years—living with one or the other of his sons and their families. His cantankerous ways will not endear him to his daughters-in-law, who will nevertheless wait on him, empty his chamber pot, and nurse his ailments until his death, although they will shed few tears on that occasion.

By the time of the wedding, the groom will have removed the cigarette from behind his ear and grown a thin moustache that will, years later, enhance his resemblance to the movie star Clark Gable. A redheaded version. The bride will soon bob her chestnut curls and wear frizzy bangs, very becoming with her turned-up nose. They will have youth and beauty in abundance, and not much else. Life will not be kind to them, and they will not live happily ever after, but their marriage will survive, at least legally and in the eyes of the community, until the groom's death. It will survive many years beyond that in the mind of the bride.

June 1933

Twelve years after their wedding, when life has thrown more at them than they ever thought they could handle, when they are much changed by time and circumstances and their world is in the middle of a depression, they will become my parents. It will be a dubious honor for all of us. It will not be a notably happy event for Red or for their two other children: Betty, who is eleven, and Jack, who is almost six. But Hazel, at least, will be cheered by the new baby—something that can be her very own since her two other children are so obviously partial to their charming but all-too-often absent father. She will make sure that such a thing doesn't happen this time. This child, she says to herself, will love her best. Even if it means he will love her only. She will see to it.

She is thinking about this as she and Red bring the new baby home in Red's old panel truck with the false wall and the hidden compartment behind the cab. Times are hard. Red is a bootlegger, and she can't think of how they could survive if he weren't, but she knows it is only a matter of time until prohibition will be repealed in Idaho. Beer is supposed to go on sale next month. That will hurt but not totally destroy Red's business. But soon, she knows, soon prohibition will be repealed. Then what? Not a particularly good year to be having babies, as Red has hinted repeatedly since she told him she was pregnant. But she is happy to have the new baby. Something of her very own. Betty has always been her daddy's girl, and Jack will be starting to school soon. Jack is . . . well . . . distant somehow and not very affectionate. "Self-contained," somebody said. Sometimes late at night, when everybody else is asleep, she cries about Jack, but she doesn't quite know why.

The house they are currently renting is a ramshackle cottage, once a farmhouse, on what everybody calls "the bench"—the first mesa up from the Boise River on the south side. The mesa has been, until recently, an area of farms and orchards. It is now becoming semi-urban as Boise continues to grow in spite of the Depression. What she likes about the place is the big corner lot it's on, with room for a yard and vegetable garden. The garden has done well this summer, in spite of the lack of rain. The irrigation ditch runs along the edge of the yard, and Red has irrigated often.

As they turn the corner, the first thing she sees is the garden with the tomatoes beginning to ripen and the corn coming into ear nicely. Then she sees Jack. He's hoeing weeds between the string beans and Swiss chard. The hoe is grotesquely too big for him, but he is strong for his size, and wiry. He handles it to good effect and is completely absorbed in what he's doing. There's something about the picture she will never forget: the child with a stern, small face and a lock of ash blond hair falling over his eyes, working like a man with a seriousness far beyond his years, as if he has never been a child and isn't one now, only a small, wizened adult. It breaks her heart, and suddenly she begins to cry uncontrollably, something she hasn't done since Jack was an infant and the doctor told her he probably would not live more than a week.

When they pull up in front of the house, she is sobbing, and her tears are falling on to the bundle in her arms. Red is confused and a little angry at her outburst.

"For Chrissake, honey, what in the hell's wrong? Are you sick? Aren't you glad to be home?"

"Yes," she sobs. "I'm glad to be home. It's just . . . it's just . . ." And she makes a vague gesture toward the garden as they hear the screen door slam and Betty runs out, screaming with excitement. Jack is running from the garden, also excited. As Red takes the baby from Hazel and hands it to Betty so she can get down out of the truck, Jack stands on tiptoe, trying to peer into the blanket-covered bundle, the hoe still in his small, strong hand. His hair is bleached by the sun and he needs a haircut. He's wearing overalls and no shirt. She reaches out and touches his hair. He ducks away, intent on seeing what's in the bundle Betty is holding. The bundle is asleep and not responding to Betty's rapturous goo-goos.

Hazel has stopped crying. She can't put into words what she is feeling, but she stares at Jack, remembering when they brought him home from the hospital as a newborn. It was summer, like this, and he was so tiny and she soon realized he was sick—very sick. She had invested everything she had and everything she was in him, in the struggle to keep him alive one more day and one more day, and she had won. But somehow, as the years went by, Jack has turned more and more toward Red, who roughhouses with him and takes him everywhere, even to his still up near Bogus Basin. Jack has become Red's shadow, and they shut her out.

She knows Red is teaching the child things he shouldn't learn. Jack can cuss like a trooper, and she has never seen a child who can take punishment the way Jack can, without tears or even words—just that stare of defiance. All you had to do was say a harsh word to Betty and she would cry, but you could whip Jack raw and it did no good. Red had seldom whipped him, but when he did there was no sound but the *whop* of the razor strap on Jack's bare butt and the sound of Red's heavy breathing. It was so unnerving that Red soon gave up whipping Jack and settled for cussing him out if he misbehaved. Sometimes, when Red was drunk, he would hit the child. When that happened, Jack would pick himself up, look daggers at his father, and say nothing. In fact, Jack seldom says very much. He is a strangely quiet child, and sometimes he seems to be older than his father.

She's lost him. She knows it now. Just as she is losing Red to the speakeasies and the women who increasingly hang out in them. Sometimes Jack allows his mother to fuss over him, but he does so in tight-lipped silence, and he escapes as quickly as possible, usually to his father. Red is teaching him to box. With Red on his knees with his fists in front of him, Jack can already throw formidable punches straight to the chin.

October 1936

Prohibition ended throughout the United States three years ago, but that had little effect on Red's business. Because of its small population, Idaho has never attracted the big-time mob figures who controlled bootlegging in other areas. Bootlegging in Idaho has been done by small, independent operators, each with his own customers, functioning, for the most part, peacefully side by side. Red's operation is typical. He and his partner maintain a still in the woods near Bogus Basin, in the mountains high above Boise. They produce, bottle, and distribute their whiskey themselves, almost never employing more than two men to run and guard the still and sometimes to help with distribution during the holidays or other peak seasons. These operations are so small and remote that the federal government has paid little attention to them.

As prohibition draws slowly and painfully to a close, the voters of the state of Idaho are divided between those who are in favor of the unregulated sale of booze and those—mostly women, temperance societies, and church groups, especially the powerful Mormon political machine—who want the sale curtailed and controlled. For more than two years, debate swirls around this, the most highly contested political issue in the state. Beer and wine go on sale in 1933, and the bars open, but the state government is still undecided about the contentious issue of "spirits."

Finally, in 1935, a compromise piece of legislation is put in place. Its purposes are twofold: to prevent the excesses and the social consequences of the previous "saloon" situation, and to generate revenue for the state. It establishes a system of state owned and operated liquor stores and a board to run this monopoly and determine the amount of tax the state can impose on hard liquor. The liquor tax, considered by many to be exorbitant, is sufficient to make it possible for the bootleggers—who charge no tax—to continue to operate at a profit by selling booze at a significantly lower price. The result of all this places the small-time bootleggers in Idaho, for the first time, in direct competition with a state revenue-generating monopoly, beginning in March 1935. Now, instead of a federal enforcement agency that generally paid little attention to them, the Idaho bootleggers have state agents to contend with, and the entire dynamic has changed.

—

It is autumn. I turned three years old in June. My mother has just put me down for my afternoon nap on the sun porch at the rear of our house on 22nd Street. The sunlight coming through the maples and elms in the backyard, and through the falling leaves, makes dappled patterns on the yellow wall. Lulled by the moving patterns, I am falling asleep. Suddenly I hear loud crashing noises. Several men in dark suits and hats have kicked in the back door, the door to the sun porch where I am supposed to be sleeping. My mother rushes to me, picks me up, and runs into the kitchen. The men are moving through the house, looking in cabinets, pulling out drawers, and dumping everything on the floor. My mother sits at the kitchen table with me in her lap. She is crying.

Now the men are in my parents' bedroom. They have swept all the cosmetics off my mother's vanity and dumped out the drawers. They are throwing clothes out of the closet and have slit the feather bed with a knife. Feathers are floating everywhere, and I can smell the perfume from the broken bottles. One of the men goes outside and comes back with an axe. *They are going to chop us! They are going to chop us!* I'm screaming. My mother tries to comfort me, but she is trembling and crying. The man begins to chop at one of the walls in my parents' bedroom. Behind the wall they find shelves with many bottles. They empty one of the bottles on to the bed and take the others away with them.

As soon as they are gone, my mother, still sobbing and shaking, takes me into the living room and sits down by the telephone with me in her lap. She dials many different numbers, and each time she says the same thing: "Is Red Shelton there? This is an emergency. It's Hazel. If he comes in, tell him not to come home. Tell him Hazel said for God's sake not to come home. They're waiting for him down the street."

JULY 1938

We are living in the drafty, old two-story house we've rented on 17th Street, with two big cherry trees and the garage out back where Red has his sign-painting equipment. In less than two months I will enter the first grade. I'm excited about it. I've been waiting to go to school for a long time, and I can already read better than Jack, who is twelve. I guess that isn't saying much. Jack can't read worth a damn, and our mother reads his schoolwork to him.

Although I don't understand it entirely, I realize we are having terrible problems about money. Red has become involved with loan sharks who are trying to take away our furniture. Our mother has told us that if we are home alone and someone knocks on the door, we should peek out the window and see who it is. If it's men we don't recognize, we should not open the door but run upstairs and hide in the closet.

Red spends several nights a week in the bars. We have supper without him. He comes home after one o'clock, very drunk. One night when the bars close, Red is so drunk and confused that he decides to bring his barfly girlfriend home to meet his family. I have never understood exactly why he did this, but I don't think he was trying to humiliate Hazel. I think he was so drunk that part of his mind had shut down and he wanted to show off his poor but beautiful family to his girlfriend.

Jack and I are sleeping in a tent in the backyard because it's so hot in the house and we like to "camp out." Red brings the woman out, and she crawls into the tent with us. She's very drunk. Jack and I are sleeping in our underwear. We get out of the tent as quick as we can and put our pants on. Red makes us go into the kitchen. When we get there, I can see the woman has chopped-off hair dyed henna-red and she is not good looking. She begins to paw us and make over us, saying how cute we are. Jack pulls away and won't let her touch him.

I try to pull away, but she gets hold of my arm. Her fingers are like claws and her fingernails are sharp and all broken off.

While she's holding on to me and I'm trying to get away, I look up and see my beautiful mother in her nightgown standing against the kitchen wall. Her face is as white as the wall. She just stands there as if she is frozen. Eventually Red takes the woman away, and we never see her again.

DECEMBER 1940

It's Christmas Eve and I'm excited. We always open our presents right after supper on Christmas Eve. I want a pair of roller skates more than anything in the world. There's a package under the tree that is about the right size and weight, but I've convinced myself that it isn't roller skates. It's a thing that I do in my head. I convince myself that I'm not going to get what I want and that way I'm not disappointed. This is the first Christmas Eve I can remember that Red has been home. Usually he doesn't come home on Christmas Eve until the bars close. Then he sits on the floor in front of the Christmas tree all by himself and opens his presents. But he's here tonight, and when he came home he brought a big box, a huge cardboard box that said FRAGILE on it. He said it was for Hazel. Betty tied a red ribbon around it, but it was too big to get under the tree, so we just put it in the corner.

After supper we take turns opening presents. Betty has torn little holes in the corners of the packages marked for her, so she already knows pretty much what she's getting. I go for the package that I don't think is roller skates first, and it's roller skates. Jack gets a BB gun. Finally it's time for Hazel to open the big box. Red has to help her. She's been drinking beer all afternoon, and she's a little unsteady. It's a set of dishes, a whole set. They're about the most beautiful dishes I've ever seen. Cream colored with apples and apple blossoms all over them. The plates aren't exactly round. They're kind of scalloped around the edges where the apples are. Hazel really likes them, I can tell. She takes each piece out, unwraps it, and sets it out on the table in the kitchen. After we've seen them all, including the big bowls and plates for serving, she puts each piece back in the box carefully.

Both Hazel and Red are pretty drunk, and I help her with the dishes because I'm afraid she'll break a plate or something, but she doesn't. Betty has been mad at Hazel for weeks because of Hazel's drinking. She started drinking beer just a few months ago, and it's already got the better of her. Red's drunk most of the time, and he can function pretty well, but she just sits down and cries. She's embarrassed Betty in front of Betty's friends.

Betty is going to a Christmas Eve party as soon as we finish opening our presents. Red tells her she has to be home by midnight or she'll be grounded again. It's funny how Red is with Betty. He doesn't seem to care where Jack or I go or when we come home, but he's very strict with Betty. All of her boyfriends hate him. Tonight, Betty doesn't argue with him. She just winks at me as she leaves, and it's her way of saying, "They're so drunk they won't know what time I come in, and I trust you not to tell them." I wink back.

Betty is gone and Jack is outside shooting his new BB gun in the dark when the fight starts. Hazel, suddenly realizing that she is very drunk, has gone into the kitchen to make coffee. She puts the coffee on and gets out an unopened can of Carnation evaporated milk, which she always drinks in her coffee. They begin to shout at one another. Red says he's leaving and turns to go. She grabs the can of evaporated milk and throws it. The heavy can bounces off his head and hits the floor. He falls to his knees, but gets up right away and turns to look at her in amazement. Then he hits her in the face with a strong right. She runs into the bathroom, leaving a trail of blood, and locks the door.

He goes to the big box of new dishes, now in the kitchen by the table. Jack has heard the commotion and comes in. Red opens the box, and Jack and I stand in the doorway and watch as he smashes each dish on the floor. When they are all smashed, he leaves to go back to the bar.

October 1951

Hazel has been sick and alone, living in the house on Holmes Street. At the end of the summer, I, her youngest child, left to attend my freshman year in college, two thousand miles away. Red has been away working on one of the dams in Hells Canyon on the Snake River. Hazel will be forty-nine next month. She is still a good-looking woman, but ill health in recent years has caused her to begin to show her age. Betty and Jack live in Boise, but they are occupied with their own growing families and trying to make a living. Hazel is pleased when her younger brother, Bob, comes to spend a few days with her. She has always been particularly fond of Bob, who was injured as a child in a logging accident and for months was not able to walk. She carried him on her back.

Bob is between marriages, a condition he has been in before and will be in again. And again. But brother Bob has an agenda on this visit. He has always resented the way Red carries on with other women behind Hazel's back—women who can't hold a candle to Hazel when it comes to good looks. He thinks that everybody in town knows Red has had one girlfriend after another. . . . Everybody but Hazel. He can't understand how Hazel can be so blind and trusting. He has forgotten, or perhaps he doesn't know, that Hazel's favorite song is "Frankie and Johnny."

So he tells her that Red isn't working on the dam in Hells Canyon, and hasn't been for more than two weeks. Red is shacked up with his latest girlfriend right there in Boise, and at night the two of them make the rounds of the downtown bars together. They usually start at the Wonderbar just off Main on 10th Street and drink their way down Main to the Nebraska Bar, always one of Red's favorites. He tells her it looks like Red is spending all the money he made while he was working on the dam, and he won't be able to pay the rent on the Holmes Street house. Then brother Bob returns to wherever he came from, having relieved his sister of her ignorance.

Hazel, who has been sick in bed for several days and is very pale and shaky, gets up and makes a pot of strong coffee. She hasn't had a drink in years, and she knows her system simply can't tolerate it, but she's tempted. There isn't any whiskey or beer in the house, and besides, she needs to keep her wits about her. Fortified with two cups of coffee, she takes a very hot bath, brushes her teeth, puts her hair up in pin curls, and plans her wardrobe. She needs a permanent, so she'd better wear a hat. Then she begins to work on her makeup. Her eyebrows have to be plucked. Just enough powder and rouge to hide the sallowness of her olive skin. A little eye makeup and lots of lipstick, the way he likes it. Very little cologne.

Smoking one cigarette after the other, in her petticoat and with her hair still up in pin curls, she goes to the closet in the little alcove off the kitchen. She has to get up on a chair to reach the shelf at the top, but she finds Red's Colt .45 where she knows it will be, unloaded as she knows it will be. The bullets are in a little box next to the gun. She has never loaded this gun, but she has watched him do it several times, and she is surprised at how easy it is. She puts the loaded gun in her fawn suede purse, which matches the fawn suede shoes and gloves she has not yet put on. The patterned silk dress, she thinks. It's the best thing she's got, and just right for this time of year. And the little black straw hat with a few tiny flowers and the veil. Red said it looked like a cow pie, but it doesn't matter. It's stylish, and she will need the veil, although it only comes down to just below her beautifully turned-up nose.

When her hair is done and her ensemble is complete except for the hat, she lights another cigarette and calls a taxi. She knows she will have time before it gets there to put on her hat, check her makeup, and make sure she has on enough eye shadow and rouge. Her hair looks OK. Her seams are straight. She's ready. When the taxi arrives, she is already halfway down the front walk. He doesn't have to honk. She is a lady from the tip of her little hat, the veil of which is now up on top with the tiny flowers, to the toes of her fawn suede sling-back pumps, and including her fawn suede purse with a kind of heft and weight to it that might be a little unusual but isn't really noticeable.

It's just past 8 p.m. She directs the taxi driver to the Wonderbar on South 10th just off Main, and he thinks it's strange that this lady, all dolled up, would be going to a dive like that, but it's none of his business and he's learned to mind his own. When they pull up at the curb, she pays him before she gets out, and then she says, "I'll only be inside for a minute. Would you please wait for me?"

He says yes he will, goes around and opens the door for her, and she gets out. She stops just before entering the bar's padded leather double doors and lowers the flimsy little veil on her hat. Then, almost as soon as she goes into the bar, the taxi driver hears what sounds like the Third World War, and he hauls ass out of there as fast as he can go.

Later, the bartender, obviously shaken up, tells the police officers that a lady, dressed to the nines, stepped into the bar, looked around, pulled a gun out of her handbag, and shot hell out of the place. Either she couldn't see very well or she didn't have any particular target in mind, although she shot the barstool out from under one customer. There were only three customers in the bar at that early hour, and nobody got a very good look at her because they were all diving for cover. When the gun was empty, she put it back in her purse and walked out the front door. He had checked on his customers first, to see if anyone was shot, and by the time he ran out to the street, she was gone. Nobody in the bar had ever seen her before.

The police believe him. Like most good lies, his story contains a mixture of truth and fiction. Actually, there are four customers in the bar when Hazel makes her appearance. Red and his girlfriend are sitting at the bar with their backs to the front door. The other two customers, Jimmy and Fred, both Red's good drinking buddies, are playing a game of pool off to the left of the front door. Jimmy, a small, quiet man, has worked as a painter with Red, off and on, for years. He's a friend of the family and very fond of Hazel. He has always felt sorry for her because of the way Red neglects her in favor of the sluts he picks up in bars.

As soon as Hazel empties the gun, she faints and falls on the floor—her beautiful dress, her cow-pie hat, her matched accessories, and the Colt .45 all in a heap on the dirty floor of the bar. Red, Jimmy, and the bartender all get to her at the same time. The bartender is also a friend of Red's, but he has never seen Hazel. Nobody is hurt, although Red's girlfriend, whose barstool took a hit not three inches from her butt, is almost in shock.

What to do? Quick! Quick! The sounds of gunfire must have been heard on the street. The cops are probably on the way now.

"My car's in the alley," Jimmy says. "Let me take her out of here. You guys can figure out what to tell the cops."

Hazel is beginning to regain consciousness. They hear a siren outside. There is no time for Red to argue.

"Can you take her to her mother's place?" Red asks. "Charlotte Beech. Down the valley past Star, about twenty miles. She's coming around. She'll be able to tell you which farm it is."

Red and Jimmy are carrying Hazel out the back door to Jimmy's car. The bartender gathers up her purse and hat and the gun, and puts everything in the car with her except the gun. "I'll keep this," he says to Red, "and you can get it later when you pay for the damages."

"I'll pay for everything," Red says. "Just get her out of here before the cops hit that door."

Jimmy drives Hazel down State Street, past the corner where thirty-one years earlier she met a handsome redhead on a motorcycle, and down the Boise Valley where her mother, now Charlotte Beech, will nurse her back to health after what Hazel will later refer to as her "nervous breakdown." Charlotte keeps her own counsel. Nobody knows what she thinks about Hazel's histrionics, but her husband, Sherman, who had been a highly decorated marksman in World War I, says very quietly, "It's a pity Hazel isn't a better shot."

⌒

When I return from my freshman year at college in the late spring, Red and Hazel are living together as if nothing had happened. As far as I could tell, that was Red's last extramarital fling. I don't believe he ever had another girlfriend, and while he drank heavily at home, he ceased spending his nights in bars.

I have always wondered about Hazel's intended target. Many times I had heard her sing "Frankie and Johnny" in a nasal voice with a slight hillbilly twang, probably in imitation of some singer she had admired as a girl. In the song Frankie goes to the barroom and shoots *right through that hardwood door,* and while the implication is that she shoots the unfaithful Johnny—*he was her man, but he was doing her wrong*—it is never stated. She might have shot his girlfriend, Nellie Bly. Added to all this was the fact that Hazel was almost blind in one eye and her veil was further impairing her vision, the bar was dimly lit, and she probably hadn't fired a gun in more than twenty years.

Did she seriously intend to kill Red or his girlfriend or both of them? Or did she intend to do exactly what she did—put the fear of the Lord into him. I will never know the answer to that question, but I have an opinion. I have never known a woman who loved a man more than Hazel loved Red. No sacrifice was too great for her to make, no humiliation would drive her away. Even after his death, she remained faithful to his memory for twenty years, until her own death. I don't believe she could have intended to kill him, but she certainly made him believe it, and that belief changed his behavior for the rest of his life.

PART II

Midwestern Interlude

The journal of Josephine Cummings Adams is written in pencil on a small, inexpensive notebook with the word MEMORANDA *embossed on the front cover. The notebook is six and a half inches tall and three and a half inches wide and opens from the top. There is a break in the entries about two-thirds of the way through and several blank pages where evidently a child has scribbled. On the first page it says Scranton, Osage, Kansas. The first entry is dated July 11, 1878, and the last is April 9, 1882. The entries run from the front to the back of the notebook until December 1880, when Josie began making entries from the back of the notebook to the front. The journal is in bad condition and very difficult to read because the writing in pencil is faded. Fortunately, at some earlier time, probably in the early 1960s, Josie's granddaughter and namesake, Hazel Josephine Shelton, made an accurate copy of the journal in ink in a small legal ledger. That copy is in excellent condition.*

JOSIE'S JOURNAL

Somewhere in Kansas, on July 11, 1878, in the eighteenth year of her life, which was not to be a long one, my great-grandmother Josie Adams, born Josephine Cummings, having been a married lady for seven whole months, began to keep a journal. It might have been because most of the women in her family kept journals and such record keeping was one of the standard duties expected of a good wife, or it might have been because she was bored. At any rate, Josie's oldest daughter and that daughter's daughter—my grandmother and mother—later kept journals of the same kind. They called them "diaries." I possess the journals of all three of these quite different women. Much of what I know about my mother's family in the late nineteenth century comes from Josie's journal.

During the period covered by her journal, Josie and her husband, James, are hard-times poor. At first they live with Josie's parents on a Kansas homestead while James does all manner of heavy work to try to get together enough money for him and Josie to obtain a homestead of their own. At times they are living temporarily in a rooming house or boardinghouse in a different community where James's work has taken him. While Josie sometimes names other towns and villages, she never feels compelled to name the community from which she is writing. She knew where she was, and if the reader doesn't, it simply indicates that Josie wasn't thinking in terms of any reader but herself, and certainly not of some confused great-grandson in Arizona in the early years of the twenty-first century. When the journal breaks off in April 1882, she and James are living in a sod shanty, which suggests they have finally acquired land of their own.

It is rural eastern Kansas in the late 1870s and early 1880s, but for Josie there is no yellow brick road and no wizard, and one of the most terse entries in her journal, all of which is noted for its terseness, is *The dog died.* If one thing could be singled out to characterize the family, it would be work: grueling labor and lots of it, with no vacations and no rest in sight. The record of the number of times Josie scrubs the floors during the four-year period covered by her journal is both astronomical and incomplete, since she does not mention such scrubbing if she has anything more important to record, like doing the washing or ironing.

Josie also works for other women in the community much of the time, scrubbing and doing whatever they require. At home, when she isn't cooking or cleaning, washing or ironing, shucking corn or canning, she makes all of the family's clothes, including her husband's overalls and her own bonnets. The journal entry for September 10, 1879, seems like high drama. *James and Ma went to Osage. Got me a dress.* But the drama is dispelled by the entry on the following day: *Sewed on my dress.* She cans everything from plums to pieplant (rhubarb). She spends weeks ripping up old rags she has collected from the women she works for and braiding them into rugs to be sold.

After they move on to their own place, James buys a few cows. Josie churns the milk into butter and announces: *I sold 13 pounds of butter. Got 30 cents a pound.* The entry stands out from the others as a veritable shout of triumph. Normally she didn't use the *I*. It was simply *Husked corn today* or *Did the wash.*

It is an understatement to say that Josie's journal is impersonal and avoids sentiment or the expression of emotion. In spite of the fact that she records the death of her first child, only twice in the entire journal does she use a word that directly describes an emotional state. Both of these come fairly early in the journal and in connection with the fact that she is left home alone for weeks at a time while her husband is working in distant places. Once, in 1878, when she has been married less than a year, she says, *Stayed home—was lonesome.* A few days later she says, *Stayed home, of course,* and there is something about the tone of those last two words that suggests a state of mind, but not directly. In 1880 she again violates the strictly impersonal tone of her journal but gives no explanation for the cause. *Stayed home. Was mad.* That's it. Otherwise, no one's feelings—including her own—are ever mentioned.

The two entries in January 1880 that record the death of her first-born, three-month-old Ina, although preceded by several references to the fact that the baby is sick, are more heartbreaking, I think, in their starkness than if she had given in to the expression of her grief on the page.

> *Fri. 23—Ina died ½ past 12 o'clock at night*
> *Sat. 24—Was buried in afternoon*

Based on the time of year, the duration of the baby's illness, and the fact that Josie was sick at the same time, I would guess that the baby died of influenza, although the time frame would also fit smallpox. If the baby did die of smallpox, Josie's recipe for a cure for smallpox, which occurs on an otherwise blank page in her journal, is a ghastly reminder of the state of medical knowledge in rural Kansas in the 1880s:

> *CURE FOR SMALL POX*
> *1 Oz Cream of Tartar*
> *Dissolved in 1 Pint Boiling Water*
> *To be Taken Often*
> *When Cold*

Josie also records the birth of her second child on September 1, 1881, but she does not give the child's name. It was Charlotte, my grandmother. Actually, Charlotta Lunetta. (There is a question in my mind now whether I would have survived or who I would have been without my grandmother Charlotte). Before Josie's early death, she would give birth to two more daughters and three sons.

Another striking example of Josie's refusal to set down her inner feelings in her journal comes in connection with a mine disaster at Carbondale, Kansas, where her husband was working as a coal miner. In May 1881 she records the following:

> *Sat. 7—Ten men killed in mine at Carbondale*
> *Sun. 8—Miners funeral today*

Mon. 9—Another funeral today of miner
Tues. 10—A picnic in the creek—raining
Wed. 11—I made a cake

Everything is given the same weight in the journal. As a literary form, it makes me think of a cross between some postmodernist poetry and a grocery list. It is the product of a writer with no literary ambitions or pretensions. It is record keeping—a record of life without the conventions of the balladeer or the journalist to dramatize it.

Such passages contrast oddly with the page, evidently used as scratch paper, on which Josie practiced her new signature: *Mrs. James Adams . . . Mrs. Josie Adams*, with quite a flourish on the *M* in *Mrs.* Suddenly she is Josie, an eighteen-year-old struggling with her identity, and she is very human. The mine disaster might, however, have been the cause of an entry about two weeks later. *James started to Rice Co. Kansas to work on the Railroad.* This would have been the young Atchison, Topeka and Santa Fe, building branch lines all over eastern and central Kansas and soon to extend its tracks at breakneck speed past Santa Fe in a race to California and the sea.

While Josie scrubs and irons at home and in the homes of others as hired help, her husband must have been one of the hardest-working males in a community of hard workers. James Adams is obviously struggling to acquire land and become independent of his in-laws. Josie's journal records how he hustles. He works as a teamster, hauling quarried stone, corn, or whatever needs hauling. He digs wells. He quarries stone. He chops corn and hires out to any farmer who needs his strong back. He works on the railroad. For a while he even tries his hand at selling some early and primitive version of a washing machine, but this is a short-lived experiment. Increasingly he works in the coal mines, often in nearby Carbondale, but sometimes in Illinois or as far away as Iowa. My grandmother told me that in middle age he became a highly skilled carpenter.

I remember all three of James Adams's sons—Alfred, Chester, and Arthur. Even in old age they were big, raw-boned men, tall and broad shouldered. Considering the way they were built and the kind of work their father did, I imagine he was built like the proverbial brick shithouse, although I doubt that he ever saw such a structure. The kind of outhouse he was most familiar with was probably a flimsy affair built of scrap lumber, leaning at a crazy angle and with an old quilt hanging over the doorway for privacy.

I have several photographs of him, all taken the same day, this man who was my great-grandfather. They were probably taken about the year I was born, which would make him seventy-nine years old. The occasion is a family get-together on somebody's lawn—I suspect it is at the farm of my great-uncle Alfred in New Plymouth, Idaho. James Adams is tall and straight, with a large white moustache and thick white hair. He is wearing dark trousers, a white shirt, and a tie. He seems relaxed, affable, almost boyish with his long arms, slender waist, and enormous shoulders. No wonder Josie was upset when a young version of this man left her at home alone.

It is of particular interest to me, although perhaps not to anyone else, that this farmhand, teamster, railroad builder, coal miner James Adams also wrote poetry. The flyleaf of Josie's journal contains two of his poems, or perhaps two sections of the same poem—it's impossible to tell. They are written in pencil in what I assume must be his hand and signed "J.A. Adams."

> *Remember me and think of one*
> *Who ever thinks of thee*
> > *When in the mines I have no time*
> *To set and chat all day*
> *The pusher comes but very slow*
> *And takes my coal away*
> *Then in my mind I think it's time*
> *To fill my coal again*
> *So when the pusher comes with alarm*
> *I will be able to fill my turn*

⌐

It is in the coal mines
That I earn my repast
But people say it is a dirty work
But I will tell you true
'Tis I that work all day
   With a lamp on my head
To dig a litel coal
To warm you up before you go to bed
At night
People say the coal miners
Are a despret crew
But they are generous to I and you

Well, I didn't say my great-grandfather wrote *good* poetry, especially in light of that last painfully twisted and misspelled couplet, although I've read worse, some of which was published at about the same period. At least James Adams didn't rely on mawkish sentimentality and florid diction to the degree that was fashionable among many poets of his day. Nor can it be said that he was a slave to meter or a rhyme scheme. In fact, he seems to have difficulty finding a rhyme scheme at all, although I feel that one was intended. But I am being picky, and as astonishing as it is that this man wrote poetry, poetry was not the artistic medium at which he excelled.

My grandmother Charlotte had a beautiful violin hanging on the wall in her bedroom, tied with a red ribbon. It was a rich, wine-dark amber, mottled to nearly black in places, and it seemed to glow from within. As a child, I begged her to play it, but she would always smile her bright, bright smile (doubly bright because it was a kind smile and because she had a gold tooth in front, which was dazzling) and say, "No. I can't play anymore. Look at these fingers, all stiff with arthritis. I haven't been able to practice for years."

Sometimes she would tell me about the past while she rolled out the dough for the noodles that were part of her famous chicken and noodle dinners, or while she worked on her tatting. "We did have some good times while my brothers and I were young and full of applesauce. I played fiddle and one of my brothers could play five different instruments. People used to write to us from miles and miles away to get us to come play for their dances and barn dances. It started when we lived in Kansas. Sometimes we would travel three counties away to play for a dance. Then when we came out here, we kept it up for a while. We played up and down the Snake River and over in Oregon, up to McCall every summer, and all around the Payette area. I always liked to go over on the Snake River. They had big outings on the river in the summer, and we would play. It was happy times for me and my brothers."

"But how did you learn to play the fiddle, Gramma? Ain't it real hard to play?"

"Oh, you bet it's hard all right, but I started young and stuck with it. Sometimes I thought my arm was going to fall off, I got so tired of practicing. My daddy taught me. His name was James, but everybody called him Jim. You should have heard him play the fiddle."

So the red ribbon on Charlotte's violin led straight back to James Adams, coal miner, farmer, railroad worker, teamster, carpenter, poet, fiddler. And I wonder, James Adams, about all the times you were away from home for long periods. Were you working in a mine or were you fiddling while Josie stayed home and kept her journal and quietly smoldered with loneliness?

What combination of genes and upbringing, of time and place and culture, creates a man like James Adams, with his poetry and his violin, and puts him in a coal mine or a stone quarry in frontier Kansas? What explanation can be given for a man like James Adams, desperately working his way *up* to a sod shanty on the American Great Plains, where he and others like him will work so hard and effectively that in another forty years they will have destroyed the land, and their children will have to leave or starve? I have no real answers to these questions, but there are clues, frail threads that can be traced and might offer a partial explanation. Might, that is, if I am willing to crawl far enough out on one limb of my family tree. But judging by my grandma Charlotte, it's a sturdy limb.

James Adams was artistically and intellectually gifted, but he lacked sufficient education, training, and time to develop his considerable gifts beyond a certain unsophisticated level. I can tell this from reading his poems and from the fact that he played the "fiddle" rather than the violin. It is not an uncommon story. But I want to know why. Where did his unusual gifts come from in the first place, and why weren't they more highly developed? I am dealing with ghosts. I can only surmise.

I have found a little mini-genealogy written in my mother's hand in one of her journals. It lists the parents of James Adams and Josie Cummings, and I assume that my mother obtained this information from her mother, the oldest living daughter of James and Josie Adams. Josie's parents were Clark and Jane Cummings, and after each name, it says *Kansas*. No maiden name is given for Jane Cummings. James's parents were Alfred and Polly Adams, and the record in my mother's hand is more informative about them. After each of their names, my mother has written *New York*, evidently where they came from before they went to Kansas. After Alfred's name the record says *Pen. Dutch*, and after Polly's name, in parentheses, it says *Barthite*, evidently her maiden name.

This is curious. The Pennsylvania Dutch were actually Germans who came to this country, mostly in the eighteenth century, to escape religious persecution. They brought with them a very high level of German culture. The German ancestors of Alfred Adams, father of James, the fiddle-playing, poetry-writing coal miner, had evidently settled somewhere in New York.

None of this is too unusual, but what I found out next was fascinating and would have been shocking to some members of my family. The name Barthite is Jewish. It refers, loosely, to a "descendent of the son of the learned rabbi David," and you can't get much more Jewish than that. Perhaps Polly Barthite was a German Jewess, since she married a German, but regardless of that, my great-great-grandmother on my mother's side of the family was a Jewess from New York. In a family as self-consciously Gentile as ours (my father was a member of the Ku Klux Klan), it is no wonder that I knew nothing about this until recently. When asked about their "nationality," my mother had always said she was Scotch-Irish and English, and my father said he was Irish. No mention of German. No mention of Jewish.

About twelve years ago I was visiting in Oregon with my mother's brother Wig and his wife, Marie, who had always been my favorite uncle and aunt. It was just a few months before Wig's death, and although he had already suffered a heart attack, he seemed to have recovered and to be in excellent spirits—pleased to have company, and more talkative than I remembered him in the past. He showed me, with considerable pleasure, a large tinted photograph in an ornate oval frame. He had obtained it from his mother, Charlotte, a few years before she died, and it was a photograph of his grandmother, Josie Cummings Adams, he'd said. She was an extremely beautiful woman with a long, elegant neck, high cheekbones, and magnificent eyes. I thought she resembled my sister Betty at about the same age, but Betty's eyes were softer, dreamier.

Then Wig told me, with a twinkle in his pale blue eyes, which always made me think of my grandmother Charlotte's eyes, that Josie had been Jewish and that she came from New York. He enjoyed dropping this little bombshell, and I enjoyed seeing him enjoy it. I was truly surprised, and I filed the information in my head for future reference. What I have been able to find out since, but unfortunately too late to tell Wig, is that he was both right and wrong. The woman in the photograph is undoubtedly Josie, although I don't see how any woman could work that hard and remain so beautiful, but Josie was neither Jewish nor was she from New York. Somehow Wig had confused what his mother told him and had applied to Josie the background of her mother-in-law, Polly Barthite Adams. He simply skipped a generation.

Because of his parents, James Adams had a culturally rich background. His father was a German, from a culture with a rich musical heritage, and his mother was Jewish, with all the religious, intellectual, and artistic layers that suggests. His parents had lived, and had probably been raised, not on the Kansas frontier, but in New York. James was born to this interesting couple in 1854, although I don't know where he was born. But I know something else that happened in 1854. That was the year Kansas began to "bleed"—the year it became a pawn in the struggle between the North and South, a struggle that was rushing the country toward a brutal and prolonged civil war.

It was the year the United States Congress passed the Kansas–Nebraska Act affirming that the people of the Territory of Kansas would determine by a future vote whether Kansas would be a free state or a slave state. The race was on. Abolitionists organized frantically to get as many northern antislavery immigrants to take up homesteads in Kansas as possible, while those in favor of slavery did the same thing in the South. Such agencies as the New England Emigrant Aid Society threw hundreds of agents into the field, agents who promised all kinds of aid and encouragement to potential emigrants from New England and other northern states. Although many of these agents were experts at chicanery, they did help thousands of settlers file on land available for homesteading. They also showed the newcomers slippery ways to get around certain provisions of the homestead laws.

James Adams's parents were probably among those settlers from the North who were rushed into the Kansas Territory by abolitionist forces to ensure that Kansas would be a free state. Those forces were successful, but the settlers paid a heavy price. James Adams could have been less than a year old when his parents left their home in New York and homesteaded in bleeding Kansas, then the rawest of frontiers. They would have left behind much of what they knew of physical comfort and culture, but they brought themselves, and they were the products of their high cultures and could pass on elements of those cultures to their children.

James was six years old when the Civil War began, and about ten when it ended. Those were bad years in Kansas. He probably received less than an eighth-grade education, possibly much less, since boys were often kept out of school to work in the fields. His poetry would indicate such a level of formal education, and in those days in Kansas an eighth-grade education for a boy was well above normal. Somebody, however, exposed him to a level of literary and musical culture that was above average for that time and place. Surely it was his German father and Jewish mother.

Because he lived on the frontier and was poor, James had to work in the coal mines; but because he had the parents he did, he could write poetry and play the violin, and he could produce a clutch of musical children, one of whom played five instruments. And at least one of his daughters, my grandmother Charlotte, went to normal school and was, for a few years, a teacher.

James's wife, Josie, was born on December 28, 1859. She died young, in her late thirties. In addition to her journal, I have one letter she wrote to her daughter Charlotte, dated July 3, 1891. According to the letter, Josie and James and all of their children except Charlotte are living on a farm somewhere near Stronghurst, Illinois. Charlotte, now eleven, is living in Hamilton, Kansas. Hamilton is the community in which Charlotte's younger sister Julia would live and raise a family many years later, and it is near Virgil, a tiny hamlet where Charlotte would later teach school and where she would meet the man who was going to be her first husband.

I do not know for sure why Charlotte, at the age of eleven, is living apart from her family, nor with whom she is living. My mother told me that Charlotte's parents were so poor they had to farm Charlotte out with relatives. This hardly makes sense to me because at this age Charlotte would have been able to be of considerable help to her mother with the five younger children. I remember that although Grandma Charlotte seldom spoke of her childhood, she once told me she had, as a child, spent much time living away from her family, and she was terribly homesick.

There is another explanation, more difficult to accept in the light of today's standards concerning children, but probably true. I don't think they farmed her out; I think they *hired* her out. Even at the age of eleven, Charlotte was probably very capable, as she was in later life. As an adult, there was very little she couldn't do. When she was in her fifties and her husband had a period of illness, she milked thirty cows by hand twice a day, and in her spare time she and her husband's niece fenced a ten-acre field. She dug the post holes and strung the wire.

She was the kind of woman who could cook for a threshing crew of twenty, can peaches, and take care of a sick grandchild all at the same time and without any apparent strain.

When her first marriage ended, she became a laundress in a brickyard in order to support herself and her four children, and eventually she became a cook on large ranches in Idaho and Oregon. Something in her early background prepared her for all this. Perhaps it was just watching her mother, Josie, work so hard all the time, work herself to death, probably; but I believe it was partly because she was hired out as a live-in servant at the age of eleven, a kind of "Little Orphan Annie" as described by James Whitcomb Riley. Such arrangements for children were not uncommon in rural America in the early 1890s.

The letter Josie writes to her daughter in 1891 is warm and loving, and she encloses a red flower. *There is a vine here that has a flower on that looks like trumpet vine and think meby it is I will try to send one in this letter. . . .* The letter is stained with an outline of the blossom. The letter also acknowledges the money Charlotte has sent to the other children, confirming my idea that she is working for wages. A few other lines are telling: *I haven't seen uncle ded's since we moved from Stronghurst. Mr Armstrong bought our place there by Bennington's. . . . Jim's time isn't out till Dec . . . papa is done plowing corn . . . it seems a long time since I saw you . . . when I come out I will fetch you some large music books.*

My interpretation of this would be that they had a farm near Stronghurst but couldn't make it and sold it to Mr. Armstrong. Since then, James has been contracted to another farmer doing farm labor, and his contract ends in December. Also, although it is not clear what Josie means by "music books," it might suggest that Charlotte reads music—unusual for someone who plays the "fiddle." There is a note of forced cheerfulness in the letter attempting to mask Josie's pain and unhappiness that Charlotte is separated from them. It's a close-knit, loving, but desperately poor family.

When she writes the letter, it has been exactly thirteen years since Josie made the first entry in her journal and practiced her new signature as *Mrs. James Adams.* Although she doesn't know it, she is nearing the end of her life, and her children will be cared for by their aunt.

After a land boom in Kansas in the 1870s—a boom spurred on by the rapidly developing railroad system spreading through the rural areas—the year 1887 was so dry the crops withered. Severe economic depression followed. During the next four years, half the settlers who had rushed into bleeding Kansas trailed back eastward, some with signs on their wagons: IN GOD WE TRUSTED, IN KANSAS WE BUSTED. James Adams and his family had evidently retreated as far as western Illinois, where rain was more dependable, but they hadn't turned tail and run entirely. Eventually they returned to Kansas, where James took up the carpenter's trade and was successful at it.

I have almost no information about them until Charlotte is married and beginning a family of her own. I have a photograph of her sister Julia's home in Hamilton, Kansas. I have the memory of a violin hanging on the wall, tied with a red ribbon. I have Josie's journal and one letter stained with a red flower.

Otherwise they are ghosts on the great open landscape of the American prairie, which they and their parents and their children and thousands like them transformed into a dust bowl in an attempt to survive. My grandmother and all of her brothers moved west and settled near the Snake River where it forms the boundary between Idaho and Oregon. Desert country, but "reclaimed" by irrigation. They had been raised on dry farming. They knew about depending on rain, and they had learned that rain does not "follow the plow," as the early Kansas boomers had promised. It was not the desert of the Snake River Plain that attracted them; it was the miracle of irrigation in a dry land.

SEARCHING FOR JOSIE

The poet Thomas Gray was right. The annals of the poor are short and simple. Not the lives of the poor. Their lives are often long, complex, and have far-reaching consequences. But what is recorded about them or what they record about themselves is often short and simple. Josie's journal is a good example. She usually records the major task of the day, often describes the weather in a word or a phrase, and almost never says anything about what she is thinking or feeling. The journals, or as their writers called them, "diaries," of her daughter and granddaughter, my grandmother and mother, are very much the same. My grandmother Charlotte excelled in the genre. Here, chosen at random, is a section from her journal of September 1950, when she was close to seventy years old.

> Mon. 25   *Quite nice. I washed. Everything got dry.*
> *Stormed in evening.*
> Tues 26   *Cloudy, windy. I made jelly and churned.*
> Wed 27   *Nice. Real cool. I ironed. frost Sherman*
> *mowed.*
> Thur 28   *Clear. Killing frost. Sherman finished mow-*
> *ing hay. I made jelly and cleaned house.*

The impulse behind each of these journals is the impulse of a woman to leave a record, to create some written history. She records her activities and those of her husband and children regardless of how repetitive those activities are, and she knows that if she doesn't do it, nobody else will, and the record of their lives as they lived them day by day will be lost. Since most of the women who maintained these journals lived or once lived on a farm, the weather is an important part of what they set down. These journals are the annals of the poor, and the fact that Charlotte continued to record her daily life in her journal long after she ceased to be poor suggests the strength of this impulse to record something each day. *Everybody's life matters to the person living it,* the journals say. *We all count, we all count for something. We don't make the big decisions and run the world, but we keep it going. We do our assigned tasks. We accomplish something every day. This is the record of some of the things we accomplished, whether anyone reads it or not. This is the record.*

My first real interest in Josie, my maternal great-grandmother, was sparked when I read her journal. Later, when I saw her photograph, I realized I had to find some trace of her, something tangible—a tombstone or a house she lived in, a window she looked out of, a road she walked along. I had to see her landscape to help me figure out who she was. I was fascinated by the almost defiant set of her small, compact head, the look in her eyes above her stiff Victorian dress, the line of her unsmiling mouth.

In early April 1996, when the impulse became stronger than I could withstand, I threw some clothes into the car, along with a cardboard box of loose documents I referred to as "research materials," although I had no idea how to go about doing real research on family history, kissed my wife good-bye, tried to ignore the accusatory looks of my dogs, and set off in search of the ghost of Josie.

⁓

I have followed the Santa Fe Trail from Santa Fe, at least as close as you can follow it by automobile. Now I have been driving across Kansas for nearly a week in search of Josie. Just about anything would satisfy me at this point: a mention in a census, a name on a church register, some reference to her family. But I have found no trace of her. All I have to go on are the place names in her journal. The names of eastern Kansas towns like Scranton, Osage City, Carbondale—for the most part little communities with more past than present and probably not much future at all. There is nothing left of her here that I can find, granted my techniques as a researcher are so primitive as to be laughable. I must be looking for her in the wrong county . . . or the wrong country. Maybe the only "annals" of her left are the journal I possess and the photograph of her that so attracts me.

I spent a miserable afternoon in a country cemetery near Scranton in the cold rain and sleet, soaked and shaking with cold, checking every gravestone because all the cemetery records had burned in a fire in 1989. I went to county courthouses, local libraries, and historical societies. No trace of Josephine Cummings Adams, my beautiful great-grandmother.

Only the landscape has kept me going. Before I started on this trip in search of the ghost of Josie in Kansas, I called Deidre Elliott, a good friend in Tucson who was born and raised in Kansas.

"Deidre, can you tell me where the scenic roads in Kansas are located?"

There was a long pause. Deidre is noted for being kind and inoffensive.

"Dick," she said finally, "I don't think you quite understand. In Kansas, when a road curves, it's considered scenic."

Flat country and great open spaces excite me, make me high. Maybe it's some genetic link to those of my ancestors who were born and lived in Kansas. I wander through a landscape in which I have never lived as excited as if I were going home after years of exile. The grain elevators stand like white castles in the distance, obscured by dust and whirlwinds, but mysteriously beautiful. The little towns that were once kept alive by the railroads are now nearly deserted. Their remaining inhabitants are mostly old and becoming increasingly vague, fading like the signs on the brick storefronts where hardware stores and mercantiles and movies have been closed for decades.

On Saturday morning the Liars' Club meets at the table reserved for them in the back of the café on Main Street in Scranton. Only one or two of them are still farming. The others were bought out by some corporation or conglomerate, and they retired years ago. But they still wear overalls and sweat-stained caps with names like *John Deere* or *Allis-Chalmers* above the brims, and they still get up very early every morning, as if they had a full day's work to do.

It's cold and rainy in Scranton as I wander down the street at 10 a.m. and try to figure out my next move. The bar across the street— the only bar in town—seems to be booming. On the street it's colder than the proverbial well digger's ass, there's no one about, and the bar seems as good a place as any to get directions. At least it will be warm. I go in and ask the bartender how to get to the graveyard. Suddenly I become the center of attention. Everyone wants to help, but there is some disagreement about exactly where the graveyard is, and even more about how to get there. Evidently this graveyard hasn't been used in recent years, and some of the patrons in the bar know its whereabouts only by hearsay. Some of the younger ones have never seen it, and most of the older ones are already too drunk to give me clear directions. But I get plenty of directions anyway, mostly contradictory.

"Now, Jess, that ain't the best way to get out there. That road's washed out, and if he gets to the bridge, he'll play hell making the turn. It's all deep mud."

"Frank, you old fart, you don't know your ass from your elbow. If he just goes straight over the bridge and turns left on the Osage Road and then follows the railroad tracks south, because that road ain't got no name, he'll see it right there on the side of the hill, as sure as shootin.'"

"Don't you listen to none of 'em. I lived here more'n fifty years. Let me tell you how to git to the graveyard the fastest and easiest way."

So it goes. With my head buzzing with various directions, I slip out of the bar as quickly as I can before a real fight gets started. Eventually I find the graveyard, after wandering down muddy roads for about an hour and nearly getting stuck several times. I am finding out that eastern Kansas isn't always flat, and although the hills are not high, they are high enough to obscure your view just when you need it.

The storm moves on, and the next day it is glorious spring in Kansas. I have to admit I'm enjoying myself in spite of my failure to find anything. Maybe it's just being on the road, but I don't think so. I think it's the landscape. I'm rolling through Kansas on the back roads with the radio blaring brokenhearted country and western songs and the car windows down, drinking in great breaths of air filled with the smell of tilled earth, last year's hay, and cow manure, and probably tons of pesticides. But in spite of everything, it smells good to me.

In terms of my "research"—whatever that is—I've come to the end of my rope in this part of Kansas, and there's no way to justify my staying around here any longer, although I'd like to. But the alternative is very unpalatable: to return home to Tucson after the expenditure of all this time and money and admit that I have found nothing. No Josie. No nothing. Can I admit that kind of defeat? Can the grandson of the indomitable Charlotte Adams Beech slink home with his tail between his legs and admit to complete failure? Of course not!

As I drive through Kansas, a plan is forming in my head. My father's family, the Sheltons, and his mother's family, the Pryors, were from western Illinois. I had asked my father about them many times, and he always refused to talk about them. Finally, in 1969, while my father was dying of cancer and I was taking care of him, I asked him again to tell me about his people. His answer was, "They were all a bunch of horse thieves and the less you know about them, the better off you'll be." That was that. And while I figured it was an exaggeration, the statement was made on his deathbed and I am just superstitious enough to believe the old wives' tale about "deathbed confessions." I assumed that his forebears must have been, at the very least, an unsavory lot.

Now, as I am rampaging through Kansas full of frustration but also a kind of crazy joy, I look at the map and notice the astonishing fact that Kansas and Illinois have nothing between them except Missouri, not counting the Mississippi River. From here, all I would need to do is cross a little of Kansas and all of Missouri and I would be in Illinois. Missouri can't be more than three hundred miles across. So why not? Surely in Illinois I will be able to find some trace of my father's ancestors, and I won't have to go home empty-handed. Of course I will have to go both ways—that's six hundred miles—and about a hundred miles north to the town my father said he was born in—Quincy, Illinois. That's eight hundred extra miles at least. *Oh, what the hell. I've come this far; I'm not turning back now.*

"Here's to you, Charlotte," I say, toasting her with my plastic bottle of warm water, and I head my little Toyota due east toward the Missouri line.

Searching for Martha

Hannibal, Missouri, seems to have become one large tourist trap. Tom Sawyer and Huck Finn have been ossified in a museum with guided tours. I stop briefly and the one thing that sticks in my mind is a sign that says skinner's barber shop. It seems to be contemporary, rather than something out of Mark Twain.

I cross the Mississippi and head north for Quincy, Illinois. Quincy makes me realize I'm not in Kansas anymore, but I'm not sure where I am—the South maybe? Another world? It's bigger than I expected and a great deal more elegant. Forsythias and jonquils are already in bloom. I drive down street after street of magnificent old mansions built between 1870 and 1900, a wild riot of architectural styles with only one common element—ostentation, and lots of it.

All the bad weather of a few days ago has passed to the east, or perhaps it simply did not dare to disturb Quincy's air of elegant gentility, where the perfect lawns around the mansions are obviously intended for afternoon games of croquet played by ladies in long white dresses with their hats secured under their chins with acres of white tulle, and gentlemen in ice-cream suits and Panama hats. It's warm and humid. The grass smells like old money.

Quincy is the county seat of Adams County. That's ironic, since the family I was looking for but couldn't find in Kansas—part of my mother's family—was named Adams. My father told everybody he was born in Quincy. It doesn't much look like horse-thief country, but I decide to start in the archives at the county courthouse. Soon I find that if my father was born in Quincy, or even in Adams County, there is no record of it in the Adams County Courthouse.

I go outside and lie down on the grass to think about things. Actually, the fine print I've been reading has given me a headache, and I need a nap. But I can't help thinking about the problem at hand, and I can't fall asleep. There is something seriously wrong with my methods or my information or my location, and I can't quite put my finger on it.

My father, Leonard Pryor Shelton, always known as "Red," obtained his birth certificate about sixty years after the fact, when he realized he would have to have one in order to get any Social Security benefits upon retirement. It took him several years of red tape to get a birth certificate, and the whole episode became a family joke. No official, it seemed, could prove or even vouch for the fact that he had been born. No one except him, of course, and he didn't seem to be sufficiently official. Since he was born at home with no doctor in attendance and no official presence at all, he simply didn't exist on paper. At that time he still had living brothers and sisters, all older than he was, and fortunately some of them were able to attest to the fact that a new baby had arrived in 1901, the last of eight children born to Charles Elmer Shelton and Martha Shelton, née Pryor, and had been named Leonard Pryor Shelton.

So Red finally got his birth certificate, and I have a copy of it somewhere. I go to the car and begin to dig through the box of maps, brochures, notebooks, mileage logs, gas receipts, dirty laundry, hiking boots, and family records in the backseat. There it is, and Red lied. I might have known. He was a master at covering and hiding his tracks. He wasn't born in Quincy; he was born in El Dara, in Pike County, the next county to the south. Why would he lie about such a thing? Was there some sinister reason? Horse thieves? Lord only knows what.

From the information I obtained in the courthouse, I should check at the historical society before I leave town. At any rate, the building it is housed in is supposed to be well worth seeing. And it turns out to be. The John Wood Mansion is very white, very Greek Revival, and very impressive, with four two-story pillars across the front and a look that says dignity, pride, and gracious living. It was completed in 1838 and housed Quincy's founder and an early Illinois governor. I would have expected to find it in Georgia. Tucked away in the upstairs back is the Historical Society of Quincy and Adams County with its library, dripping gentility. My heart sinks again. I don't think it's likely that any of the ancestors in my family will be found here. No poor farmers or horse thieves. This must be where they keep the records of the generals who fought in the Civil War and their descendants who played croquet on the lawn.

The two middle-aged women working in the library are very quiet and polite. I feel like a bull in a china closet. They direct me to *A Portrait and Biographical Album of Pike and Calhoun Counties, Illinois*, published in 1891, in which prominent male citizens are dealt with at length, and the listings are blessedly alphabetical. It's a huge, formidable volume, and I plunge in expecting nothing.

Nothing under *Shelton*. Not a single prominent citizen. Well, that figures. So I try *Pryor*. Immediately BINGO! There it is. I find something so exciting I can barely sit still in this genteel library and read the long passage to the end.

It is an extensive entry on the history of the Pryor family, focusing on William H. Pryor, my grandmother Martha's father. I am in shock. *Well, I'll be damned! I never thought I'd find anything like this on Red's side of the family.* The more I read, the more I go into shock. Then there is the large reproduction of a painting of the elegant farmhouse and its outbuildings in a kind of neoclassical style. Even the cattle and horses are immaculate. Although I know the painting is highly stylized and idealized, the property must have been pretty damned impressive, and it was evidently one of the most important pieces of property that made up a community called El Dara. It might as well have been El Dorado or Atlantis for all my father said about it, and according to his birth certificate, he was born there.

The long account of the Pryor family says that William H. Pryor's father, Isaac Pryor, who would have been my great-great-grandfather, was English and came to Illinois from Tennessee with his wife, Sarah, (Harris) and six children in 1838. He first built a log cabin, and by the time of his death, he owned 320 acres of rich land, including the Pryor spread in the picture. He was township treasurer for seventeen years and also constable. He was a Democrat, a Mason, and a Methodist. He was, in short, one helluva highly respectable dude, and rich. Reading all this, I sit a little straighter in my chair and no longer feel so out of place in this genteel mansion, but I stifle the impulse to show what I have found to everybody in the library.

Isaac's son William H. Pryor carried on the family tradition and is described as "well-to-do," "an enterprising and progressive farmer, and intelligent and reliable citizen," and "a man of excellent private character." His farm, however, had shrunk to 160 acres "of fertile and highly developed land."

In 1855 William H. married Susan E. Moyer from Indiana (hello, Great-Grandmother Moyer, I've never heard of you before), and they had seven children before she died at the age of forty-six. (Good-bye, Great-Grandmother Moyer. You didn't last too long, but you left a great deal to be remembered by.) Less than a year after Susan's death, William married Dorothea Robinson (he could have waited a little longer, dear Great-Grandmother Moyer, but then he had all those children to take care of), who died within three years, and old William again married less than a year later—this time a Miss Lyda Reeve. Like his father, William was a Mason and a Methodist, and he was obviously not a man to waste any time or cry over spilled milk. The third of his seven children by his first wife is listed as Mrs. Martha Shelton, my father's mother.

I turn to see if there are any entries on the Moyers and find two prominent families who lived in El Dara, the families of Solomon and William H., whose ages would suggest that Susan was their sister. Their parents were "Moses and Martha Moyer, of German ancestry." German? This is getting interestinger and interestinger. Once, when he was drunk, Red told me his mother was Dutch, but now it falls into place. Red used the term *Dutch* to mean Pennsylvania Dutch, which means German. (Surely he knew the difference.) And he once talked about living somewhere near a huge farm owned by Germans who raised mostly cabbage. Could that have been part of the Moyer family, relatives of his mother?

There are two foods I associate with my childhood and adolescence, and I loved both of them. They were sauerkraut and pickled pigs' feet—not exactly the delicacies my friends chose as an after-school snack, but I did. Somehow, it never occurred to me to question why I, with my solidly English, Irish, and Scotch-Irish background, should be eating sauerkraut and pickled pigs' feet. I didn't know the origins of such foods, only that each year, without fail, my father, Red, would put down pigs' feet in brine in a big crock, and he would shred cabbage and put it in another large crock to turn into sauerkraut. I remember his cabbage shredder, a long, narrow trough with a blade in it, down which a head of cabbage was forced again and again until it was all shredded. I often asked him to let me shred the cabbage, but he wouldn't, claiming that I would cut off my fingers. Now I realize that shredding the cabbage was simply one element of his childhood and culture that he could neither pass on to his children nor bear to give up.

Red was generally considered a redheaded Irishman, and this was the image he preferred to project. I have just found out that he was half German, raised in a community of Germans. But why would he go to such lengths to hide the fact that he was German? And why did my mother never mention that her grandfather, James Adams, was German? Why was all this shrouded behind the term *Pennsylvania Dutch* when it appeared in records and family Bibles? And why did Red always say he was Irish, leading his children to grow up believing they were Irish?

It's easy to ask the questions—and they are real questions—but the answers are all hypothetical. Surmises based on a treacherous history and a few remembered details. Unless they left written records, we are at the mercy of the dead. They won't tell us much of anything for sure.

I think about 1917, World War I, and the height of the anti-German hysteria in this country, when mobs roamed through areas heavily populated by Germans, killing and looting. Red would have been sixteen that year, and the effect of such a pogrom on a sixteen-year-old could have been devastating. Enough to make him hide his German ancestry for the rest of his life.

Sitting at a table in the very proper library of the historical society in the John Wood Mansion, I feel my sense of myself melting and running down a window like rain, although the weather outside is clear and beautiful. Who in the hell am I anyway? Certainly not the person I thought I was. I came here expecting nothing but the possibility of horse thieves, and I will be leaving with a knowledge of solid respectability and wealth and a whole new German patrimony that has been denied me. I thought I was Irish. Am I Irish at all? I doubt it now. Somehow it was comfortable being Irish. Being suddenly German, with all the history of two world wars, is more difficult. It's going to take me a while to adjust. But being a descendant of the eminently respectable Pryors and Moyers, when I had expected horse thieves, isn't hard to take.

After thanking the librarians and leaving a donation to the historical society somewhat larger than I can afford, I stride out of the library with my head a little higher than it was when I came in. From now on, things will be onward and upward. This research stuff isn't so hard when you get the hang of it.

~

Pittsfield, the county seat of Pike County, Illinois, is small and drowsy this afternoon. I'm getting a little drowsy myself since I didn't really get a nap on the lawn in Quincy earlier in the day. It's not hard to find the library in Pittsfield. I'm there by midafternoon, riding a wave of euphoria from my discovery in Quincy, and I'm looking for the Derry Township census records. El Dara is in Derry Township. The records for the 1890 census are not available, but those for 1880 are, and they are a gold mine for me.

One of the miscellaneous papers in the hodgepodge in the box in the car is a copy of a handwritten document compiled by the wife of one of my cousins on Red's side of the family.

It is almost entirely a series of lists, and it focuses on the family of my father's older brother, Minnis Richard Shelton, after whom I was named. (Fortunately my parents chose his middle name for me.) One of the lists is family marriages and their dates, and the first entry on that list is Charles Elmer Shelton and Martha Pryor, my father's parents, at Pittsfield, Illinois, June 3, 1880. With that date in mind, I hit the 1880 census for Derry Township, looking under Pryor, and find that although Martha Pryor probably got married in 1880, she had not yet married when the census was compiled.

> *106, Pryor, William H., 47, Farmer*
> *Susan E., 42, W*
> *Henry, 16, Son, works on farm,*
> *Martha E., 19, Dau.,*
> *Isaac, 12, Son,*
> *Wilbert, 10, Son,*
> *Shelton, Charles, 18, Hired, works on farm.*

There it is—a love story in the census records. Oh, Martha! Martha! You did it, didn't you? You married the hired hand. You jumped right off the ledge of being rich and respectable and married a penniless boy who was a year younger than you. Judging by photographs taken years later, you must have been plump and pretty at nineteen. You had bright red hair, a redhead's very fair skin, and freckles. I think of you each time I see my sister's beautiful red-headed daughter Sandy. I, too, got my red hair and freckles from you, through my redheaded father, but I also got the heavily lidded eyes you handed down to some unlucky member of each generation. And was your courtship with the hired hand conducted in the Victorian parlor of that handsome farmhouse, or was it a series of furtive moments in the barn? Was it a love match, or were you afraid of becoming an old maid?

I have a photograph of you and your husband when you are both much older. Your children, also in the photograph, are mostly grown, except my father, the youngest. You are stout but still pretty. Charles Elmer is skinny and angular, with a long, drooping moustache and no chin to speak of. I cannot imagine him ever having been handsome or dashing or anything that would have attracted the pretty daughter of the wealthy farmer William Pryor. But you married him, and your lives together were lives of dreadful poverty and hardship. You bore and raised eight children who survived, some of them to torture one another and their spouses for many years. I know you insisted that your youngest son wear his bright red hair long and in corkscrew curls that hung down his back, like little Lord Fauntleroy. Could that be why he tried so hard as an adult to prove how tough he was, that he wasn't a sissy? Could that be why, later, his heroes were the racketeers and gangsters of the day, like Al Capone and "Pretty Boy" Floyd? Did he choose to become a bootlegger because of the tough image, because that made it possible for him to carry a gun and live outside the law?

Your husband was said to be cruel, and at least one of your children (blessedly not my father) and one of your grandchildren were strangely cruel, especially when young. But your children adored you as far as I can tell. You created a family and somehow held it together in spite of extreme poverty.

In the same 1880 census report, but under the next township to the south, Pleasant Hill Township, I find the Sheltons. Nancy V. (née Duncan), age forty-seven, a widow and her eight children, of whom Charles Elmer is fifth and identified as "18, son Farm laborer." I know now for whom he was laboring—William H. Pryor, who was to become my great-grandfather. But who was Charles Elmer's father? There is no 1870 census for Pleasant Hill Township available, so I will have to go to Pleasant Hill and see what I can find. This is getting complicated. In spite of my delight at finding out *anything* in Illinois after my abject failure in Kansas, I'm beginning to think I need help. But what kind of help, and where can I find it?

I've been driving through hilly country with rich bottomlands and wooded patches of mostly oak. It's green and attractive and rich. The cicadas are making a great racket. The hills are small by Arizona standards, with pleasing contours. I call this kind of country "wrinkled." But as soon as I leave Pittsfield, I realize I am going steadily down toward the biggest river in America, as if I am being sucked into some huge vortex. Along the base of the last range of hills before the enormous flat river bottom is Pleasant Hill, a village that straddles both the hills and the river bottom. The heat and humidity have become oppressive. Something like sheer fecundity is rising from the soil of that black bottomland, and it's overpowering. The village seems to be climbing the hill to avoid it. The bottomland is divided into large acreages, cultivated, planted, fertilized, manicured. It repels me in a way I can't explain. I'm glad the small business section of town, where I'm looking for the city hall or some equivalent, is up on the hill a ways.

I've developed the habit of just walking into the city hall of a small town, explaining what I'm looking for, and asking for help. In every case, even when they had no help to give, like in Kansas, I've been met with courtesy and interest. People are always trying to be helpful. Pleasant Hill is no exception.

"Yes, there were some Sheltons living around here, I think," the man who has come from somewhere in the back of the building says. "If anybody in town would know, it would be Virginia. Virginia Hart. She lives right down the road. She's a genealogist who does professional research for people looking up their family trees. You know, lots of LDS people come here, and she helps them. Hold on just a minute, and I'll get you her telephone number. You can use this phone right here."

I do, and Virginia Hart answers, sounding a little gruff. At the mention of my name and the fact that I'm from Arizona, she sounds interested, although distantly.

"You got any relatives in Idaho?" she asks abruptly.

I tell her I was raised in Idaho and have all kinds of relatives there.

"Well, one of them wrote to me. A woman named Turner. From Twin Falls, I think. Maiden name was Shelton. That sound familiar to you?"

No, it doesn't sound familiar to me at all. It baffles me.

"Well, I did quite a bit of research on the Sheltons who lived here. In fact, I'm distantly related to that family by marriage. They lived up Ten Mile Creek. There was quite a bit of incest in that family as I recall."

Jesus Christ and all the angels! I think I've got a tiger by the tail.

Virginia talks about her charges for research at some length, both an hourly rate and a rate for the material she has already researched. The rates seem high, but I'm not about to quibble after the incest bit. (Yes, Virginia, there is a Santa Claus.) She gives me her address and directions, and when I ask if I can come over right away, she says it will have to be tomorrow. She has family responsibilities and it's almost supper time. So we make an appointment for the next morning at eight. It occurs to me that she might be stalling to whet my appetite—as if she hadn't done that already—but I'm ashamed of myself for thinking it.

I snoop around Pleasant Hill some. There isn't much to see, and I'm getting very hungry. Somehow after the big discovery at the historical society library in Quincy, I forgot to eat lunch. The only restaurant I can find in Pleasant Hill is a long, narrow, evil-looking diner. I go in and check the menu, but both the menu and the place are too grim. There seems to be no hotel or motel in Pleasant Hill, and not much to do. Maybe that explains the incest. So I am going to have to go back to Pittsfield for the night, but it's only thirty miles and I remember seeing a big hotel on the square there with what looked like a good restaurant, and also a modest motel on the edge of town that looked just right for me.

Searching for
Phebe

During the night a storm has moved in, and suddenly it's winter again. A cold, slanting rain alternates with sleet. I'm on Virginia's porch in Pleasant Hill at eight sharp, but nobody's home. I pace up and down the porch, shivering and freezing, and wait. In a few minutes she pulls up in front of the house. As we go in, she explains that she is in the process of moving to another house because she has an elderly parent to care for.

Virginia is small and ageless, somewhere between forty and sixty, but full of energy, with small bright eyes that remind me of a cactus wren's. Her darting movements and quick, direct talk—somewhere between conversation and confrontation—also remind me of that wren. She sits me down, still shivering, at the kitchen table and makes coffee. While the coffee is brewing, she rummages through several metal filing cabinets that seem to be scattered at random throughout the house.

"Here it is," she says, handing me a letter. "Linda Turner. Maiden name of Shelton. She's a Mormon from Twin Falls, Idaho, and I've been helping her with her genealogy, but we've hit a snag. Is she a relative of yours?"

"I don't know. What was her father's name?"

"Lester."

"That can't be. Lester was one of my father's older brothers. His only daughter is named Juanita and her last name isn't Turner. She lives in Boise—oops! Wait a minute—Juanita has a younger brother . . . what did they call him? Little Lester, of course. . . . I haven't seen him since I was a child—if I ever saw him then. Had forgotten all about him. This must be Little Lester's daughter. I didn't know he had one."

"She pays well," Virginia says dryly, as a not-so-subtle introduction to our next topic. After we have agreed on the terms, she goes back to the filing cabinet and returns with another folder. It looks like a rat's nest or, as Red would have said, *a Basco load of hay.* Remembering the box of stuff in the back of my car, I decide I have no right to make that judgment.

"Here's the problem," Virginia says, spreading a confusing mass of papers, letters, charts, lists, and other documents—often bad Xerox copies—in front of me. "A girl came here to Pleasant Hill about 1830. She was seventeen and had her infant son with her. His name was Benjamin. Her name was Phebe Shelton, and she called herself *Miss* Phebe Shelton. Was she the widow of a man named Shelton, or was Shelton her maiden name, making her son Benjamin illegitimate? Nobody has been able to find out for sure. And until we find out, we can't trace the line back any farther. I've been working on this for a long time, and it's a nut I can't crack. I think Phebe came here from somewhere across the river in Missouri, but I haven't been able to find out where. Maybe her family kicked her out when she had the baby. She just sort of appeared here and stayed with friends. Her son Benjamin was to become Charles Elmer's father, and if you are Leonard's son, that would make Benjamin your great-grandfather."

"Did Phebe marry after she got here?"

"Did she ever," Virginia says. "This was a frontier in 1835, and women were scarce. She married twice and was widowed once."

"Children?"

"Here's the list." Her hands play deftly over two of the papers written in pencil and the copy of a census record, making sense out of what is gibberish to me.

"In 1842 she married Robert Stewart who was from Ireland and was thirteen years older than she was. He had already been married twice and widowed twice, and he brought to the marriage with Phebe six children under the age of fourteen: one from his first marriage and five from his second. The youngest was less than a year old when he married Phebe. Robert Stewart and Phebe had six children spaced about two years apart, and Robert died in 1855, leaving her with . . . wait a minute while I count . . . ten children under the age of seventeen. The next year Phebe married Thomas Owsley and bore him a daughter before she died."

"And Benjamin was the oldest of all this brood?"

"Yes, and here's the rub—all of Robert Stewart's property went to his widow and the children of his three marriages. Benjamin evidently got nothing, in spite of the fact that he had helped raise the younger children. Look, here's a copy of the census report for 1860, the year Phebe died. Benjamin is now thirty, married, and has three children of his own, but listed in his household are two of Phebe's younger children, Emmeline and James Stewart, who were eleven and five years old. They are Benjamin's half sister and half brother, and he evidently took them to raise when his mother died. The scuttlebutt passed down through the family was that Benjamin was the rock Phebe depended on, and he helped her raise all that gang of children and got nothing for his trouble."

"What about the incest?"

She looks away quickly. "I shouldn't have said anything about that. It's only an old rumor around here and probably unfounded. Probably came from the fact that there were all those half brothers and half sisters living out there on Ten Mile Creek together. Robert Stewart's brood by his first two marriages was not even related by blood to Benjamin or to Phebe's daughter by Owsley. It was a complicated family. Maybe some of them got a little confused. Or maybe there were relationships that only appeared to be incestuous because people around here didn't understand the structure of the family."

"Do you know where Phebe is buried?"

"Nobody knows where Phebe is buried. It's a great mystery. Benjamin and his wife and some of their children are buried in the Wells Cemetery, just outside town. But I believe their son, who was your grandfather, is buried in Idaho."

"Yes, Charles Elmer and Martha are both buried in Boise, along with several of their children."

"So would you like to go and see your great-grandfather Benjamin's grave? Did you know much about him before you came here?"

"Never heard of him," I answer, "unless he was a horse thief."

"A horse thief!" Virginia is amused. "Why, my goodness no! The Sheltons were all farmers. Hardworking farmers. Whatever gave you an idea like that?"

"Just a rumor," I answer, "like incest."

———

When we get to the Wells Cemetery, it's raining, sleeting, and snowing, all at the same time. Virginia seems to be less affected by the cold than I am. Forty years in southern Arizona has diminished my tolerance for cold. My teeth are chattering audibly. I am trying to write down the names that appear on the gravestones, but my hands are blue and shaking too hard to write. I see the stone marking the grave of Benjamin and his wife, Nancy. It's polished pink granite, large and imposing but simple—the epitome of solid respectability. Something about the style suggests that it was placed there when Nancy died in 1926. Benjamin died in 1875, and Nancy outlived him by fifty-one years. Five of their children are buried near them: Richard, Emma, George, Mary, and Edgar.

Benjamin's wife, my great-grandmother Nancy Duncan, is coming into focus for me now. I hadn't paid much attention to her in the shock of discovering Phebe and her probably less-than-legitimate son. But here is Nancy, lying beside her husband under this very respectable tombstone, and I remember that she and her family figure prominently in the folder of papers Virginia xeroxed for me, although I haven't had time to digest many of them yet. I make a mental note to read the information on Nancy Duncan, and I try to write her name in my notebook, but my hands are shaking too hard, and the writing isn't legible.

I'm fascinated by the cemetery itself. It's not large, but it seems to be right in the middle of somebody's farm. Cultivated fields surround it on all sides, and there's no margin or border. One steps from the tilled field directly onto the grass of the cemetery. Close beside it is a huge grain auger, several metal farm buildings, and a silo. The cemetery is well cared for in a Spartan kind of way, but the resting place of the dead is an island completely surrounded by the farming activities of the living.

On the way back into town, Virginia points out Ten Mile Creek Road, where Phebe and Robert Stewart lived and farmed and raised their complicated layers of children, some of whom may have become a little more familiar with one another than the community felt was acceptable. "They lived up that road four miles," she says. "The house is gone, and I doubt that anybody could find the exact property. Do you want to go up there?"

"Not in this weather. I'll take you home now and then drive up there tomorrow. Maybe this storm will be over by then. This business of chasing ghosts is cold work. I think I've had about enough of it for today. I'm going back to my motel in Pittsfield and will try to make some sense of all these papers and documents. Maybe with a stiff shot of whiskey. My God, it's cold. I think it's the humidity that's getting to me."

"Sometimes," Virginia says, "it can get right nasty here in the spring, but it won't last long. It could be beautiful tomorrow."

"Do you really think Benjamin was illegitimate?" I ask abruptly. "That tombstone looked so . . . so respectable and kind of imposing."

Suddenly her hard, bright eyes turn soft and shadowy. She reaches over and pats my hand on the steering wheel. "Yes, I do believe Benjamin was illegitimate, and that tombstone was put up more than fifty years after his death. It's possible that Phebe was the widow of an older man, but it's more likely that she was the lover of a younger man who got her pregnant and abandoned her. I'm sorry. It means we can't trace Benjamin's line back any farther."

―

By morning it has cleared off and is spring again. I sleep in until eight because I stayed up late in my snug motel room reading copies of letters, pedigree charts, marriage certificates, school attendance records, and one extremely detailed will. The problem with chasing ghosts, I'm discovering, is that you never find a ghost all in one piece. There's a fact here, a hint there, a detail somewhere else, and you wind up with papers scattered all over the bed and wake up in the morning with your head on Aunt Fannie Shultz's will, but you haven't figured out who Aunt Fannie Shultz was. This family tree has entirely too many branches.

In the nineteenth-century Midwest, so many wives died and so many husbands died, and the remaining partners immediately got married again and continued to produce dozens of children.

There was typhoid (bilious fever), cholera (black vomit), dysentery, influenza, tuberculosis (consumption), small pox, and the often deadly complications of childbirth. If a man accidently cut his leg while butchering a hog, he could die of blood poisoning. When a woman's husband died and left her with ten minor children, there were almost no social services for her to turn to. Another husband, if she were lucky enough to find one, was the best—and almost the only—solution short of the county poorhouse, and marriage often brought more children. What was a farmer to do when his wife died in childbirth, leaving him six children to care for, one a newborn infant? He must either give up his children to relatives, neighbors, and friends, or find a woman to help him raise them and marry her quick.

I have breakfast in Pittsfield and head back toward Pleasant Hill but turn off the highway on the road marked TEN MILE CREEK. It's a narrow, winding road that follows the creek upstream between the curves of the hills that get gradually higher and steeper. The landscape changes fast as I leave the more open country just above the flat river bottom. Instead of the space and sunny vista, things close in. While one side of the hill is in sunshine, the narrow valley is dark, and patches of thick but stunted-looking trees, mostly scrub oak, are very dark. It's exactly what I've always imagined a "holler" to look like. It's ominous and disquieting.

The creek bed is overgrown with a confusion of trees, vines, and brambles. I can't see very many houses from the road. The cultivated fields are small and irregularly shaped, and hills cut off the view in all directions. Maybe I'm a little claustrophobic, but this place bothers me. It looks like a good place for incest—or murder. Creepy. Four miles from where I turned onto it, I stop beside the road, get out of the car, and walk along the creek for a ways, wondering exactly where Phebe Shelton Stewart and her large brood of children lived. Suddenly a cloud covers the sun, and everything turns dark. I realize I'm shivering a little, getting some bad vibrations here. I get back in the car with a sense of relief and head back down the twisting road.

From the landscape I've gotten an entirely different view of the Shelton/Stewart family that lived here. I can see how rumors of incest or something sinister could get started up in this dark hollow. It makes me think of the perfect setting for a bootlegger's still. The flat Mississippi River bottom beckons, and I want to get out into the open where I can see some distance. I've lived in the desert too long.

~

It's about twenty miles from here to El Dara. I don't know what I expect to find there, except that it's where my grandmother Martha, my father's mother, was raised, and where my father was born. Virginia explained something about that to me. She said that during the years Martha and Charles Elmer lived at Pleasant Hill, Martha always went home to the gracious farm in El Dara to have her babies, and that by the time my father was born, his parents had moved to El Dara. That tells me that Martha and her family were not totally estranged because she married the hired hand—at least not for long—although I can't imagine that old William Pryor was exactly overjoyed about it.

Last night, before I fell asleep with Aunt Fannie's will (whoever she was), I found out something about Benjamin's wife, Nancy Duncan, my paternal great-grandmother. She was born in Missouri, and nobody seems to know much about her father, John Duncan. Her mother, however, was the daughter of Richard Kerr, who was sheriff of Pike County, Missouri, and served eight years in the Missouri House of Representatives. He was a friend of Abraham Lincoln. In the papers Virginia gave me are copies of several of his letters to his brother and other members of the family, and one of the saddest has to do with four of his granddaughters, one of whom was Nancy Duncan, my great-grandmother. It is dated October 4, 1844.

My son(-in-law JOHN) DUNCAN died on the 10th of January last of winter fever and his wife (CAROLYN KERR DUNCAN) on the 15th of the same disease, leaving us 4 little girles (Nancy, Malinda, Elizabeth, and Susan DUNCAN) to raise that are entirely destitute of any means.

Nancy would have been eleven when her parents died and was probably the oldest of the "4 little girles." She is listed in another document in the hodgepodge that Virginia gave me, but I couldn't figure out its significance for a long time. When Virginia pointed it out to me yesterday, I wasn't familiar enough with the names to know what she was talking about. Now I see how one seemingly insignificant scrap of a record can tell a great deal. It's an undated school attendance record. The school is at Atlas, Illinois, just down the road from Pleasant Hill and probably the only school in the immediate area at that time. The teacher is Richard Kerr, Nancy Duncan's grandfather, who wrote the letter about the four orphan girls, a man who wore many hats and had served in the Missouri House of Representatives. The students' names are listed in a beautiful, ornate script, which I assume was the hand of Richard Kerr. Among them are the four destitute granddaughters who are now living with Richard Kerr and his wife. Three of the others on the list are the children of Phebe Shelton Stewart. Benjamin Shelton, whom Nancy would later marry, is not on the list. He was three years older than Nancy, and his formal education was probably already over. If she was eleven at this time, he would have been fourteen and working full time on the farm up Ten Mile Creek to help his mother and stepfather.

All of this intrigues me because it might point to some earlier connection between Phebe Shelton and Richard Kerr, and it might help explain why Phebe came to Pleasant Hill with her infant son rather than to some other community. There has to be a reason why she chose or was sent to Pleasant Hill. Could it be the fact that Richard Kerr, who had been a powerful member of the legislature in Missouri, as well as a sheriff, had settled in Pleasant Hill, and that

Phebe, who, it is assumed, was from Missouri, either came to him or was sent to him for support and protection? But why? It is possible that Phebe's family and the Kerrs in Missouri were friends, and that when Phebe found herself "in a family way," as they said then, Richard Kerr and his wife offered to help her establish herself and her son in a new place, where she could start over and possibly pass herself off as a widow.

And climbing farther and farther out on this limb of conjecture, was there some connection between the fact that Phebe was "in a family way" and the Kerrs in Missouri? Could the person who got Phebe into that delicate condition in the first place possibly be a relative, even perhaps a son, of Richard Kerr? Or a nephew? So that Richard Kerr, who seems to have been a very responsible, caring kind of person, would have felt obligated to help Phebe in any way he could? If the man responsible for Phebe's pregnancy were Richard Kerr's son, it would mean that Benjamin Shelton married his first cousin. If he were a nephew, the marriage would be between, I think, second cousins. Suddenly I am beginning to see that this may be the source of the rumors of incest, rather than the explanation Virginia gave me. Both, of course, could be true. If one pursues this line, it even becomes possible that Benjamin's father was that John Duncan, Richard Kerr's son-in-law, the father of Nancy, who died of bilious fever in 1844, which would mean that Benjamin married his half sister. This is the most extreme scenario, and it's highly doubtful, but why did Virginia give me all these papers concerning the Kerr family, most of which have no immediate connection to the Sheltons/Stewarts unless she was trying to see if I could figure things out for myself? And could my father have known about this? Could it be the reason he refused to help anybody, including me, pry into his family history? Horse thieves! My aunt Fannie!

As I drive toward El Dara on this beautiful spring morning, I wonder if that elegant house the Pryors lived in might still be standing, and if it is, how I can find it. El Dara is still on the map, but it's on a little-traveled secondary road off a secondary highway on the way to nowhere. The road is Highway 13. Not too auspicious.

I turn onto Highway 13 and the countryside is placid and pleasant. Low, rolling hills, sometimes wooded, with mostly cornfields and hayfields. Last year's hay is rolled into tight bundles—whole fields of peculiar little V-shaped hutches for some kind of animal. When I look closer, I see pigs coming out of the hutches. Then I notice the pigs are everywhere—rooting under the trees, piled up on top of one another, sleeping in the sunshine, their pink rumps gleaming.

This must be the pork capital of the world. It is also a land of blindingly white farmhouses with bright green metal roofs and immaculate yards and farmyards. Even the pigs look like they have just been scrubbed. I am reminded of the Pryor farm pictured in the history book. I drive around looking for it without any luck.

El Dara is truly a hamlet. A couple dozen houses scattered widely over a few square blocks, with a white Methodist church on the hill. The church seems to be closed today. Beyond that, it's farms. No business district or stores. My usual practice of going to the city hall won't work here: There isn't any. There is nobody out and about, and I know I'm becoming conspicuous, driving aimlessly around and around with Arizona license plates.

Other than the church, there's only one public building I can find, and it's a trailer—a portable library. The librarian is an attractive young woman who has her little daughter with her. The child is lying on her stomach on the floor, entirely involved in a coloring book. I ask the librarian if she knows of anybody in the community who is knowledgeable about the history of the place, especially of the families who lived here in earlier years.

"Oh, that would be J.C. Harlow," she says without hesitation. "He and Ruth live just down the road in the next-to-the-last house on the left. It's the one with a porch across the front and porch swing. It has a black roof, and J.C.'s maroon car will be out in front."

Sure enough, J.C. Harlow is sitting in the porch swing as if he were expecting me. In fact, he is expecting me. He's been watching me driving around, peering at each house, and he has a pretty good notion of what I'm up to. He also knows that sooner or later, if I have any sense, I will come to him. So he just waits on the front porch and gets up to greet me when I finally come to rest. He's middle-aged, retired, bluff, and friendly, and as soon as I introduce myself, his wife, Ruth, puts the coffee on and tells me to make myself at home.

J.C. inherited his interest in local history from his mother, who was the unofficial town historian. There are still some Pryors in the area, he says, and mentions two names. They might be the descendants of my grandmother Martha's brothers or half brothers, or then again, they might not be. It's hard to explain to J.C. that I'm not interested in bothering these people, even though they may be distant collateral relatives. I'm interested in the ghosts. He picks up on it quickly.

"The old Pryor house is gone," he says. "You're just a little too late. It sat empty for years, and they finally tore it down last year. I can give you directions to get out there, though." He brings out a big platte map of El Dara, Derry Township. "But I guess what you would want to see most would be the Hornbeck Cemetery where the Pryors are buried. It's on private property, on Steve Hoskin's place just out of town, but if you ask him, Steve will let you walk down to it. It's about a mile and a half off the road in an oak grove. You'll pretty much find all of them there, but some of the stones you can't read anymore."

I'm excited. Another cemetery, and this time I won't have to fight bad weather. It's a beautiful, crisp, and slightly windy spring day. Perfect weather for a walk to an abandoned graveyard.

Before I go, there's one more thing I need to ask J.C. Harlow, and I have a piece of paper handy. It's a plain white sheet of paper with Virginia Hart's notes scrawled on it, and in the upper right-hand corner, it says, "I read this from film. VH." I don't know what film, but it must have been records of real estate in El Dara. Whatever document Virginia was copying was dated June 13, 1900, and it says that Charles Shelton, a farm laborer who could write and speak English had rented house number 167 on Mississippi Street in El Dara. It then lists by name, date of birth, and age his wife, Martha, and his seven children. His eighth child, my father, Leonard Pryor, was to be born fourteen months later in August 1901.

"Can house number 167 be located on the platte map?" I ask J.C. Harlow, "and can I go find it, or at least where it stood?"

"No," he says. "We don't have any records of the house numbers from that period. But judging by the high number, the house was probably well out of the center of the village."

The rental document tells me that Red's father, as late as 1900, still did not have any land of his own. A few years later he and Martha would move their family west to Colorado, following the path of one of their older sons, but if they were able to obtain a homestead there, they lost it within a few years and moved farther west to the Snake River country.

J.C. Harlow gives me a handsome copy of the Derry Township platte map dated 1912. It shows the various acreages owned and by whom. The name Shelton never appears, but the names of Martha's maternal German relatives, the Moyers, pop up three times, and they jointly own 274 acres.

A notion is forming from all this. My father was the youngest of his father's eight children, and his father was still a farm laborer when Red was born. My father was raised in a rich farming community where many of his relatives were well-to-do landowners, and certainly his maternal grandfather had been affluent. The pattern of poverty my father was born into began when his grandfather Benjamin inherited no land because he had no father. His children continued with no land, and the poverty increased with each generation. Not only were they poor, but they lived in the shadow of their relatives who had land and prospered. Ultimately, I think I know what kind of effect this had on my father.

He hated the rich with a fury I could never understand, especially those who displayed their wealth. My father's sense of class, as determined by economic situation, was absolute. His litany for his children was: "Don't get above yourself. Stay in your place." When it was a matter of any of his children associating with the rich or even with members of the upper middle class, he said, "That's not for us. We don't do that. Stay in your place." He opposed any of his children getting an education beyond high school. I watched him oppose my sister Betty when she wanted to go to college, and he won—although I don't think she put up a fierce struggle.

When it was my turn, he did what he could to stop me from going to college, but by then he was so deeply compromised by alcoholism and his affairs with various women, and so alienated from me, his youngest son, that he could not put up a truly effective fight. I never asked him to help me financially, and I think he believed that I couldn't make it in college if I had no money. He came close to being right. His opposition was also weakened by the fact that my mother encouraged me to further my education. But he never approved. I think he was influenced by the fact that no one in our entire extended family had ever gone to college.

Perhaps we tend to overlook the searing psychological effects poverty can have on children in certain situations. In a community where everyone is poor, these effects might be minimal. But that wasn't the case with my father and his immediate family. His father was a landless farm laborer in a community where his relatives were landed gentry. Of course, many people who are raised in severe poverty do not grow up with the negative attitudes my father had. I assume they found support in family and community that my father did not. His attitude, it seems to me, was close to that of a European peasant in an earlier century. Beyond doing his work each day, he could not imagine any way to improve his situation. The avenues toward upward mobility sought by others were not for him or his children, and when such an opportunity would come his way, he derailed.

Whatever made him that way, whatever seared his young life so badly that he was forever after a slave to alcohol and to a dreadful feeling of inferiority that only alcohol could relieve, must have happened here in this idyllic little village where he lived until he was about ten, and I will never know for sure what it was. I can only imagine.

With directions and a map of Derry Township in hand, I set out for the farm of Steve Hoskin to get permission to see the burial place of my grandmother Martha's family. J.C. and Ruth Harlow stand on the porch and wave as I leave, as if they were saying good-bye to an old friend.

Steve Hoskin's large two-story house is situated at the top of a hill. Whoever built it there knew what they were doing. It's impressive, and it must provide a great view. I find Steve in one of the barns hosing down farm equipment. He is young, handsome, and friendly. He quickly gives me permission to visit the graveyard. There is no road to it, but he offers to drive me down there through the fields in his pickup. I tell him I'm looking forward to the walk, so he gives me directions and I drive back down the road to find the gate. I park beside the road, climb over the large wooden gate because it seems easier than opening it, and set off. The land is magnificent, sweeping down to the south in great curves. I will have only one fence to crawl through. The sun is bright, everything is green, and there is just enough breeze to keep me from getting hot. I lope down the hill like a child. This is the kind of research I was cut out for. Lost graveyards, magnificent country, and beautiful weather. To hell with all those papers and Aunt Fannie Shultz's will!

The graveyard is in a thick grove of oaks and totally uncared for. If I didn't have detailed directions, I would have passed it by without recognizing it. The gravestones have become so well camouflaged with leaf stains and lichen as to be invisible from a distance in the deep, dappled shade. It is called the Hornbeck Cemetery because it's on land once owned by the Hornbecks, the first family to settle in the area, but other families used it. The mossy ground is covered with wild jonquils not yet in bloom. The trees are not large, mostly scrub oak, but thick enough to shade and hide the entire graveyard. It's perfect for a graveyard, I think. Soft and shadowy, green and quiet, and miles from the noise of traffic or any human sound.

There are many graves of the Pryors here, and the first one I stumble upon, trying to adjust my eyes to the sudden gloom after the sunny fields, is the grave of my great-grandmother, Martha's German mother. It is a handsome mossy obelisk, but the fancy top section has fallen behind it.

> *Pryor*
> *Susan E. Moyer*
> *wife of*
> *W. H. Pryor*

died Dec. 4, 1884
aged 46 y. 7 m. 23 d.

Lone is the house and sad the hour
Since her sweet smile is gone
But oh a brighter home than ours
In heaven is now thine own

This epitaph was probably lifted from some collection of sentimental poems on death, fairly common in the 1880s. Perhaps it was chosen by Susan's grieving husband, William H. Pryor, pillar of the community, who remarried less than a year after Susan's death. Well, nobody wants to live in a "Lone" house too long. I cannot find his grave. Perhaps by the time he died, having been widowed and remarried twice after Susan's death, this graveyard was no longer in use. But his parents' graves are here.

Isaac, who was a pioneer in the region, has a fancy slab with an open book carved near the top and two lines of illegible verse at the bottom. He died January 5, 1864, at the age of fifty-two. The simple slab marking the grave of his wife, Sarah Harris, who, according to the information in the book I read in Quincy, could trace her family back to Daniel Boone, has fallen over and some kind soul has propped it up against a tree. I'd like to think that kind soul was Virginia Hart, since I know she's visited this graveyard in the course of her research. Sarah was born in Tennessee in 1808 and was thirty-two when she died. The grave of Nancy, the daughter of Isaac and Sarah, who died at fifteen, is very near the graves of her parents, touchingly near.

Isaac's second wife, Nancy, is buried nearby, as well as two of the children she bore him. She, like Isaac's first wife, my great-great-grandmother, died at thirty-two. In this family the men seemed to outlive the women, often by many years, which accounts for complicated tiers of half brothers and half sisters. I wonder if there were diseases to which the women were more susceptible or if they simply wore out from overwork and having so many children without the benefit of decent medical attention.

By the time I'm ready to leave the graveyard and hike back to the car, it's late afternoon. The graveyard is in deep shadow. Not eager to leave, I follow a little gully that meanders in the general direction of the road. I take one last look at the graveyard, dark and peaceful and full of the record of more living, more pain, more joy, more suffering, and maybe even more triumph than I have ever known or could imagine. Having spent the afternoon wandering among the tombstones, I feel fulfilled, somehow—at least for now. I can return to my life in Arizona and not be troubled by the ghosts for a while.

I feel good about what I've accomplished in the last two days. Maybe I'm not a total failure at the business of chasing ghosts. I may not be any good at genealogy, but I can make up for it when it comes to climbing over fences and hiking through fields. I'm not going to spend any more time tonight trying to figure out the ramifications of Aunt Fannie Shultz's will. I have a sneaking hunch that Virginia Hart just threw Aunt Fannie in there to confuse me. If so, she succeeded. But tomorrow morning, early, I will head west toward Arizona and home. Any ghosts who want to go with me are welcome.

PART III

GOING DOWN THE VALLEY

Flume Street

It is June 27, 2000. I am standing just outside the gate of the Pioneer Cemetery in Boise, Idaho. Nobody I ever knew is buried in this cemetery, and I haven't been in it for sixty years, but I feel as if I have been circling it all my adult life, somehow never able to go in. Each time I return to Boise, where I was born and raised, I sneak around this cemetery. Not actually in it, but around it. I've driven and walked and ridden my bicycle around it many times, but I never told anybody. They would think I was weird and Gothic. Maybe I am weird and Gothic. Still chasing ghosts.

It doesn't look like a very Gothic kind of cemetery on this summer day, with the afternoon sun flooding everything and the grass as bright green as grass can be. I left my suit coat in the rental car, but I'm aware of the heat even without it. A brilliant black-and-white magpie stalks across the lawn at a little distance with a loud *yak yak yak* and eyes me with disapproval.

Well, at least it's not a raven, I think, *croaking "Nevermore,"* and the thought almost makes me laugh and lightens my morbid mood. *Maybe it's never too late to face a ghost.*

I can hear sparrows and finches squabbling in the junipers and pines scattered through the cemetery. It's actually an idyllic and inviting place, wedged between fashionable Warm Springs Avenue and unfashionable Flume Street, a quiet and generally forgotten street of mostly old and very modest houses only a block long. The cemetery is an irregular shape, bordered by streets that run at unusual angles, and it's not much larger than a large city block, with maples and cypresses scattered through it. Across the back is an alley hidden by a tall hedge, an alley down which I have walked many times, both during the year I lived on Flume Street as a child, and more recently when I have been drawn back to circle like a bird who could not land. Well, I'm going to land this time. My brother Jack is dead.

I flew in yesterday from Arizona to attend my only brother's funeral, and I have just come from that funeral and the burial in another cemetery in a different part of town. This funeral was different from most of the other family funerals I have attended. Grandma Charlotte, Red, Hazel, Betty—they are all gone now. Ghosts. Jack's was a Mormon funeral because Jack was a very staunch Mormon, and so is his family. The funeral was longer and more elaborate, and certainly better attended than our other family funerals have been. It took the united strength of the entire Mormon community to hoist Jack into heaven, but they did it. They created a saint and sent him on his way. Since the Mormon heaven includes the pleasures of the flesh, I guess Jack's recently amputated leg will be given back to him, and without the pain it caused him for such a long time.

At the funeral, even I did a little of the lifting, Gentile though I am. My contribution was only a brief and carefully edited biographical sketch of Jack's childhood and teenage years, but I'm exhausted. All those testimonials somewhere between fiction and outright fantasy—but based on real feeling—wore me out. I loved him. At least I think I loved him. I tried to love him.

But I couldn't bear to be in the same room with him for very long. That tension lessened as we both got older, but when I was teenager, it was dreadful. I guess everything is more of a problem when we are teenagers. The moment he appeared, I would become a klutz who could screw up anything. I said I wasn't afraid of him. I tried not to be afraid of him. But I was still afraid of him. I have come directly from the funeral dinner in a Mormon gymnasium to this cemetery. I owe it to Jack and to myself to walk, at last, through the gates of the Pioneer Cemetery and confront my ghosts in the time I have left.

A sign on the gate says the cemetery was "restored during the Centennial year by Friends of the Pioneer Cemetery," but it doesn't look much changed from the way I remember it as a child except for the fancy wrought-iron fence around most of it. The sign also says that it was established as a "Masonic/IOOF" cemetery in 1872, but the first body was buried here in 1864. IOOF means Independent Order of Odd Fellows, and like the Masons, it was a powerful fraternal organization in most western mining communities. As I think *frater-nal*, I wince, remembering all the good friends who have been much more like brothers to me than my real brother ever was. Then I feel guilty at the thought, today of all days.

This cemetery is right beside the Oregon Trail, although you couldn't tell it by the looks of the neighborhood, and I want to believe that the first body buried here was some pioneer on his way to Oregon, but it's doubtful. The Oregon Trail was still in use in 1864, but by then other things were happening in this part of Idaho, things that were far more likely to have resulted in the first burial at this site.

It is easy to forget what an enormous impact the Civil War had on the exploration and development of the American West. All those draft dodgers, like Mark Twain, were mucking about in the West, intent on avoiding the front lines at Gettysburg or Chancellorsville. They did various things, but most of them prospected for gold or silver. On August 2, 1862, three of them discovered gold on Grimes Creek, about fifteen miles up the road from here, and this road, then a trail, became the highway to El Dorado. Miners came by the thousands, and the fabulous Boise Basin, eighteen square miles of gold-laden mountains, started shipping its bounty out to a waiting world.

In 1863 Idaho became a territory—the usual Civil War scenario when rich deposits of valuable minerals were found in an otherwise "godforsaken" wilderness. The Union desperately needed gold and silver to pay for the war. It could well afford to create territories in remote areas only vaguely known to members of Congress, and it could wink at the men who fled west to avoid conscription since some of them were finding exactly what the Union needed. In fact, the federal government established an army post here in 1863 to protect the miners from the Natives in the area and from one another, and to ensure that the flow of gold eastward would not be interrupted.

The first person to be buried here, in 1864, when this area was in the midst of gold fever, could have been a miner or a gambler or a soldier hastily planted beside the road to the gold fields. Or one of the "ladies" who followed the miners and gamblers and soldiers into the wilderness, or one of the wives who also followed them, usually later. It could have been just about anybody who got unlucky in the commercial headquarters of a booming mining area.

I didn't know anything about this cemetery when my family moved to the little house on Flume Street, number 204. I was six. I just knew it was a place where dead people were buried and that the quickest way to the little market on Warm Springs Avenue—the only direct way— was the path that cut through the cemetery. I absolutely believed in ghosts, but I was not so afraid of them that I didn't play in the cemetery some when we first moved into the house on Flume Street. Never at night, of course, but ghosts didn't come out in the daylight.

What I really became frightened of was the crazy old man who worked as a grounds keeper in the cemetery. It wasn't so much fright as terror, and only once in subsequent years have I ever been as frightened of anything as I was of that man. It was when I had to crawl under live machine-gun fire in military basic training.

The first time I encountered him, a fairly old man with long greasy hair and wild eyes, he chased me with a hoe, screaming that he was going to catch me and cut off my head and chop me into little pieces. Although he had a limp, he could run very fast, with a kind of hopping gait. I ran all the way home and told my mother. I don't think she believed me, but she was willing to walk back through the cemetery with me and see what happened. When we went back, nothing happened. There was just an old man mowing the grass, and he ignored us completely. Harmless. After that, nobody believed me, and as long as I went down the path through the cemetery with anybody else, even my brother Jack, who was twelve, the old man paid no attention to us. But when I hurried down the path alone on the way to the market, hoping he would not be there that day, he would chase me with a shovel or hoe or clippers or whatever he was working with, shouting the horrible things he was going to do to me if he caught me. I think there was something about my bright red hair that set him off. He always screamed at me as "you little redheaded bastard!" and none of the other children in the neighborhood complained about his bothering them.

Once, while I was running from him, I fell and broke the bottle of whatever it was I had been sent to the store to get. My story seemed to the rest of the family merely a convenient way to excuse myself from punishment. What they saw when they crossed the cemetery was a gentle old man working at a distance. What I saw was a monster, and a crafty one. He practiced the kind of adult deception I had no defense against since no one would believe me, but why the members of my family would choose to believe I was capable of making up such a horror and not believe the old man was capable of committing it, I don't know. I felt the bitter injustice of it.

It was the whole problem of gratuitous evil—evil that is directed at the helpless and vulnerable and brings no obvious benefit to the evildoer—and many of us are faced with it very young. I don't understand how that kind of evil came into the world. When I read Elie Wiesel's accounts of the Holocaust from the viewpoint of one of its victims, I see that kind of evil disguised as a political agenda, but it's still the same kind of evil.

I have entered the cemetery gate now and am wandering among the headstones almost at random, but with an ultimate goal in mind, a spot near the back not far from the little shed that was used by the gardeners to store their tools and equipment. I am breathing as deeply and as steadily as I can, practicing what little I know about how to prevent a panic attack, and feeling guilty and ridiculous about the whole thing. How can anyone still be afraid after sixty years?

I veer more to the left. I can't put this off forever, but things are getting a little difficult for me now. What if I can't find it? But I know it's in the next-to-the-last row at the back and not far from the little toolshed. That little building, I see now, has been converted into toilets. The sign on this side says MEN. Probably part of the "restoration," although I'm sure the mourners in pioneer days had at best a privy and at worst a clump of sagebrush. I guess there are a lot of things from pioneer days that we really don't want to "restore."

Here I go, ready or not. I know there is nothing to fear in this cemetery, no one to hurt me. Just me and the late afternoon sunshine and the birds and two big brown squirrels chasing each other around the trunk of a walnut tree. What little I ate of my brother's funeral dinner in the Mormon church gymnasium is sitting like a rock in the pit of my stomach. Fear flickers somewhere behind my eyes, almost like pain, flickers and flames and dies out again.

I walk quickly past the converted toolshed and down the next-to-the-last row of graves, looking straight ahead. And there it is. Somehow unexpected and right where I knew it would be. The stone is fairly large but not distinctive. Gray polished granite.

> Frank G. Ramsey
> Apr. 22, 1857—Sept. 6, 1940

Nothing else. It's just another grave in a long row of graves. Somehow, knowing the name is calming to me. I'm no longer frightened, and I'm embarrassed at having been frightened. Then something comes into my mind that makes me almost laugh. It's from *Goldilocks and the Three Bears*, sort of.

Somebody has been sleeping in my grave, and here he is. I mean no disrespect to Mr. Ramsey, who lived to be eighty-three, but it was my grave before it was his, although I now relinquish all claim to it and to the memories that go with it.

It was a late afternoon in early September. I had turned seven at the end of June. Jack and two of his friends were playing "swords" in the graveyard. I had tagged along as usual, knowing the old monster man would not menace me as long as I was with Jack. He and his friends had made their swords (which we pronounced exactly as the word was spelled) from laths whittled to a cutting edge, fitted with fancy crosspieces at the handles and painted with bright metallic colors from the paint found in my father's "paint shop" in the attic of our house on Flume Street. Although not metal, the swords had very sharp points and were formidable weapons.

Usually Jack and his friends played swords in the basement of our house, a fairly large area used for nothing but storage and laundry, where Jack had convinced me, a few months earlier, to drink gasoline out of a bottle. At this age, Jack was still my hero. He was tough. I adored him. I wanted to be like him. I was afraid of him. I did whatever he told me to do. But I was too little to play swords, and since I had no sword, I would run and hide under the stairs.

Each of the boys would take up a position with a sword. "One, two, three," Jack would say, and then turn out the lights. There were no windows. It was totally black. Everyone would begin flailing about in the dark, listening for telltale breathing or sounds of movement. It usually lasted until somebody was hurt badly enough to yell, "I give up!" Then Jack would turn the lights on and assess the damage. No one ever had an eye put out, but blood was often plentiful, and severe bruises were so common as to go unnoticed.

In the fall, Jack and his friends had started playing swords in the cemetery, leaping onto and off of the gravestones in a swashbuckling way inspired by a Three Musketeers movie. That afternoon in early September, Jack's two friends had to go home early, leaving Jack and me in the cemetery with nothing much to do. We found a new grave that had been dug in preparation for a funeral the following day. The neat squares of turf were stacked and the dirt that had been removed was in a big mound covered with fake grass.

We lay on our bellies and looked down into the grave that was so deep it scared me. "Let's pretend you're dead," Jack said. Suddenly he grabbed me by one arm and rolled me into the open grave. I dangled there for a moment, screaming. There was a tearing kind of pain in my shoulder. He let me go and I dropped to the floor of the grave.

I got on my feet as fast as I could and reached up toward him. Something was wrong with my left arm, the same one that had been mangled before and that I had worn in a cast and sling for six months. But I was more afraid than in pain. I reached up toward him and began to jump wildly. I could almost touch his fingers as he lay on his belly and extended his arms down to me. He didn't seem to be reaching down as far as he could.

Then all I could see of him was his head. He gave me one of those shy, winsome grins that was later to be so captivating to girls (although I once heard my father describe it as "a grin like a skunk eating horse manure"), and said, "So long, Tool." "The little tool" was how he normally referred to me. It meant something like "slave," only more degrading. A thing that had no will of its own. A thing that existed only to be used. A thing.

I heard his footsteps as he went away, but I knew he was just fooling. I was sure he was waiting at a little distance to scare me, and in a minute he would come back and get me out. But what if he had really gone away and I called for help and the old monster man heard me? I knew he would kill me if he found me in this hole, probably with a shovel or a rake. I could see the rake as he swung it from above and its teeth sank into my head. The old monster would shovel some of the loose dirt over me, and tomorrow, when they lowered the coffin on top of me, nobody would know I was there. Maybe I wouldn't be quite dead when they lowered the coffin on me. . . .

I started to cry, but I was afraid the monster would hear me. Maybe he was in the little house where they stored the tools. Jack didn't come back. I tried to dig footholds in the sheer wall of the grave, but it was solid clay. My fingers began to bleed, and it was no use. By then my left shoulder was hurting so bad I knew I couldn't climb up the wall, even if I had footholds. I stuck my fist in my mouth to stop the sound of my sobs. I could taste blood and clay on my hand. It was getting dark. The crazy old man was out there somewhere, listening. I knew it. There were some stars straight up, but it was very dark in the grave. I think I heard ghosts. Some kind of bird. Footsteps from somewhere. Was it the monster man? Nothing mattered except that I not make a sound. I sat in the corner of the grave. I had to be very still. I had to be very still.

> *Dear Mr. Ramsey,*
> *I never knew you, but I was in your grave for five hours,*
> *and I have been blessed that I can't remember most of*
> *that time. I hope you are in heaven. I hope none of what I*
> *experienced in that grave remained to disturb you when*
> *you were lowered into it with much more ceremony than*
> *I was. May you rest in peace. May my only brother, who*
> *was buried today, rest in peace. May we all have peace*

at last. May I be granted the ability to forgive, to forgive
without bitterness, to forgive with love and understand-
ing, to forgive completely and forever.

I don't know exactly what went on at home with Red and Hazel while I was missing. Perhaps they were both drunk. Her serious drinking had begun only recently but was getting worse every day. When it started to get dark, Red would have searched the neighborhood and perhaps talked to some of the neighbors. I wasn't the kind of child who would run away. They probably questioned Jack, and he probably lied for fear of getting in trouble. They might have discussed calling the police, but they didn't call them. In our family the police were the enemy. My father's past as a bootlegger had taught him to distrust the police, and Jack had already gotten into such serious trouble that he had been brought home one evening in a police car and had a record as a juvenile delinquent, a humiliation Hazel could barely endure. That hadn't been the first time the police had come to our house, and it wouldn't be the last. No, the police were out of the question.

I don't know if Jack finally broke down as the pressure mounted, or if Red simply thought of searching the cemetery and found me. No one ever told me because no one would ever discuss it with me. I saw a light shining down into my eyes, blinding me. I thought the crazy old man had found me and it was the end. Then I heard my father's voice, and the voice of someone with him, but I couldn't answer. I remember someone putting a ladder down into the grave and my father carrying me out.

My sister said that I did not speak until the next day, that I made whimpering sounds like a puppy, but that I was mostly very still and cold, very cold. She put me in her bed, my beautiful sixteen-year-old sister Betty, and got in bed with me and held me in her arms all night. Finally I slept. She said I woke in the morning in terror, fighting my way up and shouting, "The monster, the monster!" She soothed me and held me, not understanding what I meant, and she said, "Yes, Jack is a monster. He gets away with everything. They never punish him. I hate him for what he did to you. I hate him."

There is a green wooden bench just down the path from Mr. Ramsey's tombstone, and suddenly I feel the need to sit down. It was a corny, melodramatic little scene—me standing with my head bowed, praying in front of the grave of a man I had never seen, but I don't care. It was the prayer I should have prayed beside my brother's grave before they lowered him into it. But I couldn't. I was so aware of that empty space under the coffin that I couldn't think about anything else. Now I realize it was myself I needed to pray for.

In our immediate family, there was an amnesia curtain. We survived by forgetting. I have often heard my mother say, when one or the other of us recounted some escapade from the past, "Why, that never happened. You made that up. You have such a vivid imagination." This in spite of the fact that there were several eyewitnesses to the event. Her ability to erase or revise the past was limitless, and it was probably what kept her alive and sane in spite of everything. She lived to be ninety-two, although her mind was a little frayed around the edges during the last few years.

A few months after my unwilling occupation of Mr. Ramsey's grave, we moved away from the house on Flume Street and its attendant sorrows. The amnesia curtain was drawn over the Pioneer Cemetery and everything associated with it. In Jack's case, the amnesia curtain was much more profound than I'd realized until about twelve years ago.

On one of our infrequent trips to Boise, my wife, Lois, and I were in Jack's spacious family room with its great vaulted ceiling and comfortable "rustic" furniture, including a shotgun mounted over the fireplace, one of Jack's extensive collection. Jack's wife's name is Lillian, and I have always been fond of her, since I was thirteen and she was the most gorgeous "older woman" of eighteen I had ever seen. She was always kind to me.

I was lying on the floor, petting one of Jack and Lillian's magnificent German shepherds. Jack had a funny story to tell us. He was bursting with it.

"I ran into a contractor last week. Fellow I've known all my life but haven't seen in years. He asked me what had become of my little redheaded brother. He was one of the gang I ran with when we lived on Flume Street. He told me the damndest story about you."

Suddenly the German shepherd was on his feet, barking ferociously at me, baring his teeth a few inches from my face. I was astonished. Dogs always love me, and he and I had been lying on the floor while I petted him for at least ten minutes before this outburst.

"Get up! Get up!" Jack shouted. "He doesn't like people to be on the floor. He thinks they're hurt and wants to get them up."

I got up and sat on the couch, a little shaken, but I didn't buy Jack's explanation for the dog's sudden outburst. The dog was reacting to my sudden fear at the mention of Flume Street and some story about me. I was probably giving off all kinds of signals only the dog's sensitive nose could detect.

"Anyway," Jack continued when things had calmed down and he had put the dog outside, "it's the damndest story I ever heard. I 'bout busted a gut laughing. This guy said he'd been telling the story for years, but I don't remember it happening. About the time you peed in the fudge."

So it wasn't the story I was afraid of at all, but another one, and Jack retold it, at least as much as his friend had told him, although he left out a good deal. It had happened during the winter before my encounter with Mr. Ramsey's grave. The weather was cold and snowy, and there was no water in the flume that cut at an angle immediately behind our house, eliminating any possibility of a backyard. On the other side of the flume was a big vacant field that had been used as a dumping ground for loads of unwanted dirt and broken pieces of concrete. There were mounds of debris eight or ten feet high, with little valleys between them. In one of the valleys Jack and his friends had found an abandoned privy lying on its side. The roof and seat were gone, and what had been the bottom was now a wall of dirt. With a few improvements, it made a wonderful long, narrow clubhouse.

Although I wasn't officially a member of Jack's gang—just a little-brother tagalong—I was permitted to help with the improvements. We shoveled enough dirt off the two adjoining mounds to cover and hide the privy, also providing insulation. Then we built a crude bench along one wall and hung a tarp over the exposed end where the roof had been, which became the entrance. Somehow Jack and his friends dragged an old trash-burner stove—the kind with two lids that usually sat beside the larger cooking stove—into the clubhouse and set it up. Since the two lids were missing, the smoke from the stove came directly into the clubhouse, so the boys installed a stovepipe above the stove to vent the smoke outside, or at least some of it.

Other than the stovepipe protruding a few inches above a mound of dirt, and the old tarp like the disguised entrance into a cave, the clubhouse was totally hidden, a wonderful place to smoke stolen cigarettes, try stolen booze, tell dirty stories, look at dirty pictures, plan vast enterprises, tell lies, engage in rituals, change the password each week, and decide who was and was not currently a member of the club. I was too young to be considered, but since I was Jack's little brother, my presence was tolerated. It was the perfect boys' hideaway. It was, as I realize now, an educational institution.

One cold night, the boys decided to make fudge. My job was to stir. I stirred and stirred. It began to look like the kind of fudge we were going to have to eat with spoons, but that didn't matter. It smelled so good. Finally, by some pseudo-democratic process understood only by gangs of boys, it was decided that the fudge was done and ready to eat.

"Go home now!" Jack told me. I was not really a member of the gang and shouldn't get any of their fudge. I objected strenuously. After all, I had stirred and stirred. I was the only one who had stood over that smoky fire and stirred the fudge.

"That's what tools are for," Jack said, and cuffed me about a little. The other boys had seen this kind of thing before, and none of them would oppose Jack, no matter how they felt. He was their leader, the toughest and most daring of the group.

I stumbled out into the night air, crying a little, but more from the injustice of it than from the cuffing. I was used to being knocked around, but to be sent away just when the fudge was ready to eat and it smelled so good and I had stirred until my arms ached—that was too much for me to take.

The night was dark and crisp, but the sky was full of stars. I could see the stovepipe above the mound of dirt and a little smoke coming out of it, and I knew the pan of fudge was directly below. At first I thought about throwing dirt down the stovepipe and ruining the fudge. Then I thought of something better. So I peed down the stovepipe and ran like hell.

I could hear Jack bellowing as he came through the canvas opening, but I had a good lead and was a fast runner. Then I tripped on something in the dark and fell, but I could still have made it home if it hadn't been for the flume. The flume was about seven feet deep and shaped like a narrow V with a flat bottom. The sides were concrete and very steep. In the summer it was filled with swift-running water for irrigation, but in the winter it was empty. When empty it had once been used by one of Betty's boyfriends to approach the house when she was "grounded." She could open her bedroom window, not more than four feet from the flume, and whisper to her boyfriend who was hiding in the flume.

Negotiating the steep sides of the flume in the dark, I had to slow down, and Jack caught me as I was climbing the far side and dragged me back down into the bottom. Usually Jack tried to hit me where it wouldn't show. He had gotten into trouble with our mother over black eyes and facial bruises. She did not approve of his beating up on me, but she was also concerned about what the neighbors would think, and especially that someone might assume that Red had inflicted the damage. So Jack had learned to be careful. But this night he was so angry he lost all control. I had humiliated him in front of his friends. I had done the one thing he couldn't bear—I had outsmarted him. It was difficult to see in the dark anyway, so he just let me have it with his fists wherever he could, and when he was through and I was trying to crawl away, he kicked me a few times for good measure.

That particular beating, since its marks were so obvious, including bruises and contusions on my face, had curious and long-lasting repercussions. My Uncle Wig and Aunt Marie came to visit soon afterward. Wig was my mother's slightly younger brother. I didn't know Uncle Wig very well, but I loved Aunt 'Ree dearly. She had taken care of us a year earlier when Hazel was in the hospital. She had found my vocabulary so shocking for a five-year-old that she had washed my mouth out with red Lifebuoy soap. I can still taste it, but I loved her anyway. (It was about this same time that I was sent home from the first grade for calling the teacher, whom I hated, "a goddamned sunamidge." I had no idea what the expression meant, but I knew when to apply it and had heard Red and Jack use it many times.) Marie was one of fifteen children born to a miner and his wife in northern Idaho, and somehow she became a saint. I don't think she ever knew how important she was to me.

Wig and Marie had seen me in bad shape before, including the time my left arm was crushed in the wringer of the washing machine, but that was the result of my mother's carelessness, and Jack had nothing to do with it. Seeing me in such a condition this time, however, triggered them to make their move, and it was a well-meaning disaster that alienated them from my parents for years and made it impossible for them to help me further.

They had been married quite a few years and had no children, although they wanted children. They seriously proposed that my parents give me up and allow them to adopt me legally. I was sitting on a tricycle on the front sidewalk while this took place, and I heard the uproar in the house, but I didn't know what caused it. Mostly my father shouting, and Uncle Wig shouting back. Wig and Marie came out the front door quickly, said good-bye to me in a hurry, and left. Red shouted a lot, got drunk, and stayed drunk for three days. When he sobered up, he blamed me for letting Wig and Marie see me in my beat-up condition.

I am sure Wig and Marie knew where the abuse was coming from, but they blamed Red and Hazel for being so ineffectual as to allow it to go on. Thinking back on the whole thing, it occurs to me that my grandmother Charlotte might have been involved in the attempt to take me away from my parents, although always discreetly and behind the scenes so as not to offend her only daughter. Many years later, when Grandma Charlotte and I were larking about and we wound up in an old-time fountain having a milk shake, she said to me, "I never criticized your parents, but it was wrong to let one child run over the other one. Terrible wrong. I tried to stay out of it because of the way your father felt about me, and your mother resented me too. But it was hard, hard. All I could do was try to keep you with me on the ranch as much as I could. Oh, we had good times on the ranch, didn't we?"

Jack considered the story his friend had told him about my peeing in the fudge wildly funny, though he could not remember the actual event.

"But don't you remember any of it, Jack?" I asked.

He looked a little confused and troubled, and shook his head slowly. "To tell you the truth, Dick, I don't remember you as a child at all."

There it was. The amnesia curtain. Complete blackout, and it was genuine. For a moment I was shocked. This man who was the most important fact of my childhood, who probably had more of a negative effect on me than any other human, whom I adored and feared, who beat me brutally and taught me never to trust, never to love— this man had no recollection of me as a child at all.

Then, after the shock, I began to laugh. Nobody in the room except possibly my wife could appreciate the hilarious irony of it. I laughed and laughed. I laughed until I cried. When your bratty little brother pees in the fudge, it does make a very funny story when told many years later.

After a while I got control of myself. The dog and I reestablished our friendship, and I realized that Jack could not remember me as a child because he could not bear to remember me as a child, and it wasn't merely because of the things he had done to me; it was also because of the things that had been done to him. I realized all this in my head, but it didn't help much.

HORSE THIEVES

I leave the Pioneer Cemetery feeling much better than I did when I arrived. There's my rental car where I parked it on East Bannock Street. I think the Sheltons used to live on East Bannock, but it must have been before I was born. *Betty and Jack would know*, I think, and then remember that Betty and Jack are both dead. I'm the only one left, and I've come back to the town I grew up in and the landscape that was once my own. How strange and foreign it is now—or is it I who have grown strange and foreign? Still chasing ghosts.

I'm driving down Broadway toward the freeway and my motel. I'll be going past the big old house in south Boise where Betty and her brood lived, and where she had her nursery school next door for so many years. How hard she worked and how uncomplaining she was. She was the best of the three of us, fiercely private and proud. I was too far away to help her when she needed help, but she wouldn't have asked for it no matter what. In some ways she was the most like Red of any of us. "Never let them see you sweat," he always said, and she didn't.

When I asked her about what Red said concerning his family, that they were all a bunch of horse thieves and the less I knew about them the better off I would be, she was thoughtful and chewed her lower lip the way she had a habit of doing when she was thinking hard.

"Well," she said, "there is that period in Colorado we don't know much of anything about. I've been told that Uncle Minnis was the first to go out there, that he was hired as a wrangler on a huge ranch somewhere near Meeker. The rest of them followed him. Nobody talks about this period much. Maybe some of the Shelton boys got into a little trouble. Next thing you know, they're in Idaho. The whole family."

I found the notion of my sweet, bespectacled, hen-pecked, pot-bellied old Uncle Minnis as a horse thief or desperado so bizarre

that it made me laugh. Betty laughed too. Whenever she and I got together over the years, we made each other laugh. Suddenly I realized
that nearly all the laughter I remember as a child had its source in this
woman who, even as a girl, had hidden her troubles behind a screen
of zany slapstick humor. I like people who laugh a lot. My wife, Lois,
laughed more than anybody I know, and often at me, of course. She
had a kind of Texas cackle that was irresistible. I found myself doing
and saying dumb things just to get to hear her laugh.

During one of my recent ghost-chasing trips I had found some
horse thieves, but they were on the wrong side of the family and related only by marriage, so I guess they weren't the ones my father was
referring to. I was tracking my grandma Charlotte on her first trip
from Kansas to Idaho. She had told me the story many years earlier.

Of Josie's three daughters, Charlotte and her two sisters, the
youngest was Berenice, and she was said to be the beauty of the family. I remember a large tinted portrait of the three young women.
When the photograph was taken, they must have ranged in age
from about seventeen to twenty-one. They are magnificent-looking
women in the Gibson Girl style, their hair piled on top of their heads,
long slender necks, and delicate features. They remind one of swans.
Berenice is, indeed, the most beautiful, but Charlotte is amazing.

Berenice married a cowboy from northern Idaho who had evidently arrived in Kansas on a cattle drive. Later, Charlotte was to
marry a Kansas cowboy. I guess the Adams girls had a thing for cowboys—or maybe all the girls in Kansas at one time had a thing for cowboys, and there were plenty of cowboys around. Anyway, Berenice
didn't know that her new husband and his entire family, a backwoods
mountain clan, made their living mostly by stealing horses on one
side of the Snake River, swimming them across the river in what is
now called Hells Canyon, and selling them on the other side. It was
a type of interstate commerce, since the Snake River at that point
forms the border between Oregon and Idaho. When I decided to
check on the story, I was truly glad that they had carried on this family business in Hells Canyon because I had never been there and had
always wanted to see the place.

Although Hells Canyon is deeper than Grand Canyon and one of America's foremost scenic wonders, capitalized on and exploited by river-runner companies, outfitters, guides, and you name it, the canyon itself is hard to get to. That's probably the only blessing it has left. Since the comparison with Grand Canyon is so often made, I slipped into the expectation that it would look like Grand Canyon, but it doesn't. It doesn't look like anywhere else I have ever seen. I saw two different stretches of the canyon, and they were so different from one another that it's hard to realize they are stretches of the same river.

Years ago, in a poem, I described the Colorado River as the "saddest of all the poor damned rivers of the West." I was wrong. I didn't know much about the Snake River then, although I had been raised within a few miles of it. It was the forgotten river. It is still the forgotten river, dammed and defiled, a slave to the farmers of Idaho and a toy of the Idaho Power Company. It is the outstanding victim of greed, and it represents the worst we have been able to do to the rivers of the West. Although the mania for dam building seems to have waned, the river is still dammed. And dammed, and damned.

There are three dams in Hells Canyon that function as a unit and are controlled from a central point. The section of the canyon in which they were built is deep, narrow, and foreboding, with steep black basaltic walls. I was reminded of Baron F.W. von Egloffstein's highly exaggerated and terrifying paintings of Grand Canyon. Egloffstein produced the first painting of the Grand Canyon, and it has been called by Wallace Stegner "a picture of the artist's dismay." It could be a painting of Hells Canyon, where the dams are built, rather than Grand Canyon, which is open and sun-drenched. When I first saw this section of Hells Canyon, I, too, felt dismay.

I saw no humans at any of the dams. They are supposed to be controlled from a central point by somebody, but one has the feeling they are controlling themselves and have evolved far beyond the needs or wishes of humans. Their enormous silent presence in the black and frightening canyon is eerie. I had the feeling I was inside some huge machine run by a robot. Nothing is on a human scale. And over it all, the almost vertical black walls of the canyon lean menacingly, reflected in the dark water. Downstream from the three dams, the river narrows and becomes a series of frothing white-water rapids.

The river runs north through Hells Canyon, and the other stretch of it I saw was a few miles farther north, or downstream, at Pittsburgh Landing. Getting over the Seven Devils Mountains from Highway 95 near the hamlet of White Bird to the river is a seventeen-mile adventure on an unpaved narrow road that twists up the east side of the mountains and plunges down the west side in a series of switchbacks that are not for the faint of heart.

That night, when I checked into the Elkhorn Lodge in Grangeville and the young manager found out I had negotiated that road in a minivan without four-wheel drive, he treated me with marked respect. He told me a hair-raising story about taking a load of horses in a trailer over the same road. At one of the switchbacks the grade was so steep that the weight of the trailer pulled his truck backward off the road.

The view from the summit makes the white-knuckle drive worthwhile. The mountains, tawny and streaked with green, sweep up from the river steeply and dramatically, but there are no cliffs, no box canyons to produce gloom or claustrophobia. From the viewpoint at the summit, the river looks small and turtle green. It is smooth through this stretch.

There isn't much to Pittsburgh Landing. I was there in late May, and it was very hot. On a flat area a little above the river was a bleak campground with concrete slabs for trailers, no shade, and nobody in it. At the river's edge there was a ramp for putting boats into the river, two official-looking trailers, and two huge round tanks. A generator was making an enormous racket. A teenage boy and girl were wading at the edge of the river. She was in a bathing suit; he was in his underpants. Their sunburns were already starting to show.

In front of one of the trailers I found a man sitting in a pickup with the motor running. On the truck it said IDAHO FISH AND GAME DEPT.

"Could you tell me what those big tanks are for?" I shouted over the noise of the generator.

"Salmon," he shouted back. "Thousands of young salmon in there. We're getting them acclimated."

"Acclimated to a tank?"

"No, acclimated to swift running water so they'll survive when we turn them loose in the river."

I was too shocked to think to ask him where the salmon had been hatched and how they got to Pittsburgh Landing in the first place. I just stood there with my mouth open while the man revved up his truck and drove away.

Then I started to calculate. They would be released here, below the three dams in Hells Canyon. They would swim down the Snake and then the Columbia into the Pacific, and then, when it was time to spawn, return here to Pittsburgh Landing. Lots of luck, I thought.

There are four more dams downstream on the Snake and a whole series of enormous dams on the Columbia. Most of the salmon would be sucked into huge turbines and destroyed. A lucky few would be trucked around some of the dams. The number that survived to return here would be minuscule, if any at all made it. For this they were being "acclimated"? How were they going to get acclimated to the trucks and the turbines, the polluted water that didn't have enough oxygen, the whole shebang, as my father used to say. If any of them make it back here to spawn, they should be put in a museum, I thought.

Later, with the aid of a map, I tried to count the number of dams on the Snake River. I came up with twenty-four, which is probably not all of them. The Snake is no longer a river. Salmon are no longer fish in a river. They are ersatz creatures hatched in a hatchery, acclimated to swift running water in huge tanks, trucked around dams, and usually destroyed in turbines designed to produce electricity.

Thinking about all this, I was not a happy camper as I started back up the dusty switchbacks over the Seven Devils Mountains. I was hot and confused and bitter. It got cooler as I climbed up away from the river. I stopped at the viewpoint to get one last look at the river and the incredible panorama below. A white pickup was parked there, and below the brow of the hill, I could see a man and a little girl. I had barely gotten out of the car when a small white dog—a miniature spitz—came racing across the parking area and almost leaped into my arms. She danced around, so happy to see me that I sat down to pet her and let her lick my face. She was an exquisite little dog—happy, well cared for, and delightful.

The man and girl—only it wasn't a girl; it was a diminutive woman under a huge straw hat—came over the brow of the hill toward me, apologizing for the dog's behavior.

"Oh no," I said. "I love it. She's a sweetie."

The man grinned with relief and pride. "That's what we named her. *Sweetie.* It's silly, but it fit so well." He was very handsome—small boned, well built, and he carried a pistol in a holster on his hip. There was something remarkably compact and neat about him. His equally attractive, doll-like wife barely came up to his shoulder, though he was not tall.

If you want to meet people, travel with a dog. I guess Steinbeck and Charley proved that. With Sweetie as the icebreaker, we were talking to each other like old friends in a few minutes. Of course I had to tell them about my two big white dogs, Nikki (the nice) German shepherd and Jefe (the naughty) Great Pyrenees.

The man told me they were ranchers. Their ranch was just off Highway 95 a little south of where I had turned to come over the mountains. They had come to the viewpoint to have a picnic and look at the view that went on forever.

"My grandmother," he said, gesturing to the panorama below, "was born in a house just on the other side of the river and lived there all her life. I spent a lot of my childhood there. You can almost see it from here, in one of those valleys."

That prompted me to tell them the story of my grandmother's unfortunate sister, Berenice, who had disappeared somewhere in these hills—the story that had served as an excuse for me to come there. My grandmother Charlotte, who was then teaching school in a little town in Kansas, somehow received word that her younger sister who had married the Idaho cowboy had died in childbirth somewhere near a hamlet called White Bird, Idaho. The child, she was told, had lived. A baby girl. No details. Just that.

That wasn't enough for Charlotte, who not only taught school but also played the fiddle. She was slightly tall as compared to most young ladies of her day, more direct than most of them, and she had a smile that could give anybody the courage to try one more time. She got on a train for Idaho and then came by stage to the hamlet of White Bird, where she rented a horse and buggy and set out in search of her sister's grave and her sister's child. She never found either of them. She inquired at every remote ranch and cabin in the area, and although many of the people she talked to knew of her sister's husband's family, no one knew where they had gone. She found their last encampment, and it showed signs they had left in haste, but no sign of a grave. She felt there had been something peculiar about her sister's death, something the family wanted to hide. It might have been that Berenice had not been provided with medical attention when she needed it, or it might have been something more sinister. Charlotte would never know. After weeks of searching, she returned to Kansas, sick at heart for her lost sister and her lost sister's child.

While I told the story, the handsome rancher and his wife kept looking at one another knowingly. Finally, he said, grinning, "They're still here. It's a family that's been operating in this area since my grandmother could remember. She knew them, and I'll bet she met your grandmother too. They steal horses on one side of the river and sell them on the other. Same family all these years. Once in a while some of them get caught, but the rest of the family just carries on. They never stay in one place too long."

"It sounds like some kind of horse-thief Mafia," I said.

"It is, and they have lots of relatives and connections by marriage living in these hills. When the sheriff starts asking questions, nobody knows anything."

"Do you really think our grandmothers might have met?"

"Absolutely. If your grandmother came to White Bird looking for her sister and that family, they would have sent her straight to my grandmother. My grandmother knew everything that went on in this area."

"You mean you think my grandmother took a horse and buggy down that road?"

"She had to, but there was a ferry across the river down there in those days."

"Well, that's reassuring. Otherwise I suppose she could have just unhitched the horse, tucked up her skirts, got on, and swum it across."

"The way you describe your grandmother," the rancher's wife said, "I don't doubt that she could have."

Looking back down that awful road I had just driven up, I got a whole new perspective on my grandma Charlotte. *Would I have the guts to take a horse and buggy down that road?* I thought, but I refused to answer on the grounds that it might incriminate me.

As I was getting ready to leave, finding it difficult to say good-bye to Sweetie and these charming people, I had to ask one more question: "Is it because of the horse thieves you wear that gun?"

The rancher laughed. "This little pop gun? Why, this little gun is just practically a toy. I carry it to shoot rattlesnakes."

"Are there many rattlesnakes around here?"

"Yes, these hills are just full of 'em."

After we shook hands and I got back in the car, I thought, *Yes, I'll bet these hills are full of dangerous snakes and some of them ride stolen horses, and somewhere around here in an unmarked grave, one of Josie's daughters, the beautiful Berenice Adams, is buried. Another ghost I'll never find.*

THE RANCH

As I turn off Broadway onto Interstate 84, I don't want to think about any more graves today. Too many already. My exit will be coming up in just a couple of miles, then my motel, a shower, and bed. I think I'll just skip supper. I'm exhausted. As Red would have said, "I feel like I've been rode hard and put away wet."

Damn! I shouldn't have thought of that. When one of Red's sayings pops into my head, dozens of others come trooping behind. It's like a broken record I can't shut off, a recitation of corny, redneck, often off-color and sexist expressions. I try desperately to think of something else, but they won't let me.

> It's hotter than a festered tit.
> It's colder than a well digger's ass.
> It's so nice out tonight, I think I'll leave it out.
> I know her. We used to go up to her house and eat chicken—shit, I know her.
> She was only a horseman's daughter, but all the horsemen knew her.
> I can drink anything that's not too thick, and I'll eat that with a spoon.
> Going to get drunk again tonight. God, how I dread it.

I knew my father was considered a funny man, but I didn't appreciate most of his humor until I was older. Now his sayings haunt me. My wife, Lois, whom he adored, and several of my cousins felt that he was charming at all times, drunk or sober. I guess we all love the people who make us laugh. I don't think many people respected Red, and some must have considered him a drunken clown, but many people loved him.

He could puncture balloons of self-importance quicker than anybody I knew. The first time I ever flew on an airplane was one of those times. I was home from college for the summer and had a job that required me to commute by plane to Oregon and come back to Boise on weekends. I was feeling terribly self-important. Red got up early, fixed my breakfast, and drove me to the airport. As I was standing in line to board the plane, he yelled, "Thanks for the beer, and write when you get work!" Then he ducked out of the airport, leaving me humiliated. *Thanks for the beer, and write when you get work* has become a family mantra passed down through three generations now. Translated, it means *Don't get too big for your britches.*

The recording of my father's sayings has played itself out in my head for the time being, but I've missed my freeway exit. Damn! My motel speeds past on the left, then the airport. So here I am, driving down the freeway away from my motel, tired to the point of collapse, and I don't seem to have sense enough to get off the freeway and go back. *My only brother is dead*, I keep thinking. *Lois and I did everything we could for him, but he was a hard man to love.*

There's something about the light at this time of day in late June in the Boise Valley, one of those long, lingering summer evenings in the Northwest when it doesn't get dark until almost ten o'clock. There's not too much traffic. The rush hour is over, but the sun still has a long way to go to get to the horizon. The slanted sunlight is positively aching, filling the valley with a soft, amber brilliance. It must have something to do with the way the Boise Valley runs a little northwest by southeast and catches the light on late summer afternoons, with the tawny hills to the north and the mesas and desert to the south. The light is concentrated, palpable. I remember it from my childhood. Somehow, like those few salmon that make it back, I can tell this is where I was born. I was imprinted with this heartbreaking light, with this place where the mountains reach down tentatively into the enormous desert of the Snake River Plain.

To the north and east, the foothills rise in voluptuous curves toward a thin outline of something darker on the horizon, something hardly noticeable but a harbinger of a total change in landscape just beyond. It's the beginning of heavy timber—pine, spruce, and fir—at the crest of the hills. When I was a child, it was one of the two edges of my universe. To the south was a great desert, and to the north a dark line where the forest began. I had never been beyond either. Since then I have learned what lies beyond that first line of trees. Miles and miles of mountains, some of the most magnificent, most heavily forested, and least inhabited mountains in the world. First the Boise Mountains, then the Sawtooths and the Sawtooth Wilderness, what may be the heart of Idaho—but perhaps *heart* is the wrong term for such ruthless and unforgiving country.

Below me now, as I continue to drive west and my motel disappears like a mirage on the Sahara, is Boise and the river valley it was originally built in, although it has grown to cover the mesas to the southwest and in recent years has crawled up the sides of the foothills to the northeast. "The city of trees," it is often called, an accurate but redundant phrase since *Boise* is a later version of the original name given to it by French trappers—*les bois*, the woods, the trees.

Seen from the first "bench," or mesa, the old part of Boise in the river bottom below is hidden by trees, and in summer it looks almost as if one could step out onto a green carpet, the tops of a sea of trees. Emerging from the mountains as a narrow canyon, the valley quickly widens just where Boise begins, and it becomes expansive and fertile, with the Boise River winding through it, lined with cottonwoods and willows. In early spring, that ribbon of trees will be the palest, most delicate green, and in the fall, a twisting pathway of gold.

Most of the hamlets strung along the length of the valley—Meridian, Eagle, Star, Middleton—have either been swallowed up by rapidly growing Boise, or have turned into bedroom communities and been gentrified almost beyond recognition. Grandma Charlotte and her third husband, Sherman Beech, whom she married in 1928 when all her children were grown, owned a farm about two miles west of Star, a farm that everybody in the family called "the ranch." I spent enough time growing up there that when I went far away to college and was, during my freshman year, desperately homesick for the first time in my life, it was not my home in Boise—my parents and Betty and Jack—that I was homesick for, it was the ranch. I missed everything about it, every sight, smell, and sound, as waves of home-sickness swept over me like nausea.

I missed waking up on early summer mornings on the sleeping porch that ran across the front of the house, hearing roosters crowing and the meadowlark's liquid arpeggio, smelling coffee and bacon and eggs coming from my grandmother's clean kitchen, with its huge black-and-silver woodburning cookstove with a plate warmer on top and the big oven below and room underneath to keep a box of or-phaned piglets warm.

Her kitchen cabinets were painted lavender, and in the breakfast room that had once been the back porch but had been closed in with banks of windows running along two sides, her curtains were fields of blue flowers often swaying in the breeze. In that room she served breakfasts that were, as they tell me I once said when very young, "worth getting up for." Breakfast started with juice, cereal with cream, coffee, and fruit—either half a grapefruit or pears or peaches she had canned. I was a skinny kid, and Grandma Charlotte was always try-ing to fatten me up. So I got to drink coffee like the grown-ups, but it was really coffee-flavored cream, straight from the cows outside in the barn, each one with a name and stall assigned to it.

Then, with the preliminaries over, the meal began to get serious. She had a little grill she set on the table with a bowl of melted butter and a brush. She swabbed both sides of a thick slice of homemade bread with butter, slapped it on the grill, closed the lid for a couple of minutes, and brought out toast like no toast has ever been or will be ever again. There were at least two, usually three, kinds of jam on the table. She had grown the strawberries or blackberries or raspberries she made the jam with. The toast was served with bacon or sausage and eggs—lots of eggs—that had been gathered the afternoon before from the hen-house, or from various nests in the barn that certain independent hens preferred. The eggs were cooked sunny-side up, and Sherman ate four each morning. Grandma ate two. I usually ate two, but it depended on whether or not we had sausage. I loved the homemade sausage.

By the time we ate that breakfast, Sherman had milked thirty cows by hand and Grandma had milked one because Old Rosie, the Holstein with a broken horn, wouldn't let anybody else milk her without a fight. Grandma ran the milk through the separator and into big milk cans that Sherman or I or whichever of the grandsons happened to be there loaded onto the two-wheeled cart and pulled down the long lane to the highway to be picked up by the milk truck.

The cats sat along the wall of the milking barn in a row, and we would shoot streams of milk directly from the cow's teat into their open mouths. Once, for no reason anybody could figure out, one of the cats leaped onto the back of the cow Sherman happened to be milking and dug in. The cow went crazy, kicking the milk bucket in one direction and the milk stool in the other. Sherman managed to get out of the way, but that cat was not welcome at milking time thereafter and had to settle for catching mice in the barn, which is what the cats were kept for.

One cat raised a brood of chickens after a hen laid her eggs in a manger in the horse barn where a female cat spent much of her time sleeping. When the eggs hatched, the chicks identified with the cat and followed her everywhere. She was demoralized and tried all kinds of tricks to get rid of them, but each time she would come down from a roof or a tree, there they were, waiting for her and welcoming her back with their loud peeping.

Everyone of my age, I would guess, has that one most powerful memory of something from their childhood that has been lost to technology and can never be reclaimed. For me, it's the milking barn early on a cold morning before the use of milking machines. The cows, side by side, each in her regular place and chewing on the hay in the trough before her, provide enough heat to make the barn comfortable. There is a little green plastic radio off somewhere, creating a soft undertone of country music or someone droning on with the current price of corn or hogs. One sits on a stool that can be tilted at an angle, places the bucket between one's knees, leans one's head against the side of the ample belly of the cow, and goes at it, choosing two teats first and squeezing each of them with a downward motion and rhythm: left, right, left, right. The sound of the milk going into the bucket is regular and hypnotic. The cows chew with contentment as they are being relieved of their heavy load. The light from a few bulbs strung the length of the barn is dim. The cats are lined up on the other side of the manure trough, waiting and smelling the warm milk.

Nearly all I knew of security as a child and much of what I knew of comfort, kindness, and serenity came from that farm and those two good, wise people who farmed it. It was a refuge, a sanctuary from troubles at home in Boise as Red's alcoholism became more pronounced, Hazel began to drink heavily, and the beatings she endured became more frequent and severe. *And a refuge from Jack.* I try to put that thought out of my mind, today of all days, but I can't.

At first Jack and I were allowed to stay at the ranch together. I think that ended about the time Grandma happened upon us one afternoon in the granary when Jack thought she was in the house. He loved whips, and he had made a primitive quirt by attaching several rawhide lashes about three feet long to a short stick. He had me down in the granary and was lashing my bare back when Grandma found us. I had seen her show displeasure before, always with tight lips and a slight shaking of the head, but I had never dreamed what fury she was capable of. She was a strong, powerful woman, although she must have been sixty at the time. With one quick move she had Jack down in the wheat of the granary, pinned with her knee. Then she beat him with his own whip, beat him until he cried out in pain—Jack, who had been taught by his father never to show pain, never to flinch or cry.

Or it might have been the episode with the electric fence that caused Charlotte and Sherman to decide that Jack and I should not be at the ranch at the same time, although Jack was a good worker. He was always willing to help with the chores, and by the time he was twelve, he could help with the haying, feed the horses, irrigate some of the fields, and do some of the milking. He was strong, wiry, and willing to work. Because he helped with the chores, he knew all about the electric fences that kept the cows in the pastures. Unfortunately, I didn't.

The story is soon told. Jack simply took me out into a distant pasture that was being irrigated, made sure I was standing in several inches of water, and said, "I want you to take hold of this wire for me, and hang on tight."

Why did I do it? Stupidity, I suppose. Or some kind of trusting innocence. The same reason that I drank the gasoline in the basement. I must have been a fool, the fool Jack often said I was. I was very young, but I seemed to be incapable of learning from past experiences as far as Jack was concerned. This stunt could have been fatal. Jack ran almost a half mile to the henhouse to shut off the "juice" while I stood with the voltage passing through my body, unable to let go of the wire. As a result, I will have nothing to do with electrical wiring. I have never replaced an electrical wall outlet or the cord on a lamp, although I know these are simple tasks. I will replace a light bulb, but beyond that, I will have nothing to do with electricity.

Jack couldn't seem to see the difference between the episode with the electric fence and the time he got the chickens drunk by feeding them pieces of bread soaked in whiskey, but Grandma and Sherman must have recognized that it could have killed me. For whatever reason, Grandma Charlotte ultimately laid down the law. Jack was not to be at the ranch when I was. Jack shrugged and said he didn't care, but for me it meant months of freedom and happiness in the place I loved beyond all others. In spite of his beatings and the danger he often placed me in, Jack was protective of me in some ways. I think he was confused and lacked the intellectual capacity to handle, at such a young age, the mixed signals he was getting. Much of his confusion revolved around a father he felt great loyalty for but did not admire or approve of. Red expected Jack to lie for him, to cover for him, and in later years, to fight for him. That sense of loyalty and support created huge problems after Jack became a Mormon convert and successful paint contractor and hired his alcoholic father to work for him. That arrangement was a recipe for disaster, but it had its roots in Jack's childhood and adolescence.

When Jack was thirteen, our father came home very drunk one night with a drunken buddy, and the buddy held Hazel from behind while Red beat her horribly and left her bleeding and semiconscious on the dining room floor. I was seven. I knew exactly where my loyalties lay, and Red had indicated to me, directly and indirectly, that he cared little for me. I was knocked down quickly, but with a baseball bat in my hands after landing one good blow on my father's deserving shin. Jack, however, was old enough to suffer from divided loyalties and the terrible confusion about trying to become a man and the things men do. Red had favored him, trained him, cultivated him, and demanded his loyalty. When our father and his buddy left to go back to the bar they had come from, Jack went with them. As I lay on the linoleum floor beside my moaning mother and watched them leave, it was Jack I hated more than I hated Red. I think part of Jack died that night. I know part of me died when I saw him leave.

—

Now I know where I am going. I've just been fooling myself about missing my exit on the freeway and going to my motel to collapse. I'm going back to the ranch. It's only about twenty miles from here, toward the west. On a couple of previous visits to Boise, while Hazel was still alive, I rode my bicycle out there and saw it. It was in terrible condition—almost totally destroyed—but I feel the need to see it again. Maybe I'm just rubbing salt in a wound, or maybe I'm hoping that somebody has rescued it.

Going west, as I am, was always called "going down the valley," and suddenly an old hymn I knew as an adolescent comes back to me. It has to be the most lugubrious and monotonous song in the world, usually reserved for funerals.

> We are going down the valley one by one,
> With our faces toward the setting of the sun;
> Down the valley where the mournful cypress grows,
> Where the stream of death in silence onward flows.

Suddenly tears start running down my face. Dammit! I got through the whole day without breaking down. Through the funeral and the sight of him in the coffin with his priestly Mormon robes on top of him, through the testimonials and the songs by one of his beautiful granddaughters from her wheelchair, where she will spend the rest of her life. I got through it all without a tear. Why must this happen now?

THE CELESTIALS

Now that I know I'm going to the ranch, or whatever is left of it, I'd better get off this freeway soon, or I'll wind up in Oregon. I need to get across to old Highway 44, the Oregon Trail, which I've known since childhood, and I'll have to do it by feel since everything has changed. I have memories to guide me, but judging by what I'm seeing, they are memories of another time *and* another place.

The sign for the next exit says COLE ROAD. Bingo! That's a familiar name. It leads past the old Cole School, a rural school, and down toward Strawberry Glen Road, which winds around and crosses the river and connects with Highway 44. If I can just make the connection between Cole Road and Strawberry Glen Road, I'll be fine. But this isn't the Cole Road I remember, a quiet country thoroughfare through farmland. Now it's a horror of uncontrolled commercial development, and so are most of the major roads crossing it. I don't recognize anything and am becoming increasingly confused and frustrated, but I must be going in the right direction. I'll get my bearings when I cross the river. *Surely they haven't moved the river to make way for all this development. Don't be too sure. . . .*

There's a huge shopping mall on the left. Dillard's, Sizzler . . . it's all there, just like everywhere else in the West. Just as I'm about to give up on this nightmare road, it veers to the left and becomes something else and then something else. Mountain View Street, and then maybe Glenwood. I can't tell where one ends and the other begins. Whatever street I'm on meanders through a residential area that looks a little familiar. I must be near what they call "the rim," the edge of the first bench. I wonder who first started calling these mesas "benches." And it's curious that the distinctive mesa at the east end of town is called Table Rock. I guess the two benches go with the "table." Isn't that cute. Now I find the hill I remember leading down to the valley floor, across the main drag of Garden City, Chinden Boulevard.

In spite of the fact that this valley was named Treasure Valley by the developers or the politicians or somebody, it has not been treasured. Much of it has been trashed, and nowhere more than right here. Chinden Boulevard was named as the result of a contest in 1952 won by Neta Danzer, who received twenty-five dollars for combining the words *Chinese* and *garden* and coming up with "Chinden." But even before this verbal desecration took place, that part of the valley through which the boulevard runs—the part I am crossing now— had been destroyed.

We had always taken the Chinese gardens for granted, the way we did the river or the foothills. Acre after acre of immaculate gardens: lettuce, cabbage, radishes, onions, garlic, potatoes, turnips, peas, beans, beets, herbs of all kinds, carrots, spinach, squash, tomatoes, and on and on. Brilliant green fields laid out in well-tended rows that seemed inevitable. The Chinese gardeners peddled their produce down the alleys and streets of Boise in ancient Model T pickup trucks that often listed to one side. A truck would stop on a neighborhood street or alley in the shade of a big walnut or maple or elm, and the housewives would flock to it. It wasn't necessary for the peddler to honk his horn. The noise of the truck's motor was usually enough to alert all the women in the area. I remember a truck near our house completely surrounded by women, many of them with baskets or bags in which to carry home their fresh vegetables. The arrival of the truck created a break for them, a chance to visit with their neighbors and exchange news and gossip. In the midst of them, an old Chinese man in a coolie hat with a braid hanging down his back was handing out vegetables and doing sums on an abacus, grinning and nodding, speaking only minimal English.

This tradition of Chinese gardens had started very early. Thomas Jefferson Davis, a settler from Ohio who arrived in 1863 with the first group of soldiers sent to establish Fort Boise, brought a group of Chinese gardeners from San Francisco to cultivate an eight-hundred-acre strip of land along the Boise River, a strip of land that had been the site of the first army camp and had come to be known as "Government Island." This was the beginning of the Chinese gardens, an enterprise that would last about eighty years. A mention in the *Idaho Tri-Weekly*

Statesman in 1871 said, "the China population are planting gardens here pretty extensively." More Chinese came to work in the mines in the Boise Basin, often to rework tailings that had been processed once already. More came later to work on the construction of the railroads that crossed Idaho. The Anglos called them "Celestials," and in spite of the hideous prejudice against them that was endemic in the mining communities of the West, many of them stayed, and a thriving Chinatown grew up in Boise. Some ran laundries. Many became cooks or servants in prosperous Boise households.

But something strange happened in 1945 concerning the Chinese gardens. Rumors in Boise said that the ninety-nine-year lease held by the Chinese on the land had expired and had not been renewed. This could not have been true because they hadn't been on the land for ninety-nine years, but somehow Randall Eagleson Realty obtained much of the Chinese gardens land and began to subdivide it.

In 1949 gambling was legalized in Idaho, but the city of Boise passed an ordinance prohibiting it. Immediately a group of Boise businessmen, some of whom seemed to have been planning far ahead, petitioned to establish a village on the land to which the Chinese had conveniently relinquished their claims, and the village would include, among other somewhat shady pastimes, gambling.

The loss of the Chinese gardens not only reduced the Chinese population in Boise, but it also decimated the landscape. Where the gardens had been, Garden City sprang up, later to be incorporated. It was a gambling boomtown, a junk town, a "Hooverville," as many Boise citizens called it, with unplanned and uncontrolled growth, and incredibly ugly—a mile of neon lights, bars, and houses of prostitution. While nearly everyone in Boise complained about Garden City in those days, many Boiseans patronized its businesses after dark. It also became a haven for teenagers, since several of the bars served liquor to minors, including me and my friends.

Gambling was outlawed again in Idaho in the mid-1950s, and Garden City subsided into a quiet stretch of wreckage. Hell after the fire went out. The people who stood to gain by it had gained. The Chinese who once cultivated the land were gone. The landscape had been destroyed.

Too Long at
the Fair

At a glance, Garden City seems to be growing and prospering now, but it's still hideous. I cross Chinden Boulevard as quickly as I can. I should hit the Strawberry Glen Road any minute. Whoa! I'm on Highway 44 already, and it's a wide major artery heading due north. The Highway 44 I knew ran east and west on the other side of the river. What happened to the beautiful Strawberry Glen Road that meandered through cottonwood and willow bosques along the river? Gone. Now this highway, straight and wide enough to be the path to destruction.

At least I recognize the fairgrounds on the right with its sign, WESTERN IDAHO FAIR, although I will always think of it as the "new" fairgrounds, not the fairgrounds of my childhood. That one was at the intersection of Fairview Avenue and Curtiss Road. The memories that swirl around that fairground are so complicated I can't sort them out: violent death, the pinhead, Incredible Evelyn, disease and deadly fever, the "rocket," and always, of course, Jack, to whose care I was relegated, for better or worse. And Red, who made it all possible because he ran a concession at the fair for the Bohemian Brewery.

From about 1938 until 1940, Red worked for the Bohemian Brewery. The brewery was in a large brick building at the corner of 6th and Idaho Streets painted a bilious shade of green, and one could smell it from several blocks away. Red's job fell into the category of advertising, although I don't know what his exact title was. He painted signs and scenes on backbars and windows, and he ran the brewery's concession at the state fair each year, which was a rough plank bar running around three sides of a tent. It served cold sandwiches wrapped in wax paper and Bohemian beer on tap.

A few years before she died, I asked Betty about that job. "Of course I was too young to know what was really going on, but as I remember it, it seemed like a pretty good job. I think we had a little more money then, at least for a couple of years. Why didn't he keep the job?"

Betty looked at me for just a second as if I had been dropped on my head as a baby, which actually had happened when I was two and fell from the top of a playground slide while she was babysitting me at Natatorium Park. Her dramatic rendition of that event, with her running all the way home, screaming, with me in her arms, apparently dead, had become a family story that she was asked to perform again and again. Over the years it had become both stylized and embellished.

"Well, you know, Dick," she said finally, "he couldn't work in a *brewery*. He couldn't stay sober." Then her irresistible humor popped up as it always did. "They had to let him go because he drank up the profits, all by himself."

As usual, we are soon out of control, laughing and egging each other on.

"And it was a huge brewery."

"Thousands of gallons of beer. He worked overtime."

"He was the hardest worker they had. Sometimes he didn't come home at all."

By this time, we were helpless. She had collapsed on the couch and I was doubled up on the floor.

"Oh, we're terrible to make fun of him," she said, trying to control her laughter and looking guilty. "But the whole idea of him working for a *brewery* is the funniest thing I ever heard of."

Nobody had ever doubted Betty's love of her father or her absolute loyalty to him. Although Hazel's heavy drinking while Betty was a teenager had infuriated her, she had never criticized her father, and the bond between them was absolute. When we lived in the house on 13th Street, Red would often come home in the wee hours after the bars had closed, and he would either be too drunk or unwilling to climb the stairs to the bedroom where his wife was sleeping. He would fall asleep on the living-room floor. The house was not heated at night during the winter. The upstairs held some of the heat, but the living room downstairs was like a refrigerator. Carrying quilts, Betty would wake me, careful not to wake Jack, who was sleeping beside me.

"Get up, Dicky, get up now and help me. I can't do it alone, and I'm afraid to go down there in the dark all by myself. He's just come in. He'll freeze. We've got to cover him up."

We would creep down the dark stairs and grope for a light switch at the bottom. Red would be laid out on his back like a corpse, snoring. We would spread one quilt beside him. Betty would push on his shoulders and I would push on his legs, and with much grunting and straining, we would roll him onto one half of the quilt. Then with the other half and any other bedding Betty had found, we would cover him up.

Somehow, in spite of everything, it came as a shock to find out from Betty that Red had been fired from his job at the Bohemian Brewery. I had always imagined he was perfect for the job. After bootlegging was no longer a viable way to make a living, Red had apprenticed himself to a man named Hoffgarten who ran the most successful sign-painting business in town. Until Red's hands began to shake so badly he could no longer paint a clean line, he was an excellent sign painter.

Even before I had started school, when we lived in the tall ramshackle house on 17th Street, I remember him working on a big sign in the backyard. It had black letters on a white background: BOHEMIAN CLUB BEER. He let me snap the chalk line. "Just pull the string back and let it go." It left, as if by magic, a straight line of blue chalk against the blank background, and he followed the line to guide his letters. He used a stick like a billiard cue, padded at one end, to steady his hand. With his left hand, he pressed the stick against the surface of the sign while using it to steady his right hand, in which he held the paintbrush. He usually painted with a cigarette in his mouth, since he had no hand free, and there was often a long ash on the end of it that eventually would drop down the front of his shirt. He rolled his cigarettes from a Bull Durham pouch and papers in his front pocket. He usually smelled like paint thinner and Bull Durham tobacco.

He also painted backbars and bar windows for holidays—sentimental advertisements for the brewery. Easter meant flowers, eggs, and bunnies, and Saint Patrick's Day was a phantasmagoria of elves and leprechauns with wheelbarrows. I can't remember what was in the wheelbarrows. Probably Bohemian beer. As Christmas approached, he was busy painting acres of snow, picturesque cottages with lighted windows, Santa Clauses, bells, holly, and so on. When each holiday was over, the water-based paint was simply washed off.

Red took me to the brewery once, and I was fascinated by it—even the smell, after I got used to it. One area had an endless huge belt stretching diagonally from the ceiling to near the floor, moving fast and making a great racket. There was also a taproom, like a private bar with taps along the walls for the beer. There was no bartender. Everybody just helped himself. There were no women in the taproom.

Red seemed to have many duties in addition to painting signs. Once Jack and I found a large bag of what we took to be shelled peanuts in his panel truck. Both of us grabbed a handful and stuffed them into our mouths. They were actually little chiles, *chiltipiquínes*, the hottest chiles I have ever encountered. Red kept the bartenders in some of the saloons supplied with them. The saloons provided bowls of shelled, salted peanuts on the bar for the customers to munch on. Times were hard, however, and some men bought one glass of beer and ate as many peanuts as possible. When the bartender saw such a customer coming, he would substitute a bowl of *chiltipiquínes*, which looked much like salted peanuts, and the deadbeat customer would get the message very quickly.

Red was in his element at the Bohemian Club Beer concession at the state fair and rodeo. He was still good-looking in a Clark Gable kind of way, and once he had a couple of drinks, everybody loved him and he loved everybody. His drinking buddies flocked around the concession, and although he wasn't always too scrupulous about charging them for their beer, he did a brisk business. He opened up the concession at midmorning and stayed until it closed at 1 a.m. He took breaks only to go to the rodeo on Friday and Saturday nights, when all of us except Betty—who would have nothing to do with the fair—went with him.

Hazel and Jack and I would arrive on the bus about noon and stay until Red closed the concession. Then we either rode home with him in his panel truck, with me in the back with the drop cloths and paint buckets, or one of his friends would bring us home. It was an exciting time for me, and always at the center of it was Red with his white dress shirt, sleeves rolled up above the elbows, black leather bow tie, paint-spattered shoes, and a grin, tending bar or sitting with the customers, making wisecracks and telling stories endlessly.

> Well, there were these two privates from the backwoods of Arkansas in the trenches in France during the war. When the mail comes one day, one of them reads his letter and looks very sad. "What's the matter?" his buddy says. "You look like you got bad news." "Yes," the other one says, "my wife's down in bed with arthritis." "Oh, that's a crying shame," the other one says. "I knew them Ritus boys. Knew Arthur better than any of 'em."
>
> And did you hear the one about the old fart who had an earache, so he went to the doctor? Doctor poked around in his ear a little and pulled out a suppository. "Look here," the doctor says, "you had a suppository in your ear." "Well, I'll be damned," says the old fart. "That explains what happened to my hearing aid."

Red's little bar in a tent attracted some of the biggest stars of the rodeo, and none of them were bigger than Bill and Cassy, king and queen of the rodeo. They were trick riders, among the best of their day. I think they must have known Red from earlier times, but they hadn't known Hazel before. Hazel didn't seem to make close friends; she always maintained a certain distance.

Bill and Cassy were slender, agile, and magnificent. Cassy had the most beautiful blond hair I had ever seen. My mother said, "Peroxide," with a little sneer, but I didn't know what that meant. When I was six, I fell in love with Cassy, and the way she treated me told me she was in love with me too.

Bill and Cassy traveled with four horses: a pair of beautifully matched blacks and a pair of magnificent whites. They followed the rodeo circuit, risking their lives with every performance and loving it. On, under, or around their horses, they did the most amazing things I had ever seen.

Bill could disappear on the far side of a galloping horse and come back up only to hang suspended by one foot from the saddle horn. Cassy could do a handstand on a galloping horse, flip into the air, and land on her feet behind the saddle. The feat for which they were most famous was the Roman stand, and it was saved for the finale since nothing could surpass it for showmanship and daring. He rode the black horses and she rode the white. They entered the rodeo arena at a full gallop, standing up with one foot on each horse. They were amazing. After the first time I saw them perform, I knew what I wanted to be someday above all else—a trick rider. I think Jack felt the same way. We both became totally enamored of Bill and Cassy.

Cassy was so kind to us. She must have missed not having children, though the horses were like her children, but I guess it wasn't the same. She spoiled Jack and me, and as long as she held court at the Bohemian tent, I was always near her, often in her lap. When we arrived the first day of the fair, she was waiting for us with a big roll of tickets good for anything at the fair—hundreds of tickets, more than we could possibly use. She and Bill also gave our family box seat tickets, right down front, for the rodeo, and as they pranced by during the grand-entrance parade, all glittering in blue and silver, she always gave us a special wave and threw a kiss. I just knew it was for me.

With that roll of tickets, Jack and I could ride every crazy, thrilling contraption at the fair as many times as we wanted to and still have tickets left over. We could visit every fun house, spook house, and freak show, and finally flop down exhausted in the barns where 4-H kids were grooming their goats and calves. We became fairground junkies, never satisfied until we were in the middle of the next thrill, dangling high above the Idaho farmland as the sun went down and Jack made the Ferris-wheel chair swing madly while I shut my eyes and hung on, enjoying even my terror.

Our favorite ride was, of course, the most frightening, and it was called the "rocket." Strapped into a bullet-shaped compartment, we would plunge from a great height straight toward the ground at enormous speed. That was thrill enough for me, but Jack grew bored when we were suspended at the top while the other compartment at the bottom was being loaded and unloaded. He reached out to the row of light bulbs that circled the compartment we were in and began unscrewing them and throwing them down at the people far below. That got everybody's attention fast, and it got us kicked off that ride for the duration of that year's fair.

We went to all the freak shows, although they were not as much fun as the rides. There were about six tents of various kinds of freaks. One of the freaks, the pinhead, affected me strangely, and I am still haunted by her. Her head was conical and came to a point. There was a small circlet of hair about halfway up; otherwise she was bald. She had a fat, round belly, skinny arms and legs, and enormous feet. She did not speak but constantly nodded her head slightly. Her eyes and the way she moved her head made me think she must be very wise, a Buddha-like creature. I realize now that she was probably profoundly retarded. I went back to see her again and again, as if she were some kind of oracle with the answers I needed, but she merely stood on the platform above the crowd, silent and nodding her head slightly, as if to say that she understood everything and forgave us all.

One barker advertised dancing girls from some exotic place—I can't remember where. Only men went into that tent, but the barker took our tickets and let Jack and me in. After a boring dance routine by about six women who were not very pretty, the barker gave a spiel for Incredible Evelyn, and those who did not buy another ticket left the tent. I don't remember what the barker said Evelyn was supposed to do, but surely she was incredible, so Jack offered the required number of tickets from our roll, but we were turned down. "It's only for the men. You little punks get your asses out of here."

We went out the front of the tent and, under Jack's expert guidance, around to the back, where it was a simple matter to lie on our bellies and raise the bottom of the tent enough to see the show. Evelyn was a little too plump and no longer young, but I had never seen a naked woman before, and as far as I was concerned, she was totally incredible. And it was a show in which the audience was invited to participate, although only a few did.

After she got all her clothes off except a G-string, Evelyn rubbed her ample breasts all over the faces of several of the gaping spectators while the barker, who was smoking a cigar, kept up a running dialogue, most of which I didn't understand. Then she took off her G-string and the barker put his finger in her vagina. She seemed bored. Then several members of the audience put their fingers in her vagina. Then the barker shoved the unlit end of his cigar in her vagina, removed it, and continued smoking it, commenting on the taste. Her attitude seemed to be amused detachment. I was shocked to the bottom of my six-year-old soul. Jack made me promise I wouldn't tell anybody what we had seen. He needn't have worried. I would never have been able to tell anybody about it. In fact, I tried hard to convince myself it never happened.

Even as incredible as Evelyn was, she is not the most vivid image I have of the fair. That came later, the last year Red had the Bohemia concession. It was a Saturday night at the rodeo. Red and Hazel and Jack and I were in the box down front and center, the box that Bill and Cassy had reserved for us. The rodeo was long. After the trick-riding part, I got a little sleepy, but I was wide awake for the grand finale, led off by Bill and Cassy's famous Roman stand. Bill came through the gate first at a furious gallop, standing in a half-crouch with one foot on each of the black horses. Cassy followed on the white horses. It was as if the two horses and the slender woman with silver-blond hair streaming behind her had become one creature. They were magnificent.

They made one complete circle of the arena, passing just a few feet from us, and were on the far side coming around again when a piece of white paper, perhaps a popcorn sack, blew across the ground. Cassy's inside horse shied suddenly, and she fell between them. Then there were two white horses galloping after two black horses, but the white horses no longer had a rider. Behind them was a woman with silver-blond hair now rapidly darkening with blood, lying on the ground, very still.

Even before Bill realized what had happened behind him, while the stunned audience gasped, Red was over the rail and racing across the arena. Then he was kneeling over Cassy while Bill struggled with his horses and several cowboys ran out to help him. Then the ambulance that was always waiting at the far end of the rodeo grounds headed toward the still figure around which a crowd had now gathered. A doctor rushed in, shoving people out of the way. He was on his knees beside her for what seemed like a long time, next to Bill and Red. Finally he stood up and some men put her on a stretcher. We could see the blood then, mostly on her head. As the ambulance slowly pulled out of the rodeo grounds, Red returned to the box in the grandstand where we were waiting. He was ashen.

"Let's get the kids out of here," he said gruffly to Hazel. Then, in response to our clamor of questions, he said, "She never knew what hit her. She's gone."

We went back to the Bohemia concession. Somebody brought us coffee. I was allowed to have a mug of coffee with lots of canned cream and sugar. People stood around the concession, crying. Red filled his coffee cup from the whiskey bottle he kept hidden in a lunch pail under the bar. He arranged for us to have a ride home and said he was going to go find Bill. We knew he was going to get drunk.

What I remember most was the flash of silver-blond hair as she went down between the horses. I have never, in all these years, seen an attractive woman with that color hair and didn't think of Cassy, my first love. And it's strange—I married a woman with that color hair, even though I was old enough by then to know it came straight out of a bottle.

⁓

Soon after the last time Red ran the Bohemian Brewery concession at the state fair, Hazel developed a fever. It persisted and she grew weaker. They took her to the hospital and the illness was diagnosed as typhoid, probably contracted from drinking water from a spigot at the fair. Other cases were later traced to that source of water, and I had drunk from it too.

Children were not allowed to visit in the hospital, so I could not see her. Aunt Marie came to take care of us. She was good to us. One night right after supper Red came home from the hospital. He looked bad, like he needed a drink. He said Hazel was dying. He said he had made arrangements for the hospital to let me in to see her one last time. Jack and Betty had been to see her that afternoon. He took me to the hospital in his old panel truck, and I didn't have to ride in the back with the paint buckets and drop cloths. When we went into the hospital room, my mother held out her hand to me, but she seemed far away and she was so skinny I hardly recognized her. There was a blue hydrangea in a pot on the table beside her bed. It was a Catholic hospital. The nuns moved about with a swishing sound. I don't remember what my mother said to me. I don't think I stayed very long.

The next day Red took me to the Ogdens'. Jack and Betty stayed at home with him. My fate was the Ogdens. Eldon Ogden was a painter/paperhanger friend of Red's, one of his drinking buddies, but more respectable and successful than Red's other friends, probably because of his aggressive and dominating wife, Lorraine. Lorraine was short and extremely obese. They had one adopted son, Bobby, whom Jack and I both hated and considered a spoiled brat. I knew that if my mother had been well enough to be consulted, she would never have allowed me to be sent to the Ogdens'. She didn't like Lorraine Ogden and called her "lard ass" behind her back. But the Ogdens had a comfortable house in the suburbs on an acre of land, luxurious by our standards.

As soon as I arrived at the Ogdens', I began to feel ill. I was running a temperature, but Lorraine Ogden decided my listlessness was caused by constipation and made me drink prune juice. The prune juice gave me diarrhea, causing dehydration, and my temperature went up farther. It evidently had not occurred to anyone that I, too, might have typhoid, and I suppose the Ogdens didn't want to bother Red with any more problems.

I lay in Bobby's room at the Ogdens' while my temperature increased and the room spun around me. I don't know where Bobby was—perhaps away at school. The pattern on the wallpaper was horses. Horses jumping, horses running, horses standing still. As I became delirious, I saw Cassy riding the horses. She was riding them in the normal way, but I knew she would soon do the Roman stand and I had to warn her to stop before it was too late. I called for help, but no one came. I don't know how long this phase of my illness lasted. It seemed like weeks but was probably only one day.

At the same time, a great struggle for my mother's life was going on in the hospital. She needed blood transfusions, but there was no blood of her type available.

"Her blood type is rare," the doctor told Red. "We need to test a large number of people to find enough of the right type for several transfusions, and we don't have very much time, possibly only hours."

"I can get them," Red said, and he was out the door.

He went straight to the city fire station across the street from the Bohemian Brewery. Nearly every fireman at the station knew him because they were regular guests in the taproom of the brewery where Red spent a good deal of time drinking and being entertaining. In less than an hour there was a long line of firemen stretching down the hall of the hospital, each waiting to have his blood typed. The immediate crisis was met.

Now, thinking about this, I remember something else about those same firemen, an irony that comes with hindsight. Whenever my mother and I walked to town from the house on Flume Street— which we often did—we walked past the fire station. Several firemen would usually be sitting out in front with their chairs tipped back against the wall, enjoying the fresh air and sunshine, and invariably one or more of them would give my mother a long wolf whistle.

She would have been in her late thirties by then, but she was still a stunningly good-looking woman with an incomparable figure. Each time the firemen whistled at her, she would blush and appear to be very angry. She would take hold of my hand and hurry me along, saying, "Those awful men. They should be ashamed of themselves. You mustn't tell your father about this. You know how jealous he is." Years later it occurred to me that there were several routes to town as short as the one we took, yet we always went down Idaho Street past the fire station. I wonder if the firemen, lined up in the hospital to help the wife of their friend Red, knew that she was the babe with a knockout figure they always whistled at as she passed the station with her little boy.

The blood transfusions Hazel received from the firemen didn't save her life, but they bought her some time, and according to family folklore, it was time she needed. Penicillin had not yet been developed, but some of the sulfa drugs had, though they were not generally available. My mother told me that the first batch of sulfa drugs to arrive in Boise was rushed to her and saved her life. I don't know if this was true, but she believed it. She was in the hospital for over a month.

My recovery involved my grandmother Charlotte, who had raised four children alone in a Western frontier community by working as a laundress in a brickyard and later by hiring out as a cook on large ranches, wherever they would take a cook with four children. She wasn't one to be cowed by typhoid fever. At first she had not been informed that I was sick. Red's attention was focused on Hazel, and he had been drunk much of the time. When Charlotte and her husband, Sherman Beech, came to Boise from the ranch to visit Hazel in the hospital, they found out where I was and that I was sick.

"Well," Grandma Charlotte told me many years later after Red had died, "I was mad at your dad, but I didn't say anything. Sherman and I got in the car and drove to the Ogdens' to get you as fast as we could go. You were bad sick—sicker than anybody realized. I don't think I've ever seen a child as sick as you were. I can tell you that fat Miz Ogden was mighty glad to get rid of you. We brought you straight to the ranch. I don't think you knew where you were for a couple of days. We put you in a tub of cool water to bring your temperature down, and we worked night and day to keep you alive, making you drink water every little while. You lost so much weight there wasn't hardly room left for your freckles. But you came around pretty fast, and by the time your mother got out of the hospital, you were well again. Do you remember any of it?"

"I remember when you and Sherman came to the Ogdens' place. It was like I woke up from a nightmare and I wouldn't have to worry about those horses anymore. Then I don't remember anything else except the drumstick."

"The drumstick?"

"Yes. Somebody ate all the meat off a chicken leg and gave me the bone to suck on. I guess I was too sick to eat anything. It was delicious. I can still taste it."

"Later, when you could eat a little, you loved my chicken-noodle soup. I think that soup made you get better."

"I remember everything about it. The way you would roll the dough up, slice off the noodles, and then hang them on a little rack to dry."

"I guess that's what Leonard did when he took you to the Ogdens'—hung you out to dry. And you would have dried up and blown away if we hadn't got you out of there. I never did like that woman."

That's as much as she would say, and I was surprised she said that much, but I could tell by the way her lips set in a firm line that she felt much more than she was saying. She was the only person who called my father by his name, Leonard, and she never called him anything else.

EAGLE TO STAR

This road, which has somehow become Highway 44 without my permission, is wall-to-wall shopping centers. How many Albertsons and Dillard's can one community support? How many Pizza Huts and Mexican fast-food joints, all dispensing pure lard to an already seriously overweight population, can flourish before we realize that they are not killing us, we are killing ourselves?

At last I've come to the end of this road, whatever it is, where what used to be Highway 44 crosses it, and I turn west toward Eagle, one of those bucolic little hamlets I remember strung along the valley. Eagle's main claim to fame when I was growing up was Orville Jackson's Drug Store. Those who knew it almost never drove through Eagle without stopping to look around in the drugstore, whether they wanted to buy anything or not. Orville Jackson's was an experience, one of those rural emporiums that became famous because it met nearly all the needs of the community. It carried everything.

The drugstore had a fountain, not unusual for those days, with a marble counter top and stools a child could spin on. Orville Jackson himself, then past middle age, was often behind the marble counter mixing sodas or scooping ice cream into boat-shaped dishes for banana splits. His huge three-scoop ice cream cones were legendary. So was the store itself. It was crammed with everything the local farmer or passing motorist might need: hats, gloves, rope, chain, harness, hair dye, beds, cosmetics, ammunition, laxatives, galoshes, almanacs, lawn furniture, nails, paintings, pots and pans, candles, candy, trusses, pitchforks, condoms, glasses, overalls, and underwear, as well as all the medicines usually dispensed in a pharmacy. Merchandise was stacked to the ceiling along narrow aisles that constantly threatened to cave in and bury a customer. Things hung from every inch of the walls and ceiling. It was a rat's nest, a challenge, an adventure.

Sometimes nobody but Orville could find a particular item, and he would burrow into mounds of unsorted articles and come up with it. There also seemed to be areas of the store nobody except Orville could get to, as if he had secret passages that led him into the heart of the warren. He would disappear for a minute, one would hear a rustling and rummaging, sometimes a crash or two, and he would reappear in a different part of the store with the desired item in his hand.

I watched one of his performances when Grandma Charlotte asked him for a hairnet. He went to the rear of the store and returned with a tall stepladder, moving down the aisle gingerly, so as not to start an avalanche. He placed the ladder precisely, climbed it, and pulled from a tangle of fishing tackle and shoe boxes near the ceiling a paper packet covered with dust and containing one hairnet, invisible.

"There you are, Miz Beech," he said. "The damages today are ten cents."

As I approach Eagle, I begin to see a line of large houses on the rim of the first tier of hills to the north, indicating that Eagle has been discovered and is being developed as a bedroom community. It has also been the victim of some attempts at gentrification, possibly at different times and with peculiar results. Green metal lampposts reminiscent of turn-of-the-century Europe and a gazebo contrast oddly with the fake Western storefronts. But there it is, the sign I have been looking for: EAGLE DRUG STORE, and over the door in large white letters ORVILLE JACKSON. I have to stop. Surely Orville himself can't still be running this store. That was sixty years ago.

A sign under the store windows reads WATCHES AND CLOCKS, HORSESHOES AND VETERINARY, DRUGS, GIFTS, MAGAZINES AND HEALTH NEEDS. Judging by the wild and colorful conglomeration of things displayed in the store window, including artificial flowers, dishes, clothing, harness, furniture, and plumbing supplies, I truly believe Orville is still here, but when I go in and ask to meet the owner, I am introduced to Wayne Crosby, affable and middle-aged, who bought the store from Orville in the '70s and had the smarts not to change it any more than was necessary except to add on in order to provide more room for the astonishing collection of everything including lumber and the kitchen sink. Mr. Crosby shows me around and gives me a brief history of the store. Started as a drugstore in 1906, it was bought by Orville in 1922. He ran it for about forty years.

The store is much neater and better organized than it was when I was a child, but it is still a warren of disparate and amazing things. *Who arranges it all?* I wonder. Who determines that the ornate table lamp with a fluted shade goes next to the harness, and the baby clothes wind up with the rabbit food? It's like a really good poem— you have to accept it on its own terms, but once you have made that leap, you realize that everything is exactly where it should be. Years ago the store became much more than a commercial enterprise. It's an institution and tourist attraction, and it must figure in the childhood memories of thousands and thousands of people raised in this area, as it does in mine.

When I go outside to get back in the car, I notice a huge sign on the side of the building facing the parking lot. Like the store, it is inexplicable and seems to have been created according to its own rules of English usage:

> *REMEMBER THIS!*
> *You Can Always Get It Of*
> *ORVILLE JACKSON*

It's only a little more than five miles on to Star, and then about a mile and a half beyond that to the ranch. How many hundreds of times have I made this twenty-two-mile trip? Sometimes, even as a child, I came alone on the Greyhound bus, wildly excited, especially if I was going to get to stay all summer. Jack sometimes made the trip by Greyhound bus too. He told me about something that happened on one of those trips when he was a teenager. It struck me as somehow significant, a wildly ironic comment on the struggle between the sexes.

"When I got on the bus in Boise," Jack said, "there was this guy I knew sitting right across the aisle. Young guy about my age. We got to talking, and after the bus pulled out, I noticed that his fly was unzipped, really gaping open. So I signaled to him, and he reached down real quick and zipped it up, but there was a woman sitting next to him with a fur coat on, and she had kind of thrown her coat open. Well, the coat got caught in the zipper when he zipped his pants up, and the zipper was stuck. This guy was dying of embarrassment, and he worked to get the zipper unstuck, but he couldn't. She was getting off the bus at Eagle. He wouldn't take his pants off, and she wouldn't give her coat up. So they got off together. The last we saw of them, they were standing in front of Orville Jackson's Drug Store screaming at one another as the bus pulled out, and we were all laughing our heads off."

I made this trip so many times when I was a child that I remember every curve in the road. In summer the cattails stood stiffly in the ditches, as if waiting for a child to color them with crayons and twist them into wonderful patterns. Rows of Lombardy poplars swirling into the sky and magnificent silver maples flashing green, silver, green, silver with every breeze. Most farms had a weeping willow or two along the ditch and petunias or gladiolus near the house. In winter the colors were muted; the frozen grass along the ditch rows was gray-brown, and the light was sepia. The breath of the cows and horses steamed, and on each farm, the house, barn, and outbuildings seemed to huddle closer to one another and to the earth. When there was snow, everything got quieter, but often there was no snow, just the frozen fields, tawny frozen grass, and brown clods where the land had been plowed in the fall. The river was half a mile to the south, a line of gray, leafless willows and cottonwoods where from time to time a great flock of blackbirds rose like a dark smudge on the horizon and settled again, unheard in the distance.

Sometimes Grandma Charlotte and Sherman would come to Boise to get me. Sometimes my parents would take me to the ranch on a Sunday, stay for dinner, and then drive back without me. Red was not a particularly good driver, but since he was often drunk, he was a very cautious one, never exceeding forty miles an hour. The trip I remember most vividly was just Hazel and Red and me. I must have been eight or nine. Red was very drunk when we left Boise, and he got drunker as we drove along. Highway 44 was a two-lane highway, and not very wide. We would drift to the left, cross the center line, and almost go off into the ditch on the wrong side of the road, then we would drift to the right. Oncoming traffic had to swerve wildly to avoid hitting us, and a couple of times a speeding driver missed us by passing us in the lane we were supposed to be in, on the wrong side of the road, with their horn blaring.

Finally my terrified mother made Red stop by the side of the road. She didn't know how to drive, and there we were, stuck halfway to Grandma's. I don't know who came up with the solution, but we arrived at it somehow. I crawled into Red's lap. He worked the pedals and gear shift and I steered. I had never steered a car before, and I was very frightened each time I saw a car coming toward us, but I soon got the hang of it. I had to make only one sharp turn when we got to the ranch and turned into the lane, and that was a nightmare, but I managed it without taking out the fence, and Red had slowed almost to a crawl by that time.

I haven't thought of that frightening trip in years, but making this drive again brings it back to me. It seems almost comical, like a fairy tale. Three small children struggling toward Grandma's house through the dark woods. There were no woods, but it does seem to me that all three of us were children. I don't know exactly when I began to think of my parents as children. It was probably a gradual thing, but by the time of this drive, I must have worked things out pretty well in my head. Red was often helpless because of his drinking, and Hazel was generally ineffectual. She drank heavily for a four-year period, and after that, her health was so bad she was often incapacitated. They had both proved from the beginning that they couldn't protect me. I could not, until I was much older, understand her dependence on him when he was so obviously undependable. I learned very early on to depend on myself. It would stand me in good stead later. Perhaps it was the most valuable gift they could have given me.

～

I'm approaching the village of Star. The distance between Eagle and Star seemed like a long way when I was a child. Now I realize it's less than six miles. There wasn't much to Star then except the mercantile on the north side of the highway and a couple of beautiful houses, one on the south side with an artesian well shooting water twenty-five feet into the air. I loved Star. It was a kind of extension of the ranch in my mind, the place to which Grandma Charlotte and Sherman would drive the Rickenbacker twice a week to get meat from the frozen food locker and bring the eggs that Charlotte's chickens had laid to the mercantile where they would be sold. The mercantile was the source of ice cream cones, and the Rickenbacker was the source of endless delight.

It was a huge luxury vehicle produced briefly in the 1920s, square and heavy. When Grandma Charlotte married Sherman Beech, her third husband, in 1928, it was the vehicle in which he took her on a six-month honeymoon to Arizona and Mexico. When I was a child, it lived in the middle section of the barn and was used for the twice-weekly trips to Star, although I was allowed to play in it between trips. Sometimes I was the driver, sometimes a passenger, sometimes it was a boat, sometimes a rocket ship or train. At one end of the backseat was a built-in and upholstered square tool box, perfect for me to ride on since it put me high enough to see everything. The car had solid wheels, enormous freestanding headlights, and a gearshift almost as tall as I was, with a round marble handle and bud vases, and it had to be cranked to start. Its spacious padded interior, all plush and faded elegance, provided a sense of absolute security, and when it was rolling down the highway at thirty miles an hour, it moved majestically and always seemed to know where it was going. To a child it was a floating castle, a magic carpet.

Star hasn't changed as much as Eagle. At least I would still recognize it, although it has grown and been spiffed up some. I remember how, as we rolled into the hamlet in the Rickenbacker, people waved and called out, "Hey, Sherman! Good morning, Miz Beech. Who's that little redheaded guy you've got with you? I hear he's a terror." Charlotte looked right at home in the Rickenbacker. I have always wondered how she could manage to be quality no matter what circumstances she found herself in. That natural elegance, never self-conscious or out of place. She could shovel cow manure or clean out a henhouse without losing her dignity.

And her only daughter, my mother, could be cute or pretty or even beautiful, but never, no matter what she did, could she be elegant or even very comfortable in her own skin. When she tried for dignity, she came off as haughty and unfriendly. She never could seem to strike the right *tone* in any situation. Her anxiety showed in the way her thin hands gripped one another until the knuckles showed white.

Grandma Charlotte could step out of the elegant Rickenbacker or off the seat of a farm wagon with the same easy grace. She knew who she was. I think she always had known that since she was a little girl whose father taught her to play the fiddle and whose mother, beautiful Josie, died young. Consequently she had a good feel for who everybody else was too. Especially Red, or *Leonard*, as she insisted on calling him, but with a kindly tone. She had known from the beginning that he was fragile, and that her only daughter, who was also fragile but made of sterner stuff than *Leonard*, adored him absolutely, completely, and without reservations. Charlotte sighed. Her daughter was a goose, but she loved her nonetheless. Toward her son-in-law, who soon proved to be the victim of an uncontrollable appetite for booze and good-time women, she adopted a slightly formal attitude.

The first time Red saw her, she made a strong impression on him, although she never had the opportunity to speak to him on that occasion. He must have known, even then, that his charm and good looks would be wasted on this ex-schoolteacher who had already married two men who were charming and good-looking and found them both useless. In 1921 Charlotte was living and working in McCall, a small lakeside town a hundred miles north of Boise, supporting herself and her two youngest sons. The oldest son was already married, and Hazel, who had been on her own for more than a year, had come to McCall to spend a few weeks with her mother. Hazel had asked

Red, to whom she had just become engaged, to come to McCall to meet her mother—the big meeting between the mother and the future son-in-law.

When the weekend arrived, Red lacked the train fare to McCall from Boise, which was really no problem for him. He had traveled around the country earlier in search of work without paying any train fare, either riding inside boxcars or under them—"riding the rails," as it was called. It was dangerous and dirty, but Red was used to lying under the car of a speeding train, inches from the ground and supported by only two metal rods that were under most cars. That's how he arrived in McCall after telling his fiancée that he would arrive by train on a certain day. Only one train a day arrived in McCall, and Hazel had assumed he meant he would arrive as a regular passenger.

As the train pulled to a stop in front of the depot in McCall, he could see that a family group was meeting somebody. He looked closer and realized who they were—his fiancée, her two younger brothers, scrubbed and dressed in their Sunday best, and his fiancée's mother, a striking woman in a simple but elegant black dress and a huge hat, the inner brim of which was lined with dark feathers. There was something about the way she carried her head under that hat, something about the way she smiled at her daughter as they waited for the passengers to get off the train.

Red was dirty, sweaty, and covered with soot and cinders. He realized that if he put in an appearance, everyone would know how he had traveled from Boise to McCall. Courage was the quality Red most admired, but it was also a quality he did not have in conspicuous amounts. Generally he had to resort to a bottle to find much of it. He had no bottle at this moment, and his courage simply failed him. He slipped from under the train on the side away from the depot, and crawled under another train going back toward Boise. His first view of his future mother-in-law was prophetic. From then on, he was always slightly uneasy in her presence. And although as long as he lived, she never criticized him or his behavior, he was a little afraid of her.

THE RANCH II

From Star to the ranch is less than two miles. I have ridden it on horseback or on a bicycle or walked it many times. Now, in spite of the changes, I know every lane and most of the farms by heart, although the people who lived here then are long since gone. I remember the ghosts. There's the Kennedy place on the left. The house was a large two-story white colonial across the highway, but it burned down, so the Kennedys moved into the two-story barn, also painted white, and never rebuilt the house. The highway ran right through the middle of their farm. The Kennedys were thought to be wealthy, and they remained somewhat aloof from the rest of the community.

Mrs. Kennedy was famous for spying. She had a pair of high-powered binoculars, and from an upstairs window or the widow's walk on the roof, she could keep track of everybody's business for miles around. The favorite fishing hole for all of Charlotte's grandchildren was in a creek that ran through the Kennedy property, and it was the cause of much contention, although we all knew who would win when it came to a real struggle between Grandma Charlotte and Mrs. Kennedy. Grandma could count on the fact that Mrs. Kennedy would phone whenever any of us went fishing.

"Miz Beech, there are children fishing in the creek on my property again. I believe they are part of your relations. One of them might fall in and drown on my property, and I can't accept that liability."

"Yes, Miz Kennedy. They are my grandsons, but one of them is almost grown, and they are all good swimmers. I don't think there's any danger of their drowning, especially since the creek is so shallow. But I'll speak to them when they come home. How did you happen to know they were down there, Miz Kennedy?"

Here, a pause while Mrs. Kennedy, taken by surprise, thinks up a story.

"Why . . . why . . . our hired hand was down there at the creek, and he saw them."

"Yes, well, I hope your hired hand doesn't fall in and drown. But then I understand you keep your eye on him with your field glasses. I'll speak to the children, Miz Kennedy. Good-bye."

Charlotte was diplomatic and formal but friendly toward Mrs. Kennedy, and everybody in the community watched with great interest while the two women maneuvered like chess players. Charlotte always won. After she hung up the phone, she would sigh and say, "Well, the poor old thing just never lets up, does she? If it was the Second Coming and the Lord landed on her property, I do believe she would have him arrested for trespassing."

The telephone at the ranch was on the wall in the dining room and housed in a box made of beautifully grained oak with a little shelf for writing messages jutting out from it at an angle. Near the top of the box was a stationary black mouthpiece. In order to talk into the mouthpiece, a child had to stand on a chair or stool. Hanging from a little stirrup on one side was an earpiece on a cord. On the other side of the box was a handle that we revolved rapidly to ring up the operator. The ranch was on a party line. At different times there were between five and thirteen families on the line, and Grandma Charlotte instructed all her grandchildren in party-line etiquette.

After you got up on the stool she kept near the telephone, you picked up the earphone and listened. More than likely you would hear Mrs. Kennedy talking. In that case, you said in your most polite voice, "Mrs. Kennedy, I have to make an important call. Would you please let me have the line?" Then you hung up and waited a couple of minutes to allow Mrs. Kennedy to complete her call. Then you got back up on the stool, picked up the earpiece, and listened again. If Mrs. Kennedy had by this time hung up, you could go on with your call. If Mrs. Kennedy had not hung up, you would tell Grandma Charlotte, and she would take care of it. When she got on the line and asked Mrs. Kennedy to hang up, she did it with the utmost politeness but in a tone that no one would mistake for a request. Then, when you got the line, you would revolve the little handle vigorously.

This rang up the operator, wherever she was, and I never figured out where "central" was, and you could tell her the number you wanted to call.

The daytime operator's name was Ruth, and she knew everybody. It was considered bad manners not to chat with Ruth when placing a call, unless it was an emergency, and if the caller used that word, Ruth became a machine of efficiency who knew the number for the closest farm and could have a neighbor on the way while she was contacting whatever emergency service was required. Ruth always passed on local news to Charlotte and Sherman and asked about their health. She was particularly friendly with Sherman, and loved to tease him about his way with women. Somehow, younger women simply could not prevent themselves from flirting with Sherman Beech.

He was small boned and a little under average height, but strong and wiry, and there wasn't an ounce of fat on his body. He had sandy hair, a funny lopsided grin, and he smelled of cow manure and Prince Albert pipe tobacco. He was a quiet man who worked hard, knew what he was doing, and didn't feel the need to explain himself or his actions to anybody. His devotion to Charlotte was monumental, unquestioned. She was his first and only wife, although she had been married twice before, and he was nine years younger than she was.

Even Ruth, the telephone operator, became coy and giggly when she was talking to Sherman on the phone, and other young women responded the same way. Once while Grandma Charlotte, Sherman, and I were in the checkout line at a grocery store in Caldwell, the woman behind the cash register called Sherman "my little butter duck." I was astonished, and Grandma was suspicious for a moment, but she could tell by the way Sherman reacted and the woman's attitude that the two of them had never met before. The woman was at least twenty years younger than Sherman. Grandma Charlotte laughed and teased him about it for years.

He just had that effect on women, and he responded by blushing and studying the ground in front of him as if it contained the answer to some profound mystery. But it wasn't just women who liked him. Everybody in the family liked Sherman. No matter who was mad at whom at any given time, or who was feuding with whom among the brothers- or sisters-in-law, Sherman could ride above it and manage to stay on good terms with everybody. Part of his success came about because he was always friendly and listened to everything his wife's dozens of relatives said with his head cocked slightly to one side, but he never commented or offered an opinion, except possibly in private to Grandma Charlotte, and if he did that, nobody ever found out. He was most comfortable with dogs, horses, and cows. He respected children and listened to them with the same bemused attention he gave to adults.

When I was between six and nine, really too young to be of much help with the daily chores, Charlotte and Sherman devised jobs for me that made me feel useful. I could feed the chickens and gather the eggs each day, sometimes no small task when a cross old hen was sitting on the nest, and I had to reach under her while she made angry noises. But these were, I knew, chores that Grandma usually performed, and I wanted to do something to help Sherman—some man's work. The chore he devised for me was somehow typical of the man, and I have never forgotten how much pleasure and self-importance it gave me.

He said that if I wanted to, I could get up at dawn, when he did, and with Rowdy the dog, hike out into the back pasture, probably half a mile away from the barn, and bring the cows in for milking. Then I could do it again in the evening, since the cows were milked twice a day. I realized that this would save Sherman a good deal of time and effort. Actually, he said, all I would have to do was put in an appearance out there in the early morning light, and the cows would follow me in. And that's exactly how it worked. Rowdy and I would show up in the pasture, Rowdy would circle the cows with a couple of quick barks, and the cows would start ambling toward the barn as I led the way. I performed this task faithfully and with great pleasure for an entire summer before I realized that Rowdy normally did it all by himself.

Sherman was born on Flag Day in 1890 in Clayton, Idaho. This would suggest that his father was a miner. Clayton was a mining community at the edge of what I think of as the "heart" of Idaho, now the Sawtooth National Recreation Area. On the map it shows up as a green, almost heart-shaped splotch of magnificent lakes and wild, forested mountains, several over eleven thousand feet high, between the Salmon River and the East Fork of the Salmon River, roughly in the center of the southern part of the state, that part of the state that is widest, south of the Continental Divide. For natural beauty, this area can hold its own against any section of the West, or anywhere else.

I spent a night in Stanley, a small community in this area, early this spring when the Sawtooths were covered with snow. The play of light and color on their peaks at sunset and sunrise was dazzling. I have the notion that some grand mountains have the look of mountains that have been looked at too many times, like T.S. Eliot's roses that "Had the look of flowers that are looked at." Like the Tetons, maybe. Certainly the Alps. But somehow the Sawtooths look as if no one has ever seen them before. They are mysterious and secretive and reveal themselves each time as if for the first time.

Clayton was established as a mining camp in the 1870s near where Kinnikinnick Creek empties into the Salmon River. *Kinnikinnick* was a term widely used by Native Americans in the West to refer to the mixture of dried bark or leaves they smoked. The town had several incarnations as various silver mines boomed and busted and the accompanying smelters were established or closed. Its claim to a certain kind of fame probably lies in the fact that it was named after Clayton Smith, who owned and operated the local brothel, which was, along with the Masons and Odd Fellows Lodge, an important institution in such mining communities. The town's glory days lasted, off and on, from about 1881 until just after the turn of the century, although there are still several active mines in the area.

The fact that Sherman was born in 1890 in Clayton, at the height of the mining activity, suggests that he came from a mining family or at least that his father was a miner. But everything about Sherman suggested something different. He was the quintessential farmer, a man whose farm was a model for others and whose advice on farming matters was always sought by others. He must have been raised on a farm. Perhaps his father, like many others, was a farmer who spent a few years working in the mines. Or perhaps his father had had some other connection with mining. At any rate, Sherman was born to farming; it was in his blood.

He knew farm animals, he knew soil, and he knew water. He bred beef cattle and dairy cows to improve the strains. I saw him get truly angry only once, and that was when a neighboring farmer's bull broke through the fence and bred with several of Sherman's heifers, destroying the careful breeding plans by means of which he was trying to develop his herd. Each cow in his dairy herd had a name and recognizable personality, and he spoke to them by name and respected their idiosyncrasies.

"Old Bessie won't allow any other cow to go into the barn ahead of her," he would say, or, "Be careful about going on the left side of Cricket. It makes her nervous and she kicks," or, "Would you like to go in and tell your grandmother that Rosie's ready to be milked? She won't let anybody else touch her."

During much of my childhood, Sherman relied on two enormous work horses to pull every piece of farm equipment that moved. Their strength made their work seem effortless, and since they were a major source of energy on the farm, their welfare was always a primary concern. They were spoiled by everybody, and had one wing of the barn, called "the horse barn," for their very own, although at different times, and especially in the winter, they sometimes had to share it with sheep, and even pigs. At haying time they pulled great wagonloads of hay to the haystack while I hung on the back rail with my empty water jugs to be filled at the pump and returned to the thirsty men loading in the field. The horses' rumps were so broad I could ride on either of them sitting cross-legged like a child Buddha and never fall off. They were magical creatures, and I loved them. I am ashamed that I can't remember their names.

The bull's name was Old Pet, and he was just that, as gentle as most of the cows, with a huge shaggy head and beautiful dark, shining eyes. As far as I knew, he never menaced anyone or anything, and

I could stroke his face as if he were the friendliest of dogs. In spite of his gentleness, he must have been very effective as a bull. His services seemed to be in constant demand on many of the farms in the area, and he was always being hauled from one farm to another.

When I was about seven or eight, I blundered into the barn one afternoon while one of Sherman's cows was being bred and was astonished to see Old Pet trussed up in an elaborate harness operated by a system of chains, ropes, and pulleys. In order to get him into position to do the deed, his front end had to be lifted above the cow's back. I was too embarrassed to ask Sherman why this was necessary. It might have been to keep the cow from being damaged by Old Pet's weight, which was enormous, or perhaps he was so heavy that he simply could not get into the proper position unaided. Or perhaps, as I suspected, Old Pet was just too lazy to make the effort, although once in the right posture, he seemed to be able to manage the rest of it by himself.

Not all the male creatures at the ranch were so gentle, and two of them were real terrors, especially for a child. The ram was dreadful. He ruled one of the large pastures it was often necessary to cross, and he would attack anyone who tried to cross it. The trick to getting across was to get as far as possible before he realized you were there, and then outrun him. I would wait until he was looking the other way and then sneak as far as I could into the pasture before he saw me. Then the race was on. If I lost the race, he would strike with his curled horns and knock me down. When I got up, he would knock me down again. When I won the race, there was no time to open the wooden gate that led to safety. I learned to simply go over it like water over a dam. Even now I can go over a wooden gate with considerable speed, especially if somebody shouts "Ram!"

But the worst creature on the place, the one I truly hated as one hates a mortal enemy, was the gander. The yard around the house was fenced, but once I went through the gate into the barnyard—and it was necessary to go through the gate to get to the privy, the barn, the henhouse, the road, or anywhere—I entered the domain of the gander and his noisy flock of geese. He was evil, perfidious, always alert. I kept a large stick, almost as tall as I was, beside the gate, and never during the lifetime of that gander, which was considerably longer than it would have been if I'd had my wishes, did I step through the gate without that stick.

What I never understood about the gander was how he knew about the anatomical difference between little girls and little boys. He might peck at a girl's arm with his strong beak, or even pull her hair sometimes, but with little boys, he went straight for the crotch, and his aim was usually masterful. Nothing short of a hard blow with the stick would deter him, and even then, he circled with his long, ugly neck stuck straight out and his mean little eyes fixed on the target. I would gladly have gone without turkey for Thanksgiving if I could have seen that gander roasted and served, and I didn't care much for the taste of roast goose.

Sherman was a wizard with water and the art of irrigation, and he functioned for years as president of the ditch board, a position that commanded great respect in the community. He seemed to be able to make water run uphill, and in a valley that had been a desert, a valley whose crops depended almost entirely on irrigation, this was an important skill. The ditch that ran just behind the house was the farm's lifeblood.

After supper Sherman did the milking, and then when the chores were done, we sat in the living room and listened to the radio. I think those were the happiest times I remember as a child. Grandma Charlotte sat in her rocker that, if anybody else tried to sit in it, would turn over backward and throw them out. She would be doing embroidery or tatting. Sherman sat in his much lower rocker, across the room but closer to the radio, smoking his pipe and reading the newspaper. I curled up in a big leather wingback chair that I loved. The wings on the sides of the chair were so large they gave me the feeling of being hidden, which pleased me. We listened to the *Grand Ole Opry*, mostly, and the news. Sometimes we listened to *I Love a Mystery* or *The Pall Mall Show*. Sometimes we listened to the *Old Fashioned Revival Hour* for the music, although neither Charlotte nor Sherman professed any strong inclination toward religion. I would snuggle into that big chair that I had pulled back a little into the shadows, reading an old *National Geographic* and listening to Minnie Pearl.

I knew what to expect. I knew that the next day would be very much like today had been—no sudden threats or surprises. I would go out and bring in the cows to be milked. I would sit down to a wonderful breakfast surrounded with the peace of two people who loved each other and, I felt, loved me. I would feed the chickens and gather the eggs. I could wander along the ditch or through the fields with Rowdy and a pet banty rooster, or as I grew older, I could ride Old Paint, the big sorrel Sherman had bought for his wife's grandsons to ride, but which I considered mine alone, down the lane to the river or in the opposite direction toward the foothills, often with the banty rooster riding on the saddle horn. When we galloped down the dirt roads, the banty rooster would dig into the saddle horn, spread his wings for balance, and ride like a cowboy.

Or if the weather was bad, I could stay in the house and read a book or listen to Grandma's wonderful collection of records on what had come to be called "the dancing machine," a large Victrola in a fancy cabinet with containers like bookshelves for thick volumes of vinyl records.

Some of the platters were recorded on only one side, and some required wooden needles. The collection included the tenors of the '30s singing such ballads as "Lay My Head Beneath a Rose," as well as the humorous talking records of the same period, like *Two Black Crows in Hades*, which, if judged on the political correctness scale of today, would go clear off the chart. I listened to them so many times I could, and did, recite them when I thought nobody could hear me. And many of the labor-movement songs of the '30s:

> *Hallelujah! I'm a bum.*
> *Hallelujah! Bum again.*
> *Hallelujah! Give us a handout*
> *To revive us again.*

Of the ballads, one of my favorites began, "I'm always high, high, high up in the hills, watching the clouds roll by." I have no doubt what would be made of that today. And there was "The Gay Caballero," many generations before *gay* took on its present meaning. It was the lament of the inept but amorous Caballero who encounters what he believes to be a willing female, but things don't work out at all well:

> *She took me to her home to nestle.*
> *Each room was as big as a castle.*
> *I said, "Why so much space?" She said, "Just in case*
> *You get fresh, I need room to rassle."*

He pursues her. Presumably in order to defend her virtue—which was suspect from the beginning—she bites his ear off. All of this leads, as if inexorably, to the unfortunate rhyme of *caballero* with *earo*.

The one I remember best, which I played again and again, was a nonsense song popular at some earlier period, probably in the mid-1920s. It gave me such delight, and I sang along with it so many times that I learned it by heart. I have no idea who wrote it, but he or she was undoubtedly a crazy genius:

> *The horses run around,*
> *Their feet are on the ground,*
> *And who will wind the clock while I'm away, away?*
> *Go get the hatchet,*
> *There's a hair on baby's chest,*
> *And a boy's best friend is his mother.*

> *Looking through a knothole*
> *In father's wooden leg,*
> *Why do they build the shore so near the ocean, the ocean?*
> *We feed the baby garlic*
> *So we can find him in the dark,*
> *And a boy's best friend is his mother.*

Since the house had no indoor plumbing until I was almost a teenager, one of the rituals Sherman and I observed was going outside to pee each night just before bedtime. Grandma had to take a flashlight and cross the footbridge to the privy on the other side of the ditch, but Sherman and I could stand out beside the house and look up at the stars on clear nights, and he would point out various constellations or show me how to find the North Star. Sherman always signaled that we were going outside by saying, "Well, I guess it's time to go see a man about a dog."

He wore overalls and an old sweat-stained felt hat, summer and winter, that had long since ceased to be any particular color. I remember him also in black rubber boots worn when he irrigated, turned down to just below the knee. I never really understood the life-and-death importance of the ditch until one summer night during a severe drought. It was hot and windy and the air was full of dust. After the sun went down, Sherman set off to walk the ditch, as he often did at strange hours since each farmer's time to use the water in the ditch was rotated around the clock. But that night, instead of a shovel, he carried a shotgun on his shoulder. In the dusty twilight he looked ghostly as he disappeared down the ditch bank with a final wave. I asked Grandma, who seemed pensive, why he was carrying the shotgun.

"One of the families who live farther up the ditch," she said, "has been stealing water at night. Opening their side ditches and putting in tarps to divert the main flow of water. Since Sherman is president of the ditch board, he has to stop them. If he doesn't, we'll have a ditch war, and that would be terrible."

"But will he shoot them?"

"I reckon so," she said, "if they don't stop it. He got medals for marksmanship when he was in the war, before I met him." Then she added, "Unless they shoot him first. Now, Dickerino, do you have to go see a man about a dog before we go to bed?"

THE ROMANCE

Charlotte and Sherman's romance and marriage was the one piece of family folklore everybody except my mother found worth retelling, although each of us emphasized a different element of it. My sister Betty emphasized the romance, Jack emphasized the money, and I emphasized the car. They were married in 1928, the year Jack was born and Betty was about six. That would have put Grandma Charlotte at forty-seven, twice divorced and with four grown children, the youngest of whom was twenty. In fact, Sherman, at thirty-eight, was only nine years older than Grandma's oldest son, James, and both of them had served in World War I in France, where Sherman distinguished himself as a sharpshooter, and Jim, as everyone called him, was gassed and severely wounded.

Grandma had raised her four children by herself after their father, George Washington Ashlock, took a powder. My mother said, with some degree of bitterness, "She ran him off," but then, my mother had been extremely fond of George Washington Ashlock and also had some unresolved grudges against her mother. She could not deny that George Washington Ashlock had been a hard drinker. One of the few stories Charlotte ever told about this period of her life was enough to assure me that even if she did "run him off," she had good reason.

She said they started homesteading across the Snake River in 1903, about fifteen miles from Ontario, Oregon. One of Charlotte's brothers, Alfred, had settled on a farm not far away, in New Plymouth, Idaho. After a few years they had a Model A that wasn't paid for and four small children. My mother was the next-to-oldest of these, and the only girl. George Washington would take the Model A into town and get drunk in one of the saloons. When he didn't come home, Charlotte would have to get her four children out of bed, bundle them up if it was winter, harness a team of horses and hitch them to the wagon, and go into town, sometimes when it was snowing, to bring him home.

"Well," she said to me thoughtfully, many years later, when all those children had grandchildren, "I couldn't leave the children alone, and I couldn't let him try to drive home drunk. I did what I had to do." And she did it again and again. Finally she did something else she had to do, although it was severely frowned upon by the community. She got a divorce. George Washington Ashlock, after drifting through the West for several years, became a sheepherder in northern Idaho.

Most of the grudge my mother held in regard to Charlotte had to do with the men in Charlotte's life, the men other than George Washington Ashlock. After becoming a divorcée, Charlotte worked hard to make a living for her four children. At first she worked as a laundress in a brickyard in Pendleton, Oregon. Later she hired out as a cook on large ranches. But she was young, lively, and attractive. She played the fiddle and she loved to dance. I think my mother's account of Charlotte's affairs and live-in boyfriends was exaggerated, but it was not, in fact, without foundation, although most of these liaisons probably occurred after Charlotte's second marriage had failed, when my mother was in her early and mid-teens, a difficult time for a proper young lady whose mother seems bent on flaunting the conventions of society.

The second marriage was, by everybody's account, a short-lived disaster, although I never heard Charlotte mention it at all. His name was Blanton. All I know about him is hearsay from my mother and one of her brothers, although I have photographs that verify part of it. Blanton, it seems, was a dandy and a gambler, accustomed to fine clothes and fancy women. He evidently saw the moneymaking potential in Charlotte's children, who ranged in age from about eight to about seventeen, and three of them were boys. He leased a large tract of timberland somewhere in north-central Idaho and set about harvesting the lumber, using Charlotte's children as his crew. I have a wonderful photograph of my mother at about fourteen, plump and pretty in a pair of overalls and a man's cap at a rakish angle, on one end of a large crosscut saw. But the party ended when the youngest child, Bob, was seriously hurt by a falling tree. Charlotte divorced Mr. Blanton, her second divorce in an era when a divorced woman was judged harshly by the conservative moral code of the rural West. How she felt about it, she never told me, nor as far as I know, did she ever tell anybody else. She did what she had to do.

She'd had it with Mr. Blanton and with marriage, but she still liked men, and they still liked her. Her daughter Hazel, whom most people at that time called Josie because she had been given her grandmother Josephine's name as a middle name, found life with her unconventional mother increasingly trying. Even when she was an old woman, my mother seemed embarrassed to talk about it, and would do so only when I pressed her. I don't think she mentioned her mother's domestic arrangements to anybody but me, although she might have told Betty.

"She had different men living there with her, right in the house," Mother said. "I couldn't stand it. I got out. I was so ashamed."

Perhaps one of Grandma's boyfriends had a roving eye for his lover's pretty young daughter, or perhaps one of them even made overtures to her. Mother implied as much, although she never said so directly. Mother wanted genteel respectability above all else, but her mother had worked too hard and seen too much of life to be overly hampered by such ideas, although I'm sure she tried to be as discreet as she could without severely restricting her behavior. There was no hiding the fact that they lived in extreme poverty. It would have seemed foolish to Charlotte to adopt the hypocritical gentility of the upper middle class.

During World War I, Charlotte's oldest son, Jim, was sent home from a hospital in France as a basket case. He was placed in the veterans' hospital in Boise for a long, painful recuperation from the effects of mustard gas. Charlotte, with her two younger sons, moved to Boise to be near him.

Although I know what happened, the exact sequence of events now grows a little hazy. None of those who told me Charlotte's story, including Charlotte herself, seemed to remember what year anything happened. My mother's journals contain lists of the dates of births, marriages, and deaths, but none of the journals—Josie's, Charlotte's, or Hazel's—cover the period between World War I and 1930. To place an exact date on anything other than a birth, marriage, or death during that period is difficult at best, and often impossible. Dated photographs are of considerable help.

Charlotte remained in Boise, and so did all her children, who, one by one, married and began their families. She eventually was living alone. At some point between her move to Boise and 1928, she worked as a chambermaid in a famous Basque boardinghouse, the DeLamar. The DeLamar was named after the mining capitalist Joseph R. DeLamar, as was the mining community in the Owyhee Mountains that boomed in 1890. It was the classiest of several Basque boardinghouses in Boise, and Boise was and still is a cultural center for Basques in the Northwest.

Male Basque immigrants coming to the region to work in the mines or herd sheep on one of the huge Idaho sheep ranches usually stayed in a Basque boardinghouse in Boise until they found work. These boardinghouses were like a little bit of home to them, and they sheltered them from the worst effects of culture shock. All the boarders spoke Basque, and Basque food was served, hot and spicy. When the men returned to town between jobs, they also stayed in one of the Basque boardinghouses. One of the boardinghouses near where the DeLamar stood even had an indoor pelota court, and that building has survived, although it is no longer a boardinghouse.

The DeLamar was queen of them all, a three-story "painted lady" with a distinctive mansard roof. It was still there when I grew up in Boise, although it was run-down and looked odd in the midst of used-car lots, parking lots, and warehouses. Grove Street had once been the most fashionable street in Boise, but that was long ago. The DeLamar was torn down in a frenzy of civic renovation that destroyed many of the most significant and interesting buildings in town; however, one room—the parlor of the old DeLamar—has been reconstructed in the Idaho State Historical Museum, but it is a sad and lifeless thing. One cannot see the lace curtains moving at the open windows or hear the canary in a cage in the next room, or the two Basque sheepherders arguing over the probable outcome of tomorrow's pelota game.

My parents married in 1921. All I know about Charlotte between then and just before she married Sherman is scandal—scandal of such proportions it could have blown the entire family to pieces had it been generally known and admitted. To what degree it was known, I have not been able to find out. I suspect it was known by several members of the family who chose simply to look the other way and avoid problems. At some point after her daughter married Leonard Shelton, and for several years, as far as I can tell, Leonard's mother-in-law, Charlotte, was the mistress of one of Leonard's older brothers, who was married and had several children. My father had five older brothers, all of whom were married and had several children. I'm not telling which one it was.

To say that my mother was upset by her mother's affair with her husband's brother is a vast understatement. She was seething with anger and shame. Telling me about it, even fifty years later, when she was an old woman, was painful for her. My mother's need to project an aura of respectability, even gentility, was very strong. When it came to discussing anything sexual, she was a prude. Once when I was about eight, while I was reading the newspaper over her shoulder, I came upon the word *rape* and asked her what it meant. She refused to tell me.

In regard to her mother's illicit affair with her husband's brother, Hazel was in a terrible bind. She could barely stand to look at her handsome mother during this period, but she could not break off relations with her because to do so would be to admit that she knew what was going on. Poor Hazel. She could only suffer inwardly and hope her mother would "come to her senses." Some scars are so deep that even the family amnesia curtain can't cover them entirely.

Finally the affair ended. I have no idea why, not any more than I know the circumstances that brought it about in the first place. Perhaps Charlotte did "come to her senses," as my mother had hoped, or more probably she grew tired of her lover and the awkwardness of the situation. My uncle's wife never left him, and years later, when I was a child growing up in Boise, Charlotte and my uncle seemed to be on good terms whenever circumstances brought them together, which was seldom. My mother felt that my uncle's wife probably knew about the affair but pretended she didn't.

Whatever my mother thought, she did not openly let her mother know how displeased and humiliated she was. Charlotte continued to visit with her daughter and her daughter's family, and when Hazel was pregnant with her second child, my brother Jack, Charlotte often came to help her with the housework or to babysit Betty. She stayed with the family when Jack was born in 1928, taking care of Betty and Leonard while Hazel was in the hospital and recuperating. Charlotte's spending much of her time at my parents' house brought on the next episode in her ongoing love life, and it was almost more than my poor mother could bear.

"Your grandma Charlotte," my mother said many years later, "took up with the iceman. The iceman! You could have knocked me over with a feather. It was the last straw."

An iceman used a large pair of tongs to hoist a big block of ice onto his back, bring it into the house through the back door, and put it in the icebox. Charlotte and the iceman chatted amiably each time he delivered ice to my parents' house, and she would serve him a cold drink. He was handsome but shy. Finally he asked her to go dancing with him, and she accepted readily. The romance flared quickly, while Hazel bit her tongue and pursed her lips. "If she is still so all-fired attractive to men," my mother said to herself, "she could at least find one with a little money so she could be secure in her old age. The iceman! The very idea! At least this one is a bachelor, or says he is. That's an improvement, but not much." How could Hazel face her relatives and acquaintances who probably knew that her mother had broken off an affair with Red's married brother only to "take up with the iceman"?

The iceman's name was Sherman Beech. He was indeed a bachelor who lived with and took care of his aged mother, a widow. They lived simply, but he and his mother owned a considerable amount of property that his father had amassed. It included most of what was then the tiny community of Parker, Arizona, several homes in Boise, and land in Oklahoma. I have heard various members of my family say that Sherman owned "oil land" in Oklahoma, but I doubt that this was true. Judging by the estate he left when he died—which was a considerable estate—I imagine his Oklahoma land was range-land. Sherman was very well off, but perhaps not as rich as "oil land" would suggest. At any rate, by my parents' standard, he was wildly rich, although they would not find out about it until after Charlotte had agreed to marry him in a quiet, private ceremony. At that point, there was considerable backpedaling.

"Well, how was I to know?" Hazel would say years later. "He was just as down-to-earth as an old shoe, and he was working as an ice-man. Rich people are too eccentric. Sometimes you can't tell."

I have never found any plausible explanation for why Sherman was working as an iceman. There are hints here and there that he might have owned at least part of the ice company. This theory is strengthened by the fact that two of Charlotte's sons later worked for the same ice company.

It is entirely possible, however, that Sherman was working as an iceman simply because he enjoyed it. On hot summer afternoons the children in the neighborhood forgot about their marble games and ball games when they saw the ice truck coming down the alley, often listing to one side with little dribbles of water leaking out the back. The truck contained big blocks of ice that the iceman chopped into smaller blocks. There was always a residue of ice chips, and the iceman doled these out by the handfuls to the eager children who promptly popped them into their mouths or down one another's necks, screaming with delight. The ice had the faint taste of the saw-dust it was packed in. Often the children rode on the tailgate of the ice truck, swinging their legs and enjoying the cold air flooding out from inside the truck, until the iceman would stop in the middle of the next block and tell them the ride was over. Yes, I can see how Sherman might have enjoyed being an iceman.

The first thing Sherman did after he married Charlotte in 1928 was buy the Rickenbacker. In this the couple set off on their honeymoon, a six-month trip that took them through the West and Midwest and deep into Mexico. I have a photograph of Charlotte taken about this time. She is standing beside the Rickenbacker, slender and assured, wearing a dark patterned silk dress edged with fur around the bottom of the skirt and sleeves and one simple, long strand of pearls that reaches to her waist. From her broad-brimmed hat trimmed with feathers to her shoes, she is utterly elegant. No one could possibly believe this woman had been a laundress in a brickyard or a chambermaid in the DeLamar boardinghouse, although it was probably a matter of complete indifference to Charlotte whether anybody knew these things or not. She was who she was, and her pearls and beautiful clothes had not changed her. The real change was that she had finally found the love of her life.

During the honeymoon trip they visited Parker, Arizona, then consisting of a hotel, saloon, primitive gas station/café, and little else. It was hot, dusty, and two blocks long. Charlotte didn't much care for Parker, Arizona, and neither did Sherman, so he sold it. Actually, they didn't find anything anywhere they liked better than the Boise Valley, and Sherman wanted, above all else, to be a farmer.

⌐

I'm almost to the ranch now. There's Canada Lane, coming in from the north. It's still Canada Lane as it heads south on the other side of the highway, but everyone around here called it Turtle Dove Lane. I always thought it was named Canada after the country, but it wasn't. It was originally *Can-Ada* because it marked the line between Canyon and Ada Counties. Like the Chinden Boulevard (Chinese-Garden) trick in Garden City. To the south it was lined with big silver maples, and there's still a low line of silver-maple growth, although the parent trees are gone.

A family lived down Turtle Dove Lane with two boys about my age or a little older. Their father had them with him one day when he stopped by the ranch to see Sherman on some farm business. After the initial awkwardness, when we stood eyeing one another, ready to become enemies at the slightest provocation, I decided I liked the boys and they decided I was OK too. They invited me to ride Old Paint, the sorrel I thought of as my own, over to their place and we could all go riding together down by the river and maybe fish some. I liked the idea.

After they left, Grandma Charlotte said, "I don't want you to go to their house alone under any circumstances. And if you should go there with Sherman on farm business, you must not eat or drink anything there, no matter what they offer you!"

I was surprised and disappointed. She was very serious. It was not like Grandma Charlotte to issue ultimatums. When I asked her why, the only answer she would give me was, "They're dirty. They're dirty people, and you might catch some disease."

So I did not go to the house down Turtle Dove Lane for more than a year, but one summer afternoon Sherman and I were coming from somewhere in the wagon. Sherman had been letting me practice handling the team. All that power concentrated in the thick reins I could barely get my hands around. For some reason I do not recall, we stopped at the farm where the two boys lived.

They were cleaning out the pit under their privy. Rather than bury the old pit when it got full and dig a new one, they were shoveling the contents of the pit into tubs to be dumped somewhere. I didn't know where. Perhaps on the garden. The farmer and his two sons were standing in the pit with shovels and buckets, almost waist deep in semiliquid shit. They showed no indication that they thought their situation was at all unusual, and although they were friendly, we stayed only a few minutes. On the way home Sherman laughed and said, "Well, I guess you know what your grandma was talking about." He found the entire episode vastly amusing.

Sherman had recently built a fancy new privy. The original privy had been a simple affair, painted red and leaning a bit to one side. It never felt entirely secure. One night, when I was about five, I opened the door to the privy to see a light streaming up from below. I was too frightened even to run. At first I thought it was a ghost. Then I thought it must be the Holy Ghost, whose name I had heard mentioned on the radio. Finally I ran screaming to the barn, where Sherman was milking. He told me that his flashlight had rolled in earlier that night. After that, I was always slightly afraid of the privy, and happy when the new one replaced it. The new privy, built on the other side of the ditch, was constructed over a concrete pit that, if treated properly with lime, would probably never fill up. It was solid, comfortable, well-vented, and painted white.

It was called the "chick sales." All the neighbors called their privies the "chick sales" too, and I never knew why.

I have pulled off the highway onto Turtle Dove Lane and turned off the motor. *You don't have to do this,* something says in my head. *Turn around and go back to Boise. Why make yourself suffer? You know it's going to be bad. You've seen it in recent years.* And another voice says, *What good did you ever get out of going back to Boise? Face it! The ranch is gone. They are all gone, and you are an old man behaving like an idiot. You've come this far. Take a good, hard look and then get on with your life.*

The swale beside the road is full of cattails at just the right stage to cut, color with crayons, twist into patterns and put in a tall vase in the front hall. Somewhere out of sight a tree toad is carrying on. Cicadas are drilling my ears with their shrill racket, starting and stopping as if going over the same passage again and again, trying to get it right. I can smell recently cut alfalfa, the acrid odor of yarrow, and something sweet. It must be wild sweet peas. I don't know why I have come here. It will be worse than seeing the body of someone I loved in a coffin. It will be like seeing the body of someone I loved *decomposed*.

Then, cutting through all my morbid thoughts like the sound of a crystal bell, the song of a meadowlark reminds me that some things have not changed. My brother and sister are dead and the place I loved the most has been destroyed, but some things have not changed: the song of the meadowlark, the flash of silver maples, the smell of alfalfa being cut, the sea-foam green of a field of oats moving like waves in the wind.

I turn around in the graveled lane and get back on the highway, driving slowly toward the ranch as the sun throws long amber shadows of farm buildings across the dark green of the pastures. The Schaeffer place is off to the north. The Groom place is on the right side of the highway, and on the other side is the Froman place. And there it is, something that was once the Beech place, now shattered like wreckage floating on still water. I pull off the highway and stop. The trees are gone. The yard and garden are gone. The barn has fallen into ruin and most of the other outbuildings have been taken away. Abandoned farm equipment is scattered here and there. A small addition has been tacked on to the side of the house. It looks otherwise uncared for. It's not a place anymore. It has no integrity. The spirit of the place has been destroyed, and I know why.

Forty-three years ago today—June 27, 1957—after putting in his regular day's work, Sherman died of a heart attack. Charlotte's journal entry, the longest entry in any of her journals, departs only in its last line from her rigid policy of expressing no emotions.

> *Thurs. 27 Sherman irrigating yard and west pasture. He was feeling fine. Ate a good supper then went and turned the water off and when he got back he had terrible pains in his chest and arms and lay down and slept about half hr. Then had a heart attack and passed suddenly away at 8.10 PM. God only knows what a great loss we all suffered.*

Charlotte was seventy-six. They had been married almost thirty years. Her grief was terrible to witness because she would not give in to it, but part of her had gone away and would never come back. I had not realized how much intense grief is like shock. While she eventually resumed much of her previous outlook and intelligence, she was never again the woman I had watched dancing the schottische with Sherman, dashing the full length of the living room and dining room to put her "little foot right there." There was, in the ensuing years, a quiet fatalism about her. She was waiting to join Sherman, and everybody knew it. Neither she nor any of us realized she would have to wait twenty-six years.

Unable to work it alone, she sold the farm we all called "the ranch" to the neighbor on the adjoining farm to the west, which accounts for its dismemberment. It was no longer a "homeplace" like the other farms around it, but merely an adjunct to one of them, and the new owner was interested only in the land. He rented out the house, incorporated the fields into his farm, and allowed the barn and outbuildings that he didn't move to his place to simply fall apart over time. Charlotte moved to Boise to live with her oldest son, Jim, whose wife had just left him.

In the fall of 1969, when I was in Boise, Grandma Charlotte was living about two miles away from Red and Hazel's with Jim and Jim's second wife. I often took Charlotte for a ride in my little blue Triumph. We would drive around town some and then out into the countryside where she could tell the difference between field corn and sweet corn in the distance at sixty-five miles an hour.

Charlotte was eighty-eight. She loved the little car, especially with the top down and the wind blowing her hair, but she had some difficulty getting her feet in over the raised door sill. Actually, everybody had trouble getting their feet into that car. It simply wasn't built to accommodate a passenger's feet. Each time she struggled to get into the car she would mumble something about her "big feet." She wore a size seven shoe. Finally one day I said, "Grandma, what is all this about your big feet? You don't have big feet."

"Oh yes, I do," she said, giving me a grin and a quick flash of her gold tooth. "Terrible big feet. Why, when I was a girl, you know my mother—her name was Josephine but everybody called her Josie—died when I was young, and later I lived with my aunt. She was very worried about my future. Girls had smaller feet before the turn of the century. One time my aunt said to me, 'Poor Charlotte. You have such big feet. No man will ever love you.'" The grin was gone, but there was a decided twinkle in her eye, and her soft smile made me think of the *Mona Lisa*.

PART IV

CHARLOTTE'S JOURNALS

The journals of Charlotte Beech (née Adams) begin with an entry on January 1, 1942, and continue without interruption until September 1, 1976, the day Charlotte's oldest son, her beloved Jimmy, died. There are five journals. The first two are hardback lined ledgers. The second two are thick spiral notebooks like those commonly used by students. The last journal is loose-leaf, and except for the last few pages, it is written on yellow lined paper from a standard writing pad. The last three pages are written on various kinds of white paper, and the entire last journal is contained in a manila envelope. After Charlotte's death at the age of 102, these journals were preserved by my mother, Hazel, and upon Hazel's death, they were given to me.

THE NETWORK

The entries in Charlotte's journals would not be exciting reading for most readers, and even those events that probably were exciting are narrated in such a way as to rob them of all excitement. Like: *Mon. March 27, 1943 Got lumber for chicken house. Started building. Wind blew it down.*

In fact, many of the earlier entries would not make sense to a contemporary reader with no knowledge of farm life during the 1940s and no knowledge of the people Charlotte is referring to. Much of those early journals have become a kind of code available to fewer and fewer people, a record of a way of life that no longer exists.

What should the reader make of an entry like this? *Wed. June 24, 1944 Sherman helped Jess float.* This mysterious passage has nothing to do with swimming lessons or navigation. It means that Sherman took his team of horses and helped his neighbor across the road, Jess Froman, level his fields. They did this by dragging a heavy wooden sled, which was called a float and weighted with stones, over the plowed fields. Since the fields will be irrigated, getting them level is essential.

Beneath such a simple entry is an entire way of life. It is obvious from the journals that Sherman spends almost as much of his time working on his neighbors' farms as he does on his own. His neighbors, in turn, are always helping Sherman. Reading through the journals, one becomes aware that both Charlotte and Sherman are operating within a large network of neighbors, relatives, and friends. The complexity of that network is staggering. Such networks in rural communities have been greatly diminished, if not lost entirely, with the coming of more highly developed technology and the disappearance of the small diversified farm.

While Sherman is helping Jess Froman float, Charlotte and Jess Froman's wife are trading roosters. According to the journals, they do this repeatedly. I can see Grandma Charlotte striding down the lane and across the highway with a large red rooster held firmly under her arm.

But why? It must have been to avoid inbreeding since each rooster would otherwise be breeding with young pullets hatched from eggs that rooster had fertilized. Under many of the seemingly simple entries in Charlotte's journals during her years on the farm is a web of relationships and practices so complex and sophisticated as to baffle me now, although I was, as a child, often part of that life, and it seemed relaxed and simple at the time.

In spite of the terseness of her entries, there is a rhythm to Charlotte's journals that is pleasing. It is the reflection of the rhythm of her life. Something is accomplished every day and the relative importance of the various accomplishments—whether it is scrubbing the back bedroom or keeping a grandson out of jail—is never stated in the journal. In fact, many of the more personal family matters that most people would consider important, like keeping a grandson out of jail, are referred to so obliquely that an outsider who happened to read the journal would never know what was going on.

The network within which Charlotte and Sherman operated on the farm near Star included several layers other than the neighbors. In terms of work and the daily running of the farm, the most important layer was the Nesbitts. Martha Nesbitt, Sherman's widowed sister, and her many children lived on a farm near Eagle. Sherman had bought the farm for Martha when she became a widow, and had installed her and her children on it.

The devotion of Martha's seven grown or nearly grown children to Sherman, and consequently to Charlotte, was absolute. Sherman functioned as a surrogate father to them. One of Martha's four sons, in fact, was named after him and was always referred to as "Little Sherman," even after he was much bigger than his uncle. All of the boys—Joe, Donald, Ben, and Little Sherman—were hardworking and accomplished farmers who not only did the work on their mother's farm but were a great help to Sherman, especially when he was too ill to manage the work on his own farm. The three girls—Bonnie, Lilly, and Gladys—were of considerable help from time to time as well, especially Gladys, the oldest, the niece who had once helped Charlotte fence a ten-acre field.

Charlotte's journals are replete with references to the Nesbitts, especially to the work one or the other of the Nesbitt boys (or men) are doing for Sherman, and she and Sherman drive to the Nesbitt farm at least once each week for a visit with Martha. Considering this close relationship, as well as constant interaction with the neighbors, as well as visits by Charlotte's children and extended stays by at least one of her grandchildren, life on the farm was an elaborate dance of hard physical work, visiting, entertaining, and mundane daily accomplishments:

> *June 1943*
>
> *Thur. 10* *Sherman took calf to Caldwell. Cloudy nice cool breeze. Dan helped Jerome hay. Donald mowed our hay.*
>
> *Fri. 11* *Sherman raked. Rained in evening.*
>
> *Sat. 12* *Cloudy a bit rainy. Went to Star and to Martha's.*
>
> *Sun. 13* *Cloudy. Sheltons were down. Had a big dinner for Sherman. Rained a bit at night.*
>
> *Mon. 14* *Cloudy a bit stormy. Planted red beans.*
>
> *Tue. 15* *Beautiful day. I washed. Sherman went to Nash's and got Jackson fork. Also went to Star and to Nesbitts.*
>
> *Wed. 16* *Donald and Ben helped put up our hay.*

Life on the farm is seasonal. It's haying time. Sherman's birthday is June 14. This time Red has managed to stay relatively sober during his drive to the ranch, and once he arrives, he is magically transformed into Leonard, although he sneaks out to the car for a drink once in a while. The big meal—fried chicken, dumplings, mashed potatoes and gravy, corn on the cob, green beans, tossed salad, biscuits, iced tea, cake, and ice cream—helps keep him in condition to drive home.

The Jackson fork Sherman needs to stack hay is a huge metal jaw with long teeth that is attached to the end of the hay derrick by a set of ropes and pulleys. A wagon loaded with hay pulls up beneath the derrick. The fork is dropped onto it and scoops up a loose mouthful of hay the size of a small car. One of the men raises the derrick arm and swivels it until the fork is directly over the right spot on the haystack. The line is tripped, the jaws open, and the hay falls. A man on top of the haystack then spreads the hay so the stack will be built evenly. Evidently the farmers in the area have invested in one Jackson fork that they pass around from farm to farm as it is needed. The haystack varies in size depending on the time of year and how much of it has been used to feed the stock, but at its biggest, right after haying, it's about the size of a modest two-story house and shaped like a loaf of bread. It diminishes sometimes to almost nothing by the following summer, but during the summer the cows and horses have plenty of pasture to graze on.

The derrick looms large and stark beside the haystack, like something on a medieval field of battle. Four poles the size of telephone poles join at the top to support the arm that swivels and to which the fork is attached.

In the days when Jack and I were allowed to be at the ranch together, Jack invented a game involving the derrick that was, although extremely dangerous, something like the thrilling rides at the fair. It scared me silly, but I enjoyed it. Jack and I would climb the ladder to the top of the haystack, and he would tie the rope at the end of the derrick through my belt. He would then go to the other end of the derrick's arm and swivel me out away from the haystack where I dangled and gyrated twenty-five to thirty feet above the ground. It was most exciting when he moved the derrick arm back and forth rapidly, causing me to whipsaw through the air at great speed. Fortunately, my belt never broke. Finally Sherman caught us playing this game and put a stop to it.

It is a coincidence that the man who came to fill a position somewhere between family member, hired hand, and trusted friend had the same last name as Sherman with a different spelling. Dan Beach, or as everybody called him, "Old Dan." Dan was a bachelor, a drifter, a jack-of-all-trades—one of many such men who found their way onto the Snake River Plain, usually from the Midwest, men who seemed to thrive on loneliness, their own bad cooking, and little else.

When Sherman and Charlotte first encountered him, he was living in a modified sheepherder's trailer across the highway on Jess Froman's property. I don't know whether Dan had been a sheepherder, but his personality, way of life, and the trailer would suggest it. He might have been working for Jess, or Jess might simply have provided him with a place to put his trailer as a kind gesture.

Sherman and Charlotte took a fancy to Dan. It is partly pity, but also they felt that Dan might be handy to have around, especially if he doesn't indulge too often in the disconcerting habit of taking his teeth out in the middle of a sentence and examining them as if they were a malfunctioning piece of farm equipment. Eventually this problem is solved when he simply throws them away.

A bargain is struck and an invitation issued. Dan would move his trailer across the road and park it near one of the weeping willows beside the ditch. Sherman and Dan, with the help of the Nesbitt boys and several neighbors, would build Dan a house, or "cabin," as he calls it, just on the far side of the ditch. It is a single large room, painted white on the outside and deliberately left unpainted on the inside because Dan will soon cover the walls and ceiling with what Charlotte refers to as "Dan's junk," a fairly accurate description of what Dan collects with a steady passion, especially since he now has a place to put some of it. Dan goes to the farm sales in Caldwell and Nampa and bids on unopened boxes of whatever: farm tools, nails, harness, rope, chains, gadgets, parts of hay balers or threshing machines, plumbing supplies, old lamps, light fixtures, picture frames, or anything else that happens to be in the boxes. He accumulates enormous amounts of this material, which he sorts carefully and stores wherever he can. One of Charlotte's repeated entries in her journal is *Dan went to Caldwell. Brought back another load of junk.*

Dan's cabin quickly begins to resemble the inside of Orville Jackson's Drug Store. Walls, ceiling, and most of the floor are covered, leaving him barely room to get to his bed in the corner and his stove and table in the middle of the room. In spite of that, it is not an unpleasant room, especially on winter nights when he heats up the stove and invites any of Charlotte's visiting grandchildren in for homemade fudge.

A really significant entry concerning Dan appears in Charlotte's journal on March 17, 1942. *Dan sold trailer.* It is done. Dan would never sell his trailer, which represents his freedom and ability to roam, if he had not decided to settle in for good, nor would Sherman and Charlotte let him sell it unless they were sure the three of them were compatible. Their arrangement is now for better or for worse. Dan cooks his own meals in his "cabin" unless he is ill, and then Charlotte carries food out to him. In fact, she often takes food out to him, explaining that she cooked more than she and Sherman can eat.

To Charlotte's grandchildren, Dan's house is a magical place. Nearly anything that is needed to repair anything can be found there if one is patient enough to wait while Dan finds it, and Dan enjoys nothing better than to rummage through his treasures in search of just the right-sized piece of leather for the pocket on a slingshot or the right-sized nut for a bicycle.

The neighbors, in addition to swapping labor and equipment with Sherman, find their way to Dan's cabin to get the exact kind of valve or piece of tubing they need to fix whatever has broken down. They troop across the pages of Charlotte's journals without background or description—just names. Jess Froman, Jess Berry, Tom and Neil Shaffer, the Grooms, the Nashes, the Roes, the McGraths, the Frasiers, the Jeromes. If they aren't working on one another's farms, they are loaning or borrowing equipment from one another, or helping out with the chores when somebody is sick. Meanwhile, "Old Dan" shuttles back and forth to the sales in Caldwell and Nampa, bringing home loads of "junk" he knows will come in handy. "It was only a quarter apiece for the three boxes, and you know sure's shootin' there's things in there folks is goin' to need."

The rhythm of life on the farm was so natural, predictable, and re-laxed when I was a child that I am almost shocked reading Charlotte's journals now to see how much coming and going there was. A day when no one comes to visit or stops by to see Sherman about something is an unusual day, and Charlotte makes note of it. *Nobody came today.* Weekends often bring one group of visitors after the other, and Charlotte entertains with coffee and cake or iced tea with fresh mint while Sherman usually continues to work.

The chores include feeding and watering all the stock in the winter, when there is no water in the ditch. Enough water for about forty cows and several horses must be pumped by hand into a trough made of a huge hollowed-out log near the cow barn. A series of entries in mid-March 1942 tells the story of Sherman, who has been sick in bed, getting out of bed and going out into a cold wind to pump water for the stock. Milking is the biggest chore of all. The cows must be milked twice a day, and Sherman does it by hand until June 22, 1942. On that date Charlotte, in her usual understated way, makes an entry signifying a fact that will change their lives. *Got milking machine.*

Even before that, everything had changed, although most of us didn't realize how completely it had changed. The entries in Charlotte's journals record the broad effects of the war on the entire family. In mid-June 1942, her son Wig leaves for Portland to work in the shipyards. Eventually all three of her sons will wind up on the coast working in various shipyards. On September 5 she records Jim's departure, and on October 16, *Bob left for Portland.* Martha Nesbitt's two oldest, Joe and Gladys, join the army, leaving the younger Nesbitts to work that much harder on the farm. When Gladys comes home on leave, Sherman and Charlotte take me to the Nesbitts to see her in her uniform. She looks terrific.

Sherman is a member of the Canyon County draft board and drives to Caldwell each month to help register civilians for the army draft, including his nephews. He works harder to produce more food with less help. He listens to war news on the radio while he's milking. Even with the machine, it's one cow at a time, a long process. He thinks about handsome young Joe, who is fighting in Italy, and about his other nephews, Donald, Ben, and Little Sherman, who are almost old enough to go to war.

INTO THE WOODS

Charlotte began her first journal less than a month after the Japanese attack on Pearl Harbor, and by means of the first journal, I can trace the Sheltons' wartime peregrinations. In late June 1942, just as I am turning nine years old, Red leaves Boise to take a job as a painter on a new naval installation being built in northern Idaho near the little town of Sandpoint. I have spent most of the summer at the ranch. Grandma and Sherman listen to war news on the radio, but I am much too involved with riding "my" horse, Old Paint, swimming in the ditch, and generally having a good time to pay much attention.

Sherman has a special little calf in the front pasture—a future bull, the result of his careful breeding—and he says I can take care of it on my own. I love the calf and haul water and food to it every day. We spend hours together. The calf and I race each other around the pasture, butt heads, and play. One day I decide it would be a good idea to put a bell on the calf so I can tell where he is at all times. I find a cowbell and attach it to a loop of leather harness. While the calf is eating oats out of the pan I have given him, I slip it over his neck. At the first sound of the bell on its neck, the calf goes crazy. Wild-eyed, he runs madly around the outer edge of the pasture. The harder he runs, the louder the bell rings. I can't stop him. I'm afraid he will run himself to death. Sherman hears the commotion and comes out of the house, followed by Grandma Charlotte, and finally Dan comes running from his cabin on the other side of the ditch. It takes all of us, waving arms and hats and eventually closing in on the maddened calf to stop it so that Sherman can remove the bell from around its neck.

I am more ashamed than I have ever been. The beautiful creature I have been given to care for and cherish, I have almost destroyed. No one reprimands me. Grandma Charlotte holds me while I cry. "It's OK, Dickerino. You didn't know what would happen. The calf will be all right. Pretty soon he will drink some water and be all right."

No matter how preoccupied I am with each day on the ranch, and no matter how far away the war is, it is closing in on all of us, and some of our lives will be changed in ways too great to be measured. Betty's steady boyfriend for the past year, Monty Barnes, has gone into the air force and is stationed near San Bernardino, California. They have decided to marry. Charlotte captures the breakup of our Boise household in three lines of her journal:

Fri. Aug. 14   *Took Dick home at night. Helped Hazel with trunks.*

Sat. Aug. 15   *Hazel left with boys for Sandpoint.*

Sun. Aug. 16   *Betty left for California.*

Saying good-bye to Betty is tough, but I am wildly excited. For the first time I will travel and find out what is beyond the mountains that form the northern boundary of the Boise Valley, and also what lies beyond the desert to the south. I will see rivers and mountains bigger than I have ever dreamed of. I will ride on a train. We are going to where Red is working as a painter on a vast construction project in the northernmost part of Idaho, Farragut Naval Training Station, which will be the largest inland naval base in the world. We are going about as far north in Idaho as you can get and not be in Canada. We will get off the train at a town called Sandpoint, where Red will meet us and drive us to Lake Pend Oreille, the largest lake in Idaho. They say it is bottomless. I'm struggling with that concept, but it seems to me that if it is bottomless, the water would run out on the other side of the world.

Hazel, Jack, and I and our large German shepherd, Sandy, board the train in Boise, along with suitcases and two large trunks full of everything we will need in order to live in a tent in the woods, including bedding and pots and pans. We also have enough food in a box—fried chicken, bread, hard-boiled eggs, coleslaw, and carrots and radishes from our garden—to last us during the journey to what I believe will be the end of the world, and I am wildly, deliriously happy and eager to go.

The train leaves midmorning. The trip will last all day, all night, and the better part of the next day. Jack and I take turns sitting with

Sandy, who is not in a cage but merely tied up in the baggage car. He seems to be handling the trip pretty well, except that he barks constantly when one of us is not with him, and the men who handle baggage are afraid of him. The train chugs slowly northward through rugged country, weaving along the border, sometimes in Oregon, sometimes in Idaho, sometimes in Washington. The country changes from farmland to desert to heavily timbered mountains. There is a dining car, but Hazel doesn't think we are supposed to use it because we are traveling coach, and anyway, we can't afford it. So we hunker down in our seats and eat from our large box of food, remembering to take some back to Sandy.

Eventually we get to a place called Wallula, Washington, near the southern border of the state. I have heard of Walla Walla, so I decide this name must be some kind of joke. It seems to be one huge railroad yard with dozens of tracks going in all directions. A man across the aisle tells us that the cars in our train are being scrambled here, and some will be shunted to a different train going somewhere else. We are terrified that we will be separated from Sandy, so we all go to the baggage car and wait to return to our seats until the train is moving again. Sandy is overjoyed to see us all at the same time but unhappy when we leave. Jack sits with him for several hours and then comes and wakes me up to take my turn.

It's the middle of the night. I stumble down the aisle to the baggage car, lurching into sleeping passengers and getting an eyeful of young servicemen and their brides who must be on their honeymoons and seem oblivious to others on the crowded train. In the dimly lit coach cars they have spread blankets over themselves, but there seems to be a great deal of movement under the blankets. I am fascinated but try not to let on that I have noticed. When I get to the baggage car, where the dog is barking furiously, I lie down on the dirty wooden floor, curl up with Sandy in my arms, and go to sleep.

When we get to the Sandpoint depot where we expect Red to meet us, he is not there. The depot is all by itself with no other buildings in sight. From the platform behind the depot, there is a view of timbered hills stretching off forever. No sign of any town. Is this really Sandpoint? Our trunks and other luggage are piled on the platform and the train pulls out. It's hot, we are exhausted, and we seem to be in the middle of nowhere. Hazel is angry and frightened. I'm just frightened. Sandy is happy to get out of that baggage car and is running around peeing on every bush and tree he can find.

"They must have let us get off at the wrong place," Hazel says. "I have a terrible headache. He promised to meet us. There's no way I can call him. Oh, Lord, what are we going to do? Jack, take care of Sandy. He's peeing on one of the trunks."

"We were supposed to be here at eight o'clock this morning," Jack says. "The train was seven hours late. He probably gave up on us and hit the bars. When the bars close, he'll remember he was supposed to meet us."

A long silence. We all know Jack is right but don't want to agree with him. Finally, after more waiting, a plan emerges. There is a taxi in front of the depot. Jack and Hazel will take it into town and find a cheap hotel that takes dogs. Sandy and I will stay on the depot platform and guard the luggage. After they find a room, Hazel will hire another taxi, maybe a truck, and return for Sandy and me and the luggage while Jack goes from bar to bar in search of Red. If he doesn't find Red, we will at least have a place to sleep. If Red comes to the depot in the meantime, I'll be there to tell him what we are doing.

I'm not sure why the next two hours, while I perched on top of a trunk and looked out on a wild landscape I had never seen before and Sandy slept in the shade of our pile of luggage, have been two hours I have never been able to forget. Perhaps it was merely anxiety or the fact that I could see nothing but forested mountains on the other side of the railroad tracks. Eventually, Hazel returned, and we were able to get all the luggage, the dog, and me into town and a hotel room, where I immediately fell asleep. Eventually Jack found Red in one of the bars, which stretched for several blocks on both sides of the main drag. Red was mad. He had been meeting every train since early morning. Hazel must have made a mistake. It was her fault.

⌒

Recently, when I decided to go back to Sandpoint and revisit the woods we lived in at Bayview, I'm not sure what kind of ghost I was looking for. Maybe it was the ghost of *us*, of a family that was suffering from the tension of strong pressures to pull it apart and strong pressures to hold it together. Maybe I just wanted to see the landscape again, to assure myself that we had actually, for a little while, been a part of the wildness, the strangeness of it. The central image in my mind, the jumping-off place in this search for ghosts, was that depot in Sandpoint, where, as a child, I sat for several hours, wondering if we were lost forever.

Because of Charlotte's journal, I had a date, and beyond that, just my own faulty memory. I drove more than two thousand miles to find a depot and begin my search. It occurred to me on this trip, for the first time, that all my ghost-chasing trips, unsuccessful as many of them had been, were really attempts to find myself, to define myself by what I found at the end of the ghost trail. And in spite of my failure as a researcher, I had found out a great deal about the blood that ran through my veins and some of the people responsible for it.

When I get to Sandpoint, it turns out that the depot is in the middle of town, a handsome Victorian building of gray stone that looks like a small fortress. I know the moment I find it that I have never before seen this building. *It was more than fifty years ago. Can you trust your memory?* Yes, I say to myself. This is one memory I can trust. This isn't the right depot.

At the local historical museum I learn that there is another depot in town, serving a different railroad line. Aha! But when I get there, it is a small, nondescript building hemmed in with warehouses and industrial businesses—not at all what I remember.

Next morning I go back to the museum and find, as luck would have it, a portly, gray-haired man constructing an elaborate miniature railroad inside the museum. There is something about him—partly the angle at which he wears the cap of a railroad brakeman and partly just him—that tells me railroads are his whole life and always have been. Suddenly, without any preliminaries, I start telling him my story: the 1942 wartime journey and the phantom depot on whose platform the frightened child sat, wondering if his father was lost for good. But where was the depot? It is exactly the kind of puzzle he enjoys. He asks me for the date and, if I can remember it, the approximate time we left Boise. Then he takes me to a back room in the museum and goes to a row of filing cabinets along the wall. In these he finds timetables for several railroads, along with photographs of some of the locomotives used in the '40s.

"You would have left Boise on the Union Pacific," he says, "but that train went on to Seattle. At Wallula you would have been transferred to"—he runs his finger quickly down a long timetable—"the Northern Pacific, and at Spokane"—he shuffles through more timetables—"your car would have been shunted to the Great Northern, which explains the delay, and you would have arrived in Sandpoint . . . out at the Great Northern depot, about five miles out of town. That depot burned down years ago, but they built a new one there, a small one. Do you think you would recognize the setting? It's no wonder your father didn't meet you. He was probably waiting at the downtown depot."

"Well, yes," I say, "the downtown depot was a lot closer to the bars." The railroad expert laughs, although I know it is an uncharitable thing to say. I am amazed at this man's ability to find and negotiate those complex railroad schedules from the past, especially since he is dealing with a wartime schedule and several different railroads. But it sounds right, and I hurry out to the third depot.

I feel, even as I approach the third depot, that this is the place. It is not the building I remember. That had been the standard long yellow frame building with tan trim like hundreds of other depots in small communities throughout the West. The newer building is smaller, dark brown, and nondescript. I park my car and go around to the platform. There it is. I sat on top of a large trunk on that platform when I was nine years old, exhausted and guarding the luggage, wondering if we had been abandoned, looking at those same timbered hills rolling off to the south while a big German shepherd guarded me.

My guess now is that Hazel wired Red that we would arrive in Sandpoint by train at a particular hour. Neither of them realized there was more than one depot in Sandpoint. Then our train was delayed. After meeting several trains at the downtown depot, Red had given up and hit the bars. But why, if this railroad man in a museum more than fifty years later could figure out which depot we would arrive at, couldn't Red have found out that much in 1942? Uncharitable thought again! I am ashamed to have thought it. Again the image of children stumbling through a dark wood on the way to Grandmother's house comes to me, but this time we were stumbling away from Grandmother's house and there would be no one to help us when we arrived at our destination.

Jack would turn fourteen the day after we arrived in Sandpoint. He had finished the sixth grade the previous spring, two years behind the others of his age, having failed two grades. I don't think any of us realized it, but his formal education was over. He had spent much of the afternoon and evening going from bar to bar, looking for his father. He was used to it, and although there were more bars along Boise's Main Street in the area known as skid row, in Boise he knew which bars to look in, and so did I. Jack was wiry, quick, and very strong. He had been setting pins in the Boise bowling alley after school every night and often during the weekend for the past two years. When he got home from the bowling alley late, he would be too exhausted to do anything but punch me to move over as he crawled into bed, and I could smell the cigarette smoke on his breath. This year he didn't expect any presents for his birthday, what with our trip and all, but he would miss the big special dinner Grandma Charlotte always cooked for birthdays at the ranch, and so would I.

Red had bought a little car, a faded blue Dodge coupe, very much used. To him, raised mostly on a farm whose power source was horses, the innards of the internal combustion engine were a great mystery, although he tried to hide his ignorance as best he could. The little car—into which he now managed to get all of us and Sandy, although he would have to make a second trip for the luggage—was to be the cross we bore for the next year. I think of that little car as representative of us, a kind of symbol of our situation. It seated only three, and those three were crowded together. But there were four of us, plus a big dog. At least I counted four of us. I'm not sure Red always did. This meant that I rode on the little shelf above and behind the seat. I could neither lie on it nor sit on it. I could sort of curl up on it with my knees pressed against my stomach and my head pressed against the wall on the driver's side. There were about three inches of space between my head and the ceiling. When we were on rough roads, I learned to brace my hands against the ceiling to avoid a concussion. The night we left Sandpoint, I had no idea I was going to be required in a few months to ride from near the Canadian border to San Bernardino, California, at forty miles an hour, in that position, very much like being shipped from northern Idaho to Southern California in a trunk, only it took much longer. Poor Sandy was on the floor, underfoot and trying to avoid the gear shift.

The night we drove out of Sandpoint in that little car, however, I was filled with relief. We were saved. Red had found us—at least it seemed as if Red had found us and not the other way around—and what I saw as I peered through the little oval window in the back of the Dodge was the most spectacular thing I had ever seen, more magnificent than the foothills north of Boise covered with snow, more incredible even than Incredible Evelyn. A full moon was rising over a huge lake so dark and tranquil, I thought I was dreaming it. And we were in the middle of the lake, crossing what Red told us was the longest wooden bridge in the world. It went on for miles. The lake was Lake Pend Oreille, and we were actually crossing only a small arm of it. After we crossed the bridge, I couldn't see the lake anymore, but the moon was still bright orange. I must have fallen back to sleep in spite of the cramped position, but I woke up when we turned off the highway onto a twisty, rutty dirt road. The little car shook and rattled. I couldn't find anything to hold on to, and when Red braked, only the shoulders of the other three in the car kept me from rolling forward. Finally we went down a steep, curving hill, past some buildings and tents Red said was Bayview, climbed again, and rolled to a dusty stop in front of an old gray tent about six feet square. It was home, but I was too tired and sleepy to care.

Bayview

Bayview had been established as a logging community in 1891. Steamboats pushed flotillas of logs to the mills in the town of Hope, near the northern end of the lake. Later, somebody discovered limestone deposits two hundred feet thick near Bayview, and the town began to boom. Steamboats hauled the lime across the lake to Hope, which was on the Northern Pacific Railway. Kilns in Bayview produced lime from 1904 to 1932. In 1911 the Spokane International Railway brought in a spur line, and Bayview was on the map. But eventually the highest-quality lime was gone and Portland cement raised its standards. In 1932 the kilns stopped operating. Sleepy times returned to Bayview, and in 1936 the railroad spur was abandoned.

The town became a tiny fishing hamlet where a few people kept boats in the summertime. Almost no one stayed there in the winter. It had, as I recall, only one brick building, the post office/gas station/general store/bank. The previous period of lime production had left two or three mansions high above the lake strung along an almost impassable dirt road, abandoned lime kilns, and much abandoned superstructure and equipment to mar the view of one of the most beautiful lakes in America. Then came the war, and Eleanor Roosevelt, a mover and shaker, happened along. She was always going somewhere during the war, inspecting military facilities, exhorting, rallying, making speeches, christening ships, and traveling so much that she became known as a busybody. "Why doesn't Eleanor Roosevelt stay home and mind her own business?" some people said, but most of them said it with a kind of respect verging on awe for this new kind of woman. Everybody was telling jokes about her, but only those told by her husband's political enemies were truly meanspirited. With his nasal tone and unforgettable accent, Franklin D. was quoted as saying, "I've bean in warrr and I've bean in Eleanorrr. I'll take warrr." And this was one of the milder ones. The one about her finding out how the navy cooks make doughnuts would cause a sailor to blush.

But Eleanor, wife of the ex–secretary of the navy who had become the president of the United States, knew that Franklin and the entire War Department were preparing for the probability that military installations on the West Coast would be bombed by the Japanese. She also knew that Franklin and the War Department were looking for some inland body of water in the West, remote from cities, where they could build an enormous naval training base. Eleanor had been in Tacoma, Washington, to deliver a speech. As she was flying home over thousands of miles of seemingly uninhabited mountains in the Northwest, she happened to look down and see a magnificent lake, a spectacular lake—huge, remote, and surrounded by timbered mountains. As soon as she got back to Washington, she said, "Franklin, I have found it." "It" was Lake Pend Oreille, a lake claimed by the locals to be bottomless, a lake so blue it was sometimes violet.

And so the training facility under construction three miles from Bayview when we arrived was Farragut Naval Training Station. Bayview was where nearly everybody who was building it—hundreds of carpenters, concrete finishers, plumbers, electricians, painters, laborers, and their families and sometimes the hangers-on, prostitutes, gamblers, and con artists such a community attracts—lived. It was the ultimate boomtown, tent-town, trailer-town, shantytown for a rough-and-tumble transient population.

As soon as we arrived, Red and one of his friends, with some help from Jack and me, went to work constructing a tent-house. It consisted of a wooden floor built over logs so that it was about two feet off the ground, with board walls about four feet high. A tent was attached to the top of this wall, creating a house that had board floors and a tent roof, although the ceiling was higher than in most tents. It contained nothing in the way of furniture but two beds with sheets hung on a rope between them for privacy. The beds were shallow wooden boxes on short legs. Red built them. When he finished them, we all gathered pine branches to fill them. We put a tarp over the branches and then bedding. They were soft, aromatic beds. When the pine branches began to dry out and lose their needles, we simply replaced them.

When we had finished the tent-house bedroom, Red attached the original tent to it as a lean-to kitchen with a picnic table and wood-burning kitchen stove. Orange crates were the cupboards. The picnic table had its own benches. Otherwise, apple boxes were chairs. It was a cozy arrangement, and I loved it—living indoors and outdoors at the same time. Almost as good as living in a tree house, which I had always considered the ultimate in luxurious accommodations. At night I could hear the pines swaying and creaking in the wind, and the sound of rain on the tent just above my head was delicious. I loved getting dressed on chilly mornings in front of the stove in the lean-to with nothing underfoot but dirt and pine needles.

Communal privies had been hastily thrown up here and there throughout the sprawling camp, and the water supply was already contaminated when we arrived. Dysentery, typhoid, polio, influenza, and even cholera were in the camp. Jack and I hauled all the water the family used more than half a mile in buckets, and all of it that was used for cooking or drinking or washing dishes had to be boiled first.

Once a week for several weeks Hazel, Jack, and I took the bus over the dirt road to the highway and then south to Coeur d'Alene for shots to immunize us against the various diseases. Jack, who was so brave otherwise, simply refused to take the shots. He would go with us into the clinic, but just before his turn came, he would bolt. No amount of coaxing by Hazel made any difference. Then, on the way home, he would find some reason to hit me on my badly swollen and painful upper arms as the bus jolted along. When that happened, I hated him and hoped he would die of some disease he could have prevented by taking his shots. I never understood how someone so brave and tough could be so afraid of the needle and so slyly cruel to me because I had overcome my fear.

The only schoolhouse in Bayview, a handsome frame building with two large classrooms, a big bell in a belfry on top, and quarters across the back for two female teachers, was built between 1915 and

1917 on a pine-covered slope at what had been at that time the edge of the village. It was less than five hundred yards from our tent. Students in the first through the fourth grade met in one room, and students in the fifth through the eighth grade met in the other. It had no plumbing, no running water, and each classroom had a woodburning pot-bellied stove kept supplied with wood by a constant stream of boys hauling logs from the woodpile near the privies. The year before we arrived, before the construction of Farragut Naval Training Station had begun, the school had a total of thirteen students. In the fall of 1942, it had about a hundred. We went to school in shifts, but the number of teachers had not been increased. I don't know how those two women did it, but they managed. I remember them as relatively young and kindly. They had been hired to teach and they taught, but the sudden construction of one of the largest military facilities in the world had blindsided them. Like the majority of the civilian population caught up in one of the most extensive and catastrophic wars in all of history, they did the best they could.

Faced with the mobs of students, most of whom, like us, lived in tents, and many of whom were none too clean or well fed, they used the tried and true methods they knew, methods used in one-room schoolhouses in the West and Midwest for generations. Under the circumstances, I think their methods probably worked as well as more sophisticated ones might have. Maybe even better. The desks in each classroom were bolted to the floor in rigid rows, one desk behind the other from the front of the room to the back, but the students in a particular grade were seated across the room in parallel lines creating tiers for each grade, so that all the students in the sixth grade sat behind all the students in the fifth grade, and so on. The day was divided into equal periods, and the students in whichever grade was sitting across the front of the room recited to the teacher, listened to instructions, or read out loud for one period. Then all the students in that grade got up and moved to the seats across the back of the room, and everybody moved up one tier. Those behind the first tier were supposed to be working on their assignments, and the fact that everybody got up and moved forward every twenty minutes or so kept us from going to sleep. We carried our books and everything we needed with us as we rotated, each of us taking a seat at a desk still warm from its previous occupant, and sometimes finding a note in the desk: *Janey thinks you're cute.* Sometimes a girl, moving up to a desk just occupied by a boy, would raise the lid of the desk and be confronted with a live toad or snake.

Perhaps it's just nostalgia, but I remember that school and everything about it with pleasure. My only regrets were two: that I couldn't stay there longer, and that once, when I had been eating an apple on the playground and the big bell in the belfry began to bong away, signifying the end of recess, I threw the core of apple as far as I could without paying any attention to where I was throwing it and hit one of the teachers squarely in the face. She must have known it was an accident; I don't remember any serious repercussions. Perhaps she felt that my dreadful embarrassment and remorse were enough.

I had come a long way since I got kicked out of the first grade for calling the teacher a "goddamned sunamidge." I had come to admire some of my teachers. I spent a great deal of time reading books, and some of the teachers seemed to approve. I knew I was a "tool" and not really worth anything when compared to Jack, but teachers sometimes seemed to single me out and ask me to read to the class or they would give me the best part in the school play. Or sometimes they even praised me, and I was not used to being praised for anything.

Jack started with me in the two-room schoolhouse in Bayview, but we were in different rooms and met at different times. I was in the early morning session, and he was in the afternoon session. I can only surmise why he dropped out after two days. When the seventh-grade group was at the front of the classroom, he would have been required to read or recite in front of everybody in the room, whether they were listening or not. Jack's reading ability was minimal, and he would have been older than nearly everyone in his group. Many of the words he couldn't have deciphered. The embarrassment must have been too great. He simply announced that he wasn't going back, and that was the end of that. Hazel said he could start over when we were located in a place with a "real" school. Red found a part-time job for him with a subcontractor, cleaning up and loading construction materials. It was undoubtedly illegal for him to be working on a government construction site at that age, but it was wartime, and with so many young men in the service, such rules were often bent. Somebody was doing Red a favor, and Jack had always been a hard and efficient worker.

I was happy when I was in school, even if it was a two-room schoolhouse in the woods of northern Idaho. Especially if it was a two-room schoolhouse in the woods of northern Idaho, because school there, for me, started at 7 a.m. and lasted only until 11:30. Then I could go into the woods. We didn't use the term *wilderness* with the same strict definition we do today, but I think much of what became my playground would have qualified for that term. Thousands and thousands of acres of pristine Douglas fir, subalpine fir, ponderosa, and western white pine. And thickets of dogwood and alders, Rocky Mountain maples, whose leaves turned gold and crimson at the first hint of frost, and syringa, the Idaho state flower. Ferns and mosses, berry bushes and willows. Wild grapes and chokecherries. Aspen and birch. Fire lanes had been cut through it in places, but none of it had been logged.

Nothing in my life so far had prepared me for this, and I was mesmerized by it. If my parents objected to my wandering, at the age of nine, through the deep woods of northern Idaho not far from the Canadian border, in an area where wildcats, bears, and rattlesnakes were plentiful, and timber wolves were still seen from time to time, I have no recollection of it. Some of the time Jack and I wandered through the woods together, but much of the time I was alone, and loved being alone.

Once I came into a small open space, a kind of natural clearing, and in the middle of it was a large hollow tree that looked as if it had been struck by lightning. Sitting in front of the tree was a very old man with a long white beard. He wore nothing but a kind of loincloth made of some material I couldn't recognize. Several birds of various kinds were perched on his shoulders and head. There were squirrels playing over his legs and rabbits beside him and in his lap. He remained absolutely motionless, but his strange eyes shifted to recognize my presence and he smiled slightly. I froze, terrified. I had never seen a face like that. It was completely surrounded with a wild nimbus of silver hair, and it seemed to gather up all the light filtering through the trees and reflect it. In spite of his slight smile and lack of any threatening gesture, I was frightened, but for several seconds I couldn't seem to drag my eyes away from that face. Then I bolted through the woods for home. When I told my story at home, Red amazed me by knowing something about the old man. I had stumbled on to a legend and hadn't had sense enough to stay and get acquainted.

"It was the hermit," Red said. "I heard about him in the bars in Sandpoint. All the locals around here know about him. They say he goes into Sandpoint every few years and walks down the street and looks around and then leaves. Once he had a wolf with him. That would've been somethin' to see. A guy told me that when this hermit was a young man he was a lunger, you know, he had TB, and the doctors pretty well gave him up for dead. So he went into the woods and lived alone, just with the animals. Doesn't wear any clothes to speak of, summer or winter. They think he has a hut somewhere or lives in a hollow tree."

I tried, several times, to find my way back to where I had seen the hermit, but when I finally found the place again, the hollow tree was just a hollow tree and there was no indication that he had been living in it. I never saw him again, although I often looked for him. Somehow, knowing he was there made me feel more comfortable roaming through the woods. I encountered a few rattlesnakes, but they were honorable creatures and warned me of their presence, and once, when I was picking blueberries, I came around a boulder and met a large black bear doing the same thing. I don't know which of us was more frightened, but we ran in opposite directions as fast as we could go. I lost my berry bucket and was too frightened to go back and get it. From then on, when I picked berries, I just did as the bear did—I ate them as I picked. Sometimes I would sit at the base of a tree and try to hold so still that the birds would land on my head or the squirrels would come up to me, but no matter how long I sat there, it never happened, and I couldn't sit still very long because there were too many things to see, too many trails I had never taken.

Jack and I found a switchback trail up one of the steep mountains that surrounded the lake. It had once been a primitive road, and we could see the ruts made by narrow wheels in some places, but it had been abandoned and overgrown and trees had fallen across it. We had to follow it and find out where it went. About three miles up the trail we found a clearing with the ruins of a small house and several outbuildings. In one of the outbuildings was the wreck of a one-horse shay, a light carriage with a leather top or bonnet that could be lowered or raised, much like the top on a convertible car. The house was littered with broken glass, but many small glass vials were still intact, and some were labeled. They had held various kinds of medicines. It appeared that a doctor had lived there. There was also a spring, icy cold and clear. The water came out of an old pipe in the side of a hill and was caught in a round metal container about three feet deep. It was delicious.

Jack and I were excited about our find and could talk about little else. As soon as we got back to the tent-house, we convinced Red to accompany us back up the mountain the following Sunday and see it for himself. When he agreed to do it, Hazel said she wanted to go too. Red and Jack didn't think it was a good idea, and even I admitted she would slow us down, but I sided with her, and finally Red grudgingly agreed. We could leave Sandy to guard the camp, and we knew no one would bother anything.

The real problem was that we didn't know what condition Hazel would be in, especially on a Sunday. For the past couple of years, she had adopted a new strategy in relation to the husband she adored, though I don't know if it was the result of a conscious decision or if she had just drifted into it. She, who had previously been a teetotaler, had decided to drink with him. The result was disastrous. While Red was a complete alcoholic, he had remarkable survival instincts. In his view, there were people who knew how to drink and people who didn't. He did and Hazel didn't. He had certain rules and a kind of discipline that made it possible for him to survive and even make a living of sorts. He never drank on a job. He never drove over forty miles an hour, and when seriously drunk, he drove slower and slower. He usually drank in bars where he had friends who could get him home if he couldn't make it on his own. He came, increasingly, to depend on Jack in various ways when he was incapacitated.

But Hazel, who had not grown up drinking and whose body was totally unaccustomed to the effects of alcohol, was another matter. For the last year and a half, when we lived in the house on 13th Street, her bouts of drunkenness were sporadic but severe when they occurred, and sometimes devastating. Betty came home from school one afternoon with a friend and found her mother lying unconscious at the bottom of the basement stairs in a pool of blood. Red would sometimes take her to the bars with him but, ironically, would be ashamed of her because she couldn't "hold her liquor." Once, when I was with them in a bar, as I often was, she fell off a barstool and Red refused to help her up, which resulted in a terrible fight and Hazel and me being put in a taxi and sent home, with her sobbing and threatening all the way.

The times he took her and me along to the bars were not nearly as bad as the times she got drunk and we went looking for him. Those were the times I dreaded most. It would begin when Red did not come home from work. Hazel would go to the grocery store on the corner and get two quarts of beer. By eight o'clock she would have drunk them both and would have changed her housedress for something fancier and put on her makeup and usually a hat. Then we would head for skid row in a taxi.

As soon as he realized what she was doing, Red began to change the bars he frequented so she couldn't find him. Her pride would not allow her to simply go in a bar and look for him or ask for him and then leave. Nobody must know that she was looking for him. So we would go in a bar and sit down, and she would have a glass of beer, hoping she would see him there. After the third or fourth bar, she could barely walk, and I would be partly supporting her. Because of all the beer, her bladder would make sudden demands. One night, while we were weaving our way down the street to the next bar, she had to pee so urgently that we turned into an alley and she squatted—hat, high heels, and all—in clear view of anybody who might happen to be passing. I was so humiliated I couldn't speak to her for hours, although I continued to help her get from bar to bar.

In Bayview, Hazel stayed sober and coped with the difficulties of camp life during the week. But weekends, when Red was drinking most heavily, were a problem for her, and she often became either boisterous or morose and would lie on the bed in the tent and cry. There was no sense in dressing up in the camp. She usually wore blue jeans rolled up to just below the knees, an old shirt, and one of Red's paint caps or a bandana tied around her head like a turban because her hair was dirty and she had no facilities to keep it clean.

She was by then drinking whiskey because it was more readily available and we had no facilities to keep beer cold, but it irritated Red because it was his whiskey. She had good days and bad days. On her good days she cooked and took care of the camp, boiled the water, did the laundry, heated water for washing and bathing, and sometimes even went to the lake with Jack and me when we went swimming, although she never went into the water above her knees. On her bad days she was neurasthenic and stayed in bed most of the time, complaining of various ailments and pains. On those nights Red was a passable fry cook and I helped, although I could happily survive on peanut butter and crackers. As far as meals went, I think the bad days were hardest on Jack. He had what was always referred to as a "weak stomach."

Many years later, when Red was dying of cancer and I was taking care of him, his stomach would not tolerate many kinds of food, and it reminded Hazel of something. She told me a story about Jack I had never heard before. "When Jack was born," she told me, "he had something wrong with his stomach and the doctor didn't know what it was. He couldn't keep anything down. Instead of gaining weight the way babies are supposed to, he lost a little more weight every day. We tried everything. The doctor had me mix up terrible concoctions, and none of them did any good. He would lie there and cry for food, and as soon as you gave him something, he would throw it up. He was dying.

I thought I would go out of my mind watching him starve. So finally I said I didn't care what the doctor said, and I gave him a sugar tit."

"A what?"

"A sugar tit. You just make a mixture of sugar and water and soak a rag in it. Then you let the baby suck on the rag. Haven't you ever heard of a sugar tit?"

"Well, I guess I have, but I thought it meant something else. Never mind. What happened?"

"He got better. Gradually, gradually he got so he could tolerate milk, but if it hadn't been for the sugar tit, he would have died. His stomach was always weak. You remember there were so many things he couldn't eat when you were kids."

Remember? How could I forget? When I was five or six, I had to eat by myself in the corner behind the water heater because my table manners made him sick. He couldn't stand to have a bowl of gravy on the table because it made him sick. Yes, I remember eating all the food he wouldn't eat, and learning to eat almost anything. Even today I clean everybody's plate. But he could certainly tolerate candy. I suppose because of the sugar tit. When Red and Hazel went out and left him to look after me, they often gave him some change for candy and made him promise to share. He would buy a sizeable sack of penny candy, several varieties, at the little store on the corner and ride away on his bike with it, laughing. I remember running after him and finally giving up and going home, hating the injustice of it and myself for believing things would be different this time.

"Yes," I told her, laughing. "That explains everything. A 'weak stomach' and a sugar tit." But it did help to explain a good many things. They thought he was going to die when he was an infant. Betty and I had been healthy infants. It must have been a dreadful, wrenching time for them, and they got into the habit of giving him anything he wanted. And later, how could they discipline him when they remembered how close he had come to dying. Give him a sugar tit. It explained a good many things.

But in Bayview, on Hazel's bad days, there was no store or café to go to, and Jack had to eat his father's greasy fried potatoes and pork chops, or nothing. Hazel might well have cooked the same thing if she were able, but it wouldn't have been as greasy.

So we planned to go up the mountain on Sunday, when Red wasn't working, and show our parents the old cabin and the shay and the spring and everything, and we just had to hope it would be one of Hazel's good days. I hoped it would be really good, going on an outing together, all of us, like a family—something we hadn't done for a long time. As it turned out, it was one of the worst days of my life. For years I had nightmares about it. Years? I had nightmares about it for several decades.

Climbing the mountain was hard for them. Neither of them was in good shape. Red carried a canteen full of whiskey. About halfway up the mountain, she asked for some of it and he told her she couldn't have it and she fought him and took it away from him and drank a long, thirsty swallow. They shared it the rest of the way. Most of the way up, Jack and I went on ahead and they followed. I was worried. I think Jack was worried too, but his attitude seemed to be to hell with her, the way she was acting.

Finally, we got to the old cabin. They looked at everything and agreed that a doctor must have lived there, but Red was impressed mostly by the spring. The water was as cold as ice water and delicious. We rested by the spring before starting back down the mountain. Hazel was very drunk. She had finished off the whiskey while Red and Jack and I were exploring. She was also argumentative and feeling sorry for herself. Red's drunk had reached a belligerent stage. It was a bad combination.

I can't remember what the substance of the argument was. For Hazel it was probably the accumulation of things—all the times she was left alone, all the other women, how he had been showing her for years that he didn't really care about her. Finally she badgered him until he hit her, as she knew he would eventually, but it wasn't a very hard hit, more of a slap on the side of the head. Jack and I had both seen much worse and had seen her with bruises and black eyes. This was nothing compared to what he might have done if he were drunker, but she turned away quickly, went into a kind of half crouch, and threw herself over a cliff at the edge of the road. Later, of course, when anyone told the story, she slipped and fell, but I saw her jump over the cliff, which was only about a six-foot drop, though I don't think she could have known how far it was to the bottom.

We all rushed to the edge of the cliff and looked down. She must have landed on her knees; they were both bleeding, and one leg was twisted under her at a strange angle. I think she was as surprised at what she'd done as we were. She just sat there at the base of the cliff, staring straight ahead, not even crying. If she had wanted to get Red's attention, she had succeeded, but his reaction was disgust. He, too, had seen that she'd done it on purpose.

We clambered around the edge of the cliff and got down to her. She was scratched and bleeding some, and nothing seemed to be broken, but her left knee was discolored and swelling rapidly. She had wrenched it badly. Getting her back up onto the trail took all three of us, and because of her knee, she wasn't able to help much. The question was whether or not she could walk, and if she couldn't, what were we going to do? We were at least three miles from the base of the trail near our tent-house.

"I can walk if I have some help," she said, looking toward Red. No response from him. She was very pale and almost sober now. "I just need somebody to lean on."

"Lean on Dicky," Red said. "He's just the right height. Me and Jack are going on down. We'll see you when you get there."

Hazel began to cry. Even knowing that Red's usual way of dealing with her was to leave the house and go to the bars, I was shocked and angry as Red and Jack disappeared down the trail.

"He could have at least left Jack to help us," she sobbed.

Finally, she put her arm around my neck and, using me as a crutch, began to hobble down the mountain. I was very worried, but I didn't want her to know. I wanted to be a big brave boy of nine helping his mother down from the mountain, but I was worried about the time. It was already late afternoon. The trail was completely in shadow. I tried to hurry her, but she couldn't go any faster, and often she had to sit down on a rock to rest. Getting over or under the fallen trees would cause her to cry out in pain. The idea of being on that mountain after dark terrified me. I had heard the mountain lions almost every night. They didn't come close to the tent-house like the coyotes and foxes did, but I could hear them on the mountain, screaming like a woman being murdered. I had also heard stories about them, that they stalked people and sometimes jumped out of trees and killed them. I didn't like the idea of the fresh blood on Hazel's knees and what it might attract. All we could do was keep going at our snail's pace as it got dark.

As the light began to fail, I became aware that something was following us. I looked back up the trail as we rounded a curve and saw a silhouette above in the middle of the trail. It could be a dog, I kept telling myself, or a coyote. Surely it couldn't be what I thought it was. *Lord, don't let it be what I think it is,* I prayed. A few minutes later we heard it, and there was no denying what it was. A long, horrible, unearthly scream. Then Hazel knew too.

I was half dragging her now, and there were no more stops to rest. There was enough of a moon that we could see the trail fairly well. She began to cry, quietly. She finally realized why I had been hurrying her so much and that we were in terrible danger. Several times I looked back and saw the mountain lion's eyes reflected by the moonlight. It was closer each time. It never screamed again. I don't know if we could have stood that. I had picked up a stout stick about three feet long and was pretending to use it as a walking stick, but I don't think Hazel was fooled. I thought about making a loud noise. Perhaps that would frighten it away. They said it worked with bears, but I decided to wait until it got closer, to save the noise as final defense strategy. They also said never to show your fear. That was a useless piece of advice. How do you avoid showing your fear when you are being stalked by a mountain lion down a trail in the dark and all you have to protect yourself with is a stick, and you're nine years old and your mother is crippled and bleeding and can't run?

We hobbled on. It seemed like hours. Finally I saw the dirt road below, white in the moonlight, and I knew we were getting close to tents and cabins. Somehow, I didn't think the mountain lion would attack us on the road, but the last few hundred yards of the trail led through a deep stand of pine and fir. I was so frightened I was shaking. I couldn't bear to look back. I didn't want to know how close the mountain lion was. Hazel had become very quiet. I was afraid she was going to faint.

As soon as we got to the road, we began to shout and call, and Sandy came running down the road to meet us. Then we could see the kitchen tent and the fire. Red and one of his drinking buddies, Old Man Denker, were sitting at the table with a bottle between them. Jack had gone to bed. Hazel got a cup and took a long drink of whiskey. We could hear a mountain lion screaming somewhere on the mountain.

BACK TO BOISE

By mid-October the maple and aspen were bursting into patches of crimson and yellow flames. At school we decorated the classrooms with colored leaves. Squirrels were storing nuts and seeds frantically all around the tent-house. The days were getting shorter and cooler. Mornings were cold. Jack and I would run out in our underwear and dress in front of the fire in the kitchen lean-to. One morning, as I ran up the hill to school, it was spitting snow, although it didn't stay on the ground. It was obvious that we couldn't live in that tent-house all winter. Soon the serious snow would come.

I don't think Red had ever intended to spend the winter in Bayview. The idea had probably been to work long hours and make as much money as possible before the snow began to fly, and then head south. Evidently the workforce at the base was being cut back during the winter. Others were leaving the camp as well. One day Red came home from Sandpoint with a two-wheel open trailer with wooden sides about four feet high. We were going to haul our stuff in this behind the little Dodge. And one more thing, Red told us. We were going to be traveling with the Denkers.

The only Denker I had seen was the one called "Old Man Denker," evidently to distinguish him from the other two, his grown sons, Ed and Larry. For a bad moment I had visions of all of us trying to get into the little Dodge coupe. Old Man Denker was a smelly, chain-smoking old drunk. Then I thought maybe that was why Red had got the trailer, for the Denkers to ride in. It was a trailer much like the one Sherman hauled the calves and pigs in when he took them to the sales in Caldwell. If it would be good enough for Sherman's calves and pigs, I said to myself, it'll be good enough for Old Man Denker, and if his sons are anything like him, it'll be good enough for them too.

"The Denkers have a better car than we do," Red said, destroying my fantasies, "and I'll feel better that way if we should have car trouble. I'm not too sure the Dodge can make it, especially pulling the trailer. And I can build a cage in the front end of the trailer for Sandy."

As it turned out, the Denkers had a big, heavy 1939 Chevrolet sedan. Half of the back seat was packed to the ceiling with their gear, but the car was much newer than ours and many times more dependable. The Denker sons, or "the boys," as everyone called them, turned out to be a big surprise. They were in their early to mid-twenties and as different as two young men could be. Ed, who was the younger of the two—although not by much—was a big, muscular blond with a great smile and a strong jaw. He had a quiet, well-mannered way that didn't hide the fact he could take on just about anything that came along.

Larry was a puzzle to me. Looking back, I realize he was gay, but the term hadn't been invented yet, and even if it had, I wouldn't have known what it meant. So he was a puzzle, but I liked him. He was a little pudgy and not nearly as handsome as his brother, but wildly, hilariously funny. Everything was a joke to Larry, and he made fun of himself constantly, exaggerating his effeminate gestures for effect and then going into crescendos of squealing laughter. He had a "hope chest," which he talked about half joking and half serious. But he was good-hearted, kind, and helpful, and everybody seemed to accept him. If they didn't, they might have to deal with Ed's fists, which were large and obviously capable. Both of the boys treated their father, who was quietly and helplessly drunk much of the time, with great gentleness and solicitude. And so we began. We were going back to the ranch to get ourselves together and decide where else Red might find work. We were going back to Grandma Charlotte's because it was the only place we knew of where we wouldn't have to pay rent and we would be welcome.

Highway 95, which finally united northern and southern Idaho in spite of the rough terrain in between, had been completed and paved in 1938. It would have been the logical, shortest, and most direct route to Boise. Instead, we went west to Spokane, Washington, and then south by a somewhat winding route to Pendleton, Oregon, and then southeast at an angle back into Idaho and the Boise Valley. Why we took this circuitous route with four of us crammed into a little car that broke down about every 150 miles, I do not know; and since I've undoubtedly outlived everybody else who was on that trip, I'll never be able to find out for sure. We did no sight-seeing as such, visited no relatives, and Red did not inquire about work anywhere along the way. We were just trying to get to where we were going. There were times when I thought we never would.

Perhaps Red was trying to avoid Highway 95 because he was afraid of it? The fact that there had been no highway connecting northern and southern Idaho until 1938 says something about the terrain that highway passes through. Or perhaps Red felt that the little Dodge pulling a trailer couldn't make it over the formidable mountains that Highway 95 crossed. At any rate, he was willing to go several hundred miles out of his way to avoid that highway.

The little Dodge broke down the first time at Athol, less than twelve miles from Bayview. Red had already told us that he believed Athol was named by a man with a speech impediment. The next time it broke down was somewhere south of Spokane. This time it required unhitching the trailer and towing the Dodge into the nearest town. Jack and Sandy and I stayed with the trailer on the side of the road. After the repairs were made, it became apparent that the Dodge couldn't pull the trailer without overheating, so we hitched the trailer to the Denkers' Chevy and went on.

Then we had two problems within a couple hours of each other. We were following the Denkers, who were now pulling the trailer with Sandy in it. They had a tendency to want to go faster than Red would go. Sometimes they would get far ahead of us and stop and wait for us to catch up. We had not seen them for about an hour and were trying to catch up with them when we came around a curve and saw them ahead of us, but the trailer was on fire. Flames were shooting from the back part of the trailer, and the Denkers were driving along completely unaware of it. Evidently Old Man Denker had tossed a lit cigarette out the window.

"Sandy!" Jack and I both shouted at once. "He's in there."

Red broke his rule about never driving over forty miles an hour, honking madly, and we were able to catch up with them and get their attention. They stopped as soon as they saw the flames, and we pulled up behind them. We made a dash for Sandy and got him out. He was unhurt but terrified. The fire was in the rear of the trailer and his cage was in the front end. That had saved him.

The tarp was blazing, and we didn't have any water to put it out, but Old Man Denker had a case of beer in the backseat of the Chevy. We opened the bottles of beer as fast as possible and poured beer on the fire. When we got the fire out, nearly everything in the trailer was either wet with beer, burned, or at least scorched. It smelled horrible. Old Man Denker was upset over the loss of his case of beer. Red was mad at him for causing the fire. Sandy smelled of smoke and refused to get back into his cage in the trailer.

It was decided that for the next stretch, until the Dodge broke down again at least, I should ride with the Denkers, since without the beer there was more room in the backseat, and Sandy could ride on my shelf in the Dodge. That's why I happened to be in the Denker car when the wheel came off the trailer. I looked out the window on the passenger side as we were going down a slight hill and saw a wheel rolling along beside us and passing us before it wound up in the ditch. I had no idea where it came from until I heard Red honking behind us. Somehow the trailer axle had not yet hit the road, and I don't think it ever did because we were able to reattach the wheel and go on.

Ultimately, after another breakdown outside Pendleton, Oregon, we made it back to the ranch. It took us two days and we drove most of one night. We arrived at the ranch after dark, exhausted, with our trailer full of smelly, beer-soaked, half-burnt clothes and bedding. The Denkers went on to Boise. Because of the nature of her journal entries, it is hard to tell whether Grandma Charlotte was happy to see us or just resigned to the inevitable. Her entry for Monday, October 19 reads: *Beautiful day. I washed. Sheltons came.* I read that now as tired resignation. I knew we would not be able to stay at the ranch very long, but I had traveled enough to last me for a while, and for me, the ranch had always been home.

O! California

We stay at the ranch only three days, long enough for Hazel to wash on one day, iron on the next, and go into Boise to buy more clothes for everybody on the third. Most of this is the result of the fire in the trailer and our novel way of putting it out. Charlotte records Hazel's activities in her journal but does not mention any other members of the Shelton family during this visit. Red and Jack are building another cage on the trailer in addition to Sandy's. It's for Jack's pigeons, or as they have come to be called by most of us, "those goddamned pigeons."

Before we left Boise the first time, while we were living in the house on 13th Street, Jack had begun to raise homing pigeons. He and Red had built an elaborate series of cages for them on the side of the garage. Before Red went to Bayview, he and Jack had transferred about fifteen of the pigeons and some of their cages to the ranch, where Old Dan seemed pleased to take care of them. Now Red and Jack are building cages for the pigeons across the front of the trailer above Sandy's compartment, making the trailer look like a rolling chicken coop. Sandy does not like the pigeons, has never liked the pigeons, and is deeply offended at having to share his space in the trailer with them. But Jack wants to take the pigeons to California, and so to California they are going, whether Sandy likes it or not. I privately agree with Sandy. Because they are homing pigeons, it occurs to me that if they accidently get loose along the way or after we get to California, they will fly back to Idaho, and we will be rid of them. I am ashamed of myself for thinking such a thing, but not very much.

The work on the trailer gives me an idea, and I ask Hazel about it. "Let me ride in the trailer in Sandy's cage. It's long enough that I could stretch out in, and he wouldn't mind sharing with me."

Hazel is shocked. "No! You can't ride back there. The Denkers are going to be pulling the trailer. What if we got separated? What if the trailer caught on fire again? It's out of the question."

"But it would be cool back there because it's just wire mesh, and if we get separated, Ed and Larry will take care of me until we get back together. And if it's cold, I can wrap up with Sandy in a quilt and he will keep me warm. If the trailer catches on fire, I can get me and Sandy out quick, and we can jump off. Please don't make me ride on that shelf anymore."

My request is not considered seriously.

The entry in Charlotte's journal for Friday, October 23, 1942, is: *Sheltons left for Cal. Cool breeze.* And with no more fanfare than that, we are off again and the Denkers are still with us, or we are with them. For us, the arrangement is undoubtedly a good thing, especially if Old Man Denker doesn't set fire to our trailer again. We are going to cross the desert now. In fact, we are going to cross two of the most formidable deserts in America. Even with the Denkers' dependable car to push, pull, and carry us through the rough spots, we will barely make it. Without them, I doubt that we could have. The Denker sons must know they can make it to Southern California by themselves in less than half the time it will take them with us. Even if our car doesn't break down regularly, there is the matter of Red refusing to drive faster than forty miles an hour across the Nevada desert, where even the slower drivers will be doing sixty. Also, they must know that the sooner they arrive in Southern California, where the government is building air bases and army installations at a furious pace, the sooner they will find work.

But they stay with us. Sometimes they take either Jack or me in their car and speed on ahead, cruise around some small town, and then return to the highway and wait for the little blue coupe to come slowly along. If it doesn't come along soon, they will know it has broken down somewhere and go back to look for it. They must have decided soon after we left Bayview that we were the burden they were going to bear, and they would bear it with as much grace as possible. Ed would protect us and Larry would make us laugh in spite of our problems along the way. Beneath it all, of course, they must feel sorry for us. Red and their father are friends. It probably seems to the boys that our father is only slightly less helpless than theirs, and they are used to taking care of Old Man Denker.

Our destination is San Bernardino, or "San Berdoo," as we will learn to call it. None of us have ever been there before, but Betty is there, and we miss her fiercely. She is married to her fly-boy, Monty Barnes, who seems to have been grounded because of an inner-ear problem. He is working in the payroll office at the air base, and Betty has been working as a cashier in a Thrifty drugstore but will soon take a job in an office at the air base where her handsome husband is stationed. She has written that there is much government construction in the area, and industry is booming. She is sure Red can find work there. On the map, San Bernardino is a long way down the road, or as Red says, "way to hell and gone," and I dread getting back on my little shelf in the Dodge. Sandy dreads getting back in his compartment in the trailer, too, especially with "those goddamned pigeons."

With the exception of the first fifty miles, I have no idea what the country will be like ahead, and I know about the first fifty miles only because it is infamous and everybody in southern Idaho knows about it. It is the dreaded Mountain Home desert, the Bermuda Triangle of Idaho. For some reason that nobody understands, the Mountain Home desert always means trouble. If your car is going to break down or if you are going to have a flat tire, it will happen while you are crossing the Mountain Home desert. The horror stories about this stretch of highway are legion. It is hotter in the summer and colder in the winter than anywhere else, and so on.

The Mountain Home desert is part of the Snake River Plain that forms the northern boundary of the Great Basin Desert. At that time, the Mountain Home desert was nearly all a sea of gray sagebrush, a flat, unprotected country exposed to the worst of the weather. The mountains, for which it evidently would have made a good home, are far in the distance, mocking.

Every boy who grew up in Boise in the '30s and '40s heard the story of the two little brothers who were hooky-bobbing and wound up in the Mountain Home desert. In winter, when snow was packed on the roads, hooky-bobbing was our favorite sport and means of transportation. We would crouch behind a hedge or tree until a car slowed down at an intersection, then, bending down so the driver couldn't see us in the rearview mirror, run out and grab the rear bumper, hunker down, and slide on the soles of our shoes, allowing the car to pull us. Getting on wasn't too difficult, but sometimes getting off, if there was much traffic, was a problem. If the car pulling you didn't slow down enough and you had to let go at a fairly high speed, you might roll into the path of an oncoming car that couldn't stop quickly on the snow-covered road.

We were told that hooky-bobbing had been made illegal because of the two little brothers who had hitched a ride on the back bumper of a big truck on Capitol Boulevard. The truck went up the depot hill and turned onto the highway to Mountain Home. As the truck picked up speed, the boys were afraid to let go. They hoisted themselves up onto the back bumper and rode into the Mountain Home desert. They called out, but the driver couldn't hear them. When he finally slowed down enough for them to get off, they wandered into the sagebrush and froze to death. They were found dead in one another's arms. I almost never hooky-bobbed without thinking of the Mountain Home desert waiting out there for the unwary, and if a car ever started up the depot hill, I got off in a hurry.

There were other stories as well. Hitchhikers had murdered whole families who had stopped to pick them up in the Mountain Home desert. Motorists stranded in the heat of summer had died from drinking the water in their radiators. Rattlesnakes hiding in the sagebrush attacked anyone so foolhardy as to stop beside the road to pee. Because of these stories, I imagined a map much like some of the medieval maps, where what is very near is enormous, and everything else is small and insignificant. I thought the real problem of getting to California was getting across the Mountain Home desert, and after that, it would be easy, but the Snake River Plain was just a tiny hint of the Great Basin Desert that was to come, the largest desert on the continent, and after that the Mojave, the most severe of the North American deserts.

While we are crossing the Mountain Home desert, my anxiety level is so high I am almost holding my breath, afraid something will go wrong. When the adults decide to stop at a roadhouse about halfway across the fifty-mile stretch of desert and have a beer, I am devastated. They are flirting with disaster and don't seem to realize it. We have to get through this dreadful place as quickly as possible. How dangerous to stop here! I can feel something menacing all around us. Everybody else goes into the roadhouse. I sit on the running board of the Dodge and worry. Sandy lies at my feet. He looks worried too, but it might be the pigeons he is worried about.

Finally they all come out, and we drive through the rest of the Mountain Home desert and on to Twin Falls without incident. I can't believe it. The car didn't even break down. It's some kind of miracle. I have grown so accustomed to problems along the way that I feel somehow unsettled when they don't occur. Hazel says I'm a worrywart. Jack says I'm a pain in the ass. Red just looks at me sideways like I'm something he'd rather not look at.

At Twin Falls we turn due south and head for Nevada. We will cross the entire state from north to south, and all of it will be desert. Although it's October, it gets warm. The heat in the little Dodge, with all of us almost literally on top of one another, becomes oppressive. We stop to have lunch beside the road. Grandma Charlotte had cooked fried chicken for us and Hazel had fixed deviled eggs. A freight train goes by in the defile just below us. Someone takes a picture of Jack and me posed on the guardrail with the train passing in the background. Jack is grinning and has thrown his arm around my shoulder as one sometimes does when a picture is being taken. I am squinting and looking down. It is a photograph I cherish because it is the only one I have in which Jack and I are touching each other.

Most of the trip is ghastly. I remember only bits and pieces. Low hills covered with cedars and at one point, in the middle of the night, somebody wakes me up to see a herd of deer on the side of a hill. The little Dodge does not like the desert. It breaks down several times, but we finally limp into Las Vegas in the middle of a hot afternoon.

Las Vegas is a wonderland to us, an oasis with tall palm trees such as we have never seen before and grass and cool shade. We pull into a downtown park where we can park the cars in the shade and let

Sandy run. All the adults head for the nearest casino, leaving Jack to take care of me and Sandy. As soon as they are out of sight, Jack and I get the change we have been hoarding since we left the ranch. We have hidden it in a sock in the sack of pigeon feed. More than three dollars in nickels and dimes. We put it all in our pockets and head for a casino with Sandy, hoping it will not be the one Red and Hazel and the Denkers are in.

I am amazed and excited by the casino. All the noise and lights and bells. We try to make Sandy wait for us outside, but he won't. He uses the trick Jack had taught him for getting into the movies. In Boise, when Jack and I would go to the movies, Sandy had learned to wait outside until we had time to get into our seats. Then he would dash in past the ushers and hide under a seat in the dark. After the commotion had died down and the ushers had stopped looking for him, he would sneak up and down the aisles until he found us, and we would hide him under our seats. This usually worked fairly well unless there were barking dogs on the screen. In that case Sandy would leap up, put his paws on the seat in front of us or on whoever happened to be sitting in it, and bark. Then an usher would come and throw us all out.

In Las Vegas, the ploy gets Sandy into the casino, but as soon as he is inside, he is confused by the lights and bells and all the people milling around. He can't find us and runs frantically through the casino. Jack and I have about five good minutes on nickel slot machines before we are spotted by an overzealous security guard.

"Get out of here, you little punks!" he shouts at us. "Minors aren't allowed in here."

To me, the term *minors* means somebody who works in a mine. "But we aren't miners," I say to him. This angers him even more. He takes hold of each of us by an arm and is almost dragging us out when Sandy finds us. The timing is terrible. Sandy thinks the security guard is hurting us and attacks him. The guard lets go of us and tries to protect himself from Sandy, who has torn his coat and is leaping for his throat.

"Help!" the security guard shouts. "Get him off me!"

Jack grabs Sandy by the collar and we all three run like hell, dodging through a crowd of frightened gamblers. The security guard chases us until we get outside and are running down the street. I don't think he wants to have anything more to do with Sandy. Sandy is proud of himself for rescuing us from the evil kidnapper. We go back to the park and wait for the others. We've lost most of our money in the slot machines, but we had a good time.

The next evening, after we have crossed into California and are somewhere in the Mojave Desert, the Dodge breaks down in the middle of nowhere. A few creosote bushes and Joshua trees and not much else. It's been comfortable all day, but the night is cooling off fast. It's going to be cold. There is a gas station and what might be a motel just down the road. The motel-like place looks deserted, but the gas station is open and the attendant says there will be a mechanic on duty in the morning. We are exhausted. Red goes to see if he can raise anybody at the motel. He comes back and says it's OK. We can stay there. The Denkers decide to go on to the next town to find a better place to stay and come back in the morning.

I don't think anyone has stayed in this motel for years. I'm not even sure it is a motel. It might be a haunted house. It's a long, low adobe building, very old and badly in need of repair. It must have about six or seven rooms and no hallway. Each room simply opens into the next. Most of them open out on to a covered porch that runs the length of the building. The floors are hard-packed dirt. Old towels are hung over the windows, some of which won't close all the way. The ancient woman, who seems to be the only person in the place and who takes us to our rooms, can barely walk. She shuffles silently over the dirt floors. I don't know if she is mute or if she doesn't speak English, but she never speaks. I think she is a witch. She shows us two cavernous rooms with one bed in each and almost nothing else.

When we turn back the sheets, we find that everything is covered with fine sand or silt. We have to take all the bedding outside and shake it before we can go to bed. In spite of that, we have grit in our teeth all night. In the one bathroom, water comes out of the tap red, almost the color of blood. Red says it's rust from the pipes. Nobody dares to mention things like scorpions or tarantulas. We have seen several tarantulas today. They were lumbering along steadily down the side of the highway, one after the other, evidently going somewhere important. We stopped to look at them, but nobody got out of the car. We are convinced they can jump four feet in the air and that the slightest contact with such a creature will mean instant death.

After Jack and I are in bed and about to go to sleep, I hear Red go back out to the car to get something. In the morning, when we get up, I see his pistol on the table beside his bed. O! California, we have arrived in the promised land.

SAN BERNARDINO

I fall in love with San Bernardino at first sight. Its streets are lined with palms and eucalyptus, and its old houses are overgrown with lush shrubbery. It has an old Spanish look about it. To a boy from Boise, it's wildly exotic. We are all impressed with the incredibly tall palm trees with no leaves except at the very top. "I hope they didn't plant them for the shade," Red says. A young woman in shorts and a halter top goes by. "If she paid for the material in that outfit by the square foot," Red says, "it must have been free."

We rent a little house close to the downtown area on Lucas Street in a depressed neighborhood behind an old cemetery. The cemetery must have been a fashionable place for the rich to bury their dead until the 1920s, but it seems to have been almost forgotten since then. The roofs of some of the elaborate aboveground crypts have fallen in on their occupants.

The first thing I notice about this house when we pull up in front of it is that all the paint is peeling off the outside. In some places the wood is bare and gray with age; in others, remnants of cream-colored paint hangs in shreds. The house is a square divided into four rooms, all the same size and without hallways. Each room has doorways into the two adjacent rooms. The floors are covered with linoleum in several floral patterns, and they slope at various angles. Across part of the back is a long, narrow lean-to bathroom that was added after the house was built, and there is an open porch across the front and across part of the back. The privy is out back but is now used for storage. The house is owned by two old Mexican brothers who have previously lived in it but now rent it out and live in a much smaller structure at the back of their long lot that borders the old cemetery. Everything about the place is Mexican. Along the path that leads from the rear of the house beside the cemetery is a huge eucalyptus tree with a broken branch. The branch is still attached but swings in the wind, making an eerie creaking sound, like the voices of the dead. Many nights I go to sleep listening to it, and I have come to find it comforting, nonthreatening.

Behind the house is a large area of hard-packed earth instead of grass, several unidentifiable outbuildings, a ramada covered with a grapevine, and dozens of containers for plants, including old tires painted white, large galvanized washtubs, and a kitchen sink. Inexplicably in the midst of all this are segments of two white marble columns, each about five feet high, one standing upright and one lying down. They must be at least four feet in diameter, as big as the marble columns in the state capitol in Boise. I never find out where they came from or how they got there. When I ask my mother, she just shrugs and says, "It's California."

I feel comfortable in this house. It's a family house where families have lived. It has a big round table in the kitchen for family meals, rockers on the front porch, and a hammock under the ramada. The beds sag, the floors slope, and the faucets drip, but there is something about the place that says *home*.

There are good family dinners around the big kitchen table. Betty and Monty have taken an apartment only two blocks away from the house on Lucas Street, and they are often at the table at dinnertime, and always on weekends. Monty is handsome and charming and quickly becomes a member of the family. He drinks with Red, flirts with Hazel, scuffles with Jack and me, and takes me to the movies and, once, the wrestling matches. When he tells me the wrestling matches are faked, I can't believe it.

Betty is more beautiful than ever. She has altered the color of her hair slightly and now wears it over a rat in a high pompadour, the current fashion. It becomes her. She dresses better and looks absolutely glamorous. I think she could be a movie star. Sometimes I sit and stare at her, trying to remember what she looked like before she came to California. The biggest change is probably because she has won a beauty contest. It was a beauty contest for the wives of all the men on the air force base where Monty is stationed, and she won it. Betty is one of those women who needs to win a beauty contest to make her understand that she is beautiful. There is now a something about her, a glamour or sophistication, that wasn't there before. Yet at any moment she can turn into a clown and start doing impressions.

There is also much drinking around that table at night, especially on Saturday nights because Red doesn't have to go to work on Sunday. Old Man Denker is there much of the time, and sometimes his son Ed. Others Red has met at work or in the bars gravitate to that round table where the whiskey bottle, usually paid for by Red, sits in the middle and is available to everyone, but it's usually an exclusively male club. Hazel is still drinking, but not as much as she had been, and she doesn't stay up at night and drink with the men around the table. Perhaps it is because Red is now holding court at home rather than in the bars or because she realizes her attempts to keep Red from straying by drinking with him simply didn't work. Her health is not good. In photographs of this period, she looks sallow and gaunt.

So the nightly round table of drinking is usually made up only of Red and his cronies. They sit around the table and talk or argue, tell jokes, stories, and lies, sometimes until dawn. One of Red's buddies is a large fat man with a totally bald, shiny head. He is an ardent Catholic and a serious drinker. At the end of a particularly long Saturday night, when everybody else has gone, he passes out with his head on the table. Red gets several of Hazel's lipsticks and draws, in great detail, an obscene picture on the fat man's bald head.

Early Sunday morning the fat man wakes up and rushes off to Mass. He returns later, waving a pistol.

"I'm going to kill him. I'll go to hell for it, but I'm going to hell anyway. They threw me out of the church and won't let me back in. I'm going to shoot that bastard and enjoy watching him die. Stay out of my way, Hazel. Where is he?"

"He left about a half hour ago."

"So help me, Hazel, if you're lying . . ."

"I swear it. You can search the house."

Red, evidently expecting something of the kind, has slipped out. When the fat man knelt to receive communion that morning, the horrified priest accused him of deliberate sacrilege and ushered him out of the church with instructions never to return. We later get a full account from one of Red's other cronies. It is possible that what Red drew on the fat man's head was both obscene *and* sacrilegious. Red never tells any of us what it was. The fat man doesn't shoot Red, but he never comes back to the house again. We wonder if maybe he has quit drinking entirely.

Hazel enrolls me in the grade school about six blocks from the house. It was built to look like a Spanish mission and is severely over-crowded. We have air-raid drills every day. Everyone in California, it seems, expects to be bombed any minute by the Japanese. If we are in the classroom when the siren sounds, we are supposed to get under our desks. If we are in the hall, we lie down almost on top of each other along both walls. On the playground we are supposed to lie down in a dry ditch. "Above all," the principal explains, "do not get near the eaves or try to go in or out of the building during an air raid. Those red clay tiles on the roof will come down in sheets if we are bombed. If you are under the eaves, they will cut you in half." The fourth graders handle this advice pretty well, but the first graders have some trouble with it and tend toward hysterics each time they hear the air-raid siren.

It has become customary for the older boys to use these times of close body contact, when everyone is lying on the floor or under the desks, to grope the girls as much as they can. Nine years old and far from pubertal, I'm not sure why I'm doing it or what I'm supposed to get out of it, but the older boys seem to think it's the thing to do, so I do it too.

In the second week of school, when I am on my way home for lunch, five Mexican boys from school, my age and older, seem to come out of nowhere. One jumps down on me from the branch of a tree. I'm used to having a fight or two each time I enter a new school, mostly because of my red hair, but I've never been set upon by a gang before. They have me down on the ground before I realize what's happening and pound me thoroughly. I manage to get home, but in a sorry condition.

In a last-ditch effort to keep Jack in school, Hazel has enrolled him in the junior high school. The school is very large, closer to downtown, and in a rough neighborhood. During the first week Jack is accosted by three Mexican boys with switchblades, but he is quick and agile and manages to outrun them. He will not go back to school, though Red and Hazel don't realize it for several weeks. Five mornings a week he will get up early, eat breakfast, take the sack lunch Hazel has prepared for him, and leave the house on his bicycle. In the evenings he will return, exhausted. Finally Red and Hazel figure it out. He has got a job instead of going to school.

Jack told me a few years ago that he got a job breaking wild horses at a ranch in the hills just outside of town. Since he couldn't remember me as a child, he couldn't remember that he took me to the "ranch" one Saturday morning. It was in the hills just outside of town all right, but it was a riding stable where people rented horses by the hour or day. I don't know exactly what Jack did there, but I don't think it was "breaking wild horses." He was an excellent rider, but I think he also spent a good deal of time saddling horses and shoveling horse manure.

There is little fuss at home when it becomes known that Jack is no longer in school, especially since he didn't go to school at the beginning of the school year in Bayview. Hazel is the most concerned and pleads with Jack, but Red says, "If the goddamned Mexican hoods carry knives to school," he doesn't see why Jack should have to go. Red has only a sixth-grade education, and he figures that's good enough for Jack too, especially since Jack had so much trouble in school and hates it so much. Hazel has a better grasp on the real problem. Jack can't read well enough to get much of anything out of books. She spends hours reading to him at night, hoping it will encourage him to read on his own. I get to listen. She reads the Jack London dog stories. I love them. I tell Sandy he should listen too, because it's about dogs, but he just falls asleep with his head in my lap.

So Jack's formal education has ended, but he is learning about life in wartime Southern California, much of which he would be better off not knowing. I guess I'm learning quite a bit too, but I learn most of it secondhand from Jack. Sometimes, though, I'm more closely involved.

"A man sold me some good homing pigeons," Jack says to me. "They're in a cage about a mile away, and I need to go pick 'em up tonight. Do you want to go with me?" That's all there is to it. No coercion or bribery. Not even any questions. I simply hop onto the handlebars of his bicycle with a burlap bag and off we go. Jack has the wire cutters. It's hard for me to believe now, but I didn't question why he would need them. I was nine years old and either very naïve or very stupid—probably both.

We stop in an alley in an old but posh neighborhood. It's very dark. Jack tells me to wait for him and be absolutely quiet or I will frighten the birds. He takes the burlap bag and the wire cutters and disappears down the alley. I wait with the bicycle. I wait a long time. I'm scared in the dark all alone. Finally he comes back with the burlap bag full of pigeons. The bag is tied at the neck. I can't tell how many are in there, but it's quite a few. It's heavy.

I get back on the handlebars and he hands me the sack of pigeons. I manage to hold it on my lap with one hand while holding on to one handlebar with the other. When we get home, we put the pigeons in a cage Jack has ready for them. They are upset at being hauled around in a gunnysack, but by the light of a flashlight they seem OK. Jack says they are really expensive first-class homing pigeons, but I can't tell the difference. They just look like more "goddamned pigeons" to me.

The next morning is Saturday, and Betty is there for breakfast. Red has already gone to work. He works Saturdays whenever he can because of the overtime pay. Jack feeds the pigeons and then takes off somewhere on his bicycle. I'm on the couch in the living room reading a book. Sandy barks. There's a cop car in front of the house and two men in suits coming up on the front porch. Hazel and Betty go to the door. I hold Sandy to keep him quiet.

I can't hear everything that is being said. Hazel and Betty have gone out on the front porch to talk to the two men. I hear the word *pigeons*. Then Betty goes off like a skyrocket. Betty almost never explodes, but when she does, it's something to see. She seems to grow much taller than her five-foot-four, and her voice takes on a resonance and authority—the authority of righteous indignation.

"You are accusing," she hisses, "my little brother, who has more purebred pigeons with long pedigrees than he knows what to do with, of stealing somebody else's pigeons? You are suggesting that MY little brother would do such a thing? You have the gall to come here and stand on our front porch and accuse my innocent little brother, in front of his dear mother here, of theft?" Betty is getting into it now, warming up like a pitcher in the last game of a tied World Series. She knows her brother is innocent and she has all the power of wronged innocence on her side. The two detectives stand on the porch just in front of the steps, to the edge of which Betty has backed them, rocking back and forth on their highly polished black shoes that are creaking audibly. They are sweating pretty bad.

I want desperately to hear the rest, to hear Betty deliver the final verbal blow that will send them back to their car and down the road in shame, but I know there is something more important I have to do. Naïve as I am, the truth hit me as soon as I saw the cop car in front of the house. The truth had been hovering in the back of my mind, but I forced it away. Now I know what I have to do, and I hope Jack doesn't come home while the detectives are here. He will only foul things up, and they will take him away to jail, and probably me too.

I slip out the back door, careful not to let the screen door slam, and run to the pigeon shed. There, on the bench where Jack left them the night before, are the wire cutters. The tool looks so huge and obvious. *Quick! Quick! Where to put them?* I look around frantically and see a gunnysack of birdseed recently opened. I jam the wire cutters as deep as I can into the birdseed and fold the top of the sack back the way it was. I start to release the pigeons, but there isn't time to get the silly things out of their cage. I can hear Betty and Hazel and the two detectives coming around the side of the house, with Betty still giving it to them. She is doing her Queen Victoria impression, for which she won an award in high school, and she is magnificent. Even knowing what I know, I halfway believe her.

"Of course you can look at his pigeons. My little brother has nothing to hide. But we do not appreciate this intrusion." Just as we get to the cage full of pigeons that I carried in the gunnysack last night, Jack arrives on his bicycle, grinning. *That's it*, I say to myself. *Betty could handle it, but now we're sunk.* And we are. Jack tells them a lame-brained story about a Mexican boy on a bicycle who brought the pigeons in a sack and sold them to him. He calls on me to verify it. I do, but the detectives press me for a description. I make up the bicycle pretty well, but have more trouble with the boy. It's hard to make up people without any warning. The detectives obviously don't buy Jack's story. One of them shakes his head, and the other one is grinning like a toad. Betty carries the fight gallantly, but she is losing. My vague description of the Mexican boy who doesn't exist has not helped. Finally, it boils down to a steely-eyed confrontation between Jack and the detectives.

"The pigeons in this cage," one of them says, "match the description of the stolen pigeons. You have no bill of sale for them, and you were seen hanging around their owner's cage several days ago. All you have to do is release them. If they are yours, they will return to their cage. If they are the pigeons in question, they will fly to the cage of their owner. If you didn't steal them, you have nothing to lose."

Jack is very quiet. Because of his hesitation, Betty is beginning to realize the truth. Hazel just looks helpless. I think she has known the truth from the beginning. Suddenly, I have to go to the bathroom. It's urgent. My bowels have turned into a liquid eruption, but sitting on the toilet in the bathroom next to the back porch with the window open, I can hear it all.

Jack is showing some spunk of his own, and I am momentarily proud of him. "To hell with you," he says, and I can hear him opening the door of the pigeon cage. Through the high window in the bathroom I see the birds rise one or two at a time, group themselves, wheel in the beautiful morning light, and head for home. And I know they don't have far to go. I don't hide in the bathroom, although I want to. Jack and Betty have shown their spunk, and I have to show mine. As soon as my bowels seem to be under control for a while, I walk out onto the back porch and expect to be arrested along with Jack. But I guess arresting people is like fishing—you throw the small ones back in. As long as Jack sticks to his story of the Mexican boy on a bicycle who sold him the pigeons, a story nobody believes, I must not tell the truth. To admit my involvement in the theft is to admit his guilt. There it hangs. They take him away in the police car.

I expect them to keep him in jail for a long time, but the legal matters are worked out very quickly. He is home before dark. Because the owner of the pigeons receives his valuable property back, not much worse for the wear, and because the person who stole the property is only fourteen years old and has no record, at least in California, the owner of the pigeons chooses not to press charges. The nine-year-old who carried the pigeons in a gunnysack is never mentioned. I have Jack to thank for that, I think, but later I realize it would have made matters worse for him to admit that he had involved his nine-year-old brother.

Thinking of it now, after so many years, what I remember best is Betty's magnificent performance. We could fight amongst ourselves and do severe physical damage to one another, but when any of us was seriously threatened from outside, we hung together, and we did it with considerable style. I think the style was what we inherited from Red. Maybe the loyalty too. Years earlier, when I was five and we lived on 17th Street, I had seen an example of both, and again it was Betty.

She would have been fifteen and in the ninth grade. I had not yet started school. My great treat on some afternoons was that I was allowed to go to meet her as she was walking home from school. It was about five blocks, and I was always careful crossing the streets. One afternoon, as I approached a vacant lot near Betty's school, I could hear a great roaring noise. As I got nearer, I saw a big crowd of students shouting and screaming in a circle around something. I pushed my way through and saw what was causing all the excitement. Betty and another girl, both with bobbed hair fashionable at that time, were rolling in the dirt in a violent struggle, punching, gouging, scratching, and pulling hair. Many of the other students were cheering for one or the other of the fighters by name. Soon Betty had the other girl on her back and was delivering repeated blows to her face. The girl screamed, "I give up!" Betty let her go, and her friends helped her up. The defeated girl was crying and had a bloody nose.

Betty's excited girlfriends surrounded her with congratulations and tried to make her as presentable as possible. Her skirt was torn and she had scratch marks and dirt on her face. She saw me and hugged me and said I must not tell what I had seen. She knew I wouldn't. She was breathing hard.

"You really showed her, Betty," one of her friends said. "That'll teach the bitch to say things like that about your little brother."

Then, in response to my stricken look, Betty put her arms around me and said, "Not you, Dicky. It wasn't you." So she had been fighting a girl who had said something bad about Jack. And in 1943, as a grown-up married lady who had won a beauty contest, she was still fighting for him.

Back to Boise II

In the late 1980s I took one of my nostalgic ghost-hunting trips, this time to San Bernardino. I had passed by it on the freeway between Phoenix and Los Angeles several times, always wanting to stop and see if I could find the old house we had lived in, although at the time I couldn't remember the name of the street. Finally, on one of my trips back to Tucson from Los Angeles, I took the freeway to San Bernardino and drove into town. As I got off the freeway on a confusing grid of streets and finally found the main downtown drag, which I wouldn't have recognized, I decided to operate on pure instinct. I knew the house hadn't been too far from the downtown area. I had walked the distance many times as a child. If the house was gone, I might be able to find the cemetery or the school. I drove slowly along past an elaborate movie theater that seemed a little familiar, and after a few blocks, something said turn right at this corner. I did. It was a major thoroughfare going east and west. About the fourth street to cross it was Lucas, and all the bells rang. I turned right, then two blocks and knew I was there. Everything except a couple of houses across the street was gone. In its place was a county office complex, but the street dead-ended, just as it had in 1942–43. The house had been the last one before it dead-ended at the cemetery.

Maybe I'm wrong, I thought, *maybe this isn't it at all. Find the cemetery.* So I drove back the way I had come and circled around the county office complex and parked in its parking lot. I've always been able to find things better on foot or on a bicycle. Within ten minutes I found the stone retaining wall that had separated the cemetery from the streets on two sides. I had sat on that wall so many times that even my butt would recognize it. The cemetery was gone, paved over, and there were several nondescript government buildings scattered over the area where it had been. *I wonder if they just paved it over or if they moved all the bodies.* It had been so beautiful, quiet and shady, with palms and eucalyptus and overgrown with all manner of green blooming things. I had spent many hours in that cemetery, being alone, lying on the grass reading a book. It was all gone. In its place was an ugly assemblage of government office buildings and a parking lot.

This one really hurt. An important part of my childhood had been spent in San Bernardino, and it seemed like we lived there for years, but it had been only seven months while I was nine years old. But why did we leave Southern California after only seven months? I find a bench in a shady spot beside one of the ugly office buildings and sit down to try to remember. When we first arrived in San Bernardino, Red worked as a painter at the Kaiser Steel Mill. I think the mill or some part of it was under construction. Was that job completed? Later he worked on a new military installation being built at Victorville, more than forty miles to the north. But why did we leave suddenly in April 1943, while the war industry was booming, only to return to Idaho, where work was scarce? Had Red and Hazel intended to stay in Southern California only during the worst of the winter? Did Red and Hazel realize that while he was making more money than he had made in Idaho, the high cost of living was eating it up and they were no better off than they had been? Or were they simply homesick for all that was familiar?

I don't know what the reason was, but there is another possibility I hope was the reason because it would show an awareness and concern that I didn't, at the time, credit them with. Jack was in terrible danger. Getting him out of Southern California was the smartest thing they could have done.

Perhaps our parents knew more about Jack's activities than I thought they did. Certainly I didn't tell them, and Betty didn't know about what he was doing. Maybe Red and Hazel just surmised things by his behavior and the hours he kept. Maybe, in spite of drinking and fighting and struggling to make a living, they just figured it out. That's what I want to believe.

As a couple of newcomers from Idaho, Jack and I both encountered gang violence in wartime Southern California, but because he was older, Jack's encounters were much more serious. He responded by forming or joining a gang of his own. It was not some well-organized group with its own language and symbols, like today's gangs. It was just a group of Anglo boys, between fourteen and sixteen years old, probably about eight of them, who organized themselves into a unit for mutual protection and, as it turned out, profit and mayhem.

I first became aware of what they were doing when Jack took me to their "clubhouse," an abandoned one-room shack hidden in a thicket of vines, bushes, and eucalyptus deep in a ravine. Inside, the walls were lined with cartons and loose packages of cigarettes, hundreds of them—*Pall Mall, Wings, Old Gold, Domino, Camel, Lucky Strike*. I had heard about the thriving black market in cigarettes, and I knew without being told that Jack and his friends were helping to supply it, but where were they getting all those cigarettes?

Finally one of Jack's friend's younger brothers explained it to me. They were breaking into gas stations late at night when the stations were closed, emptying the cigarette machines, and taking any cartons of cigarettes stored in the station. The cigarette machines were also sources of cash, and they sold the cigarettes to shady characters who dealt in black-market items.

I was frightened by the danger all this placed Jack in, especially after the episode with the stolen pigeons, but what really shocked me to the bottom of my prudish nine-year-old soul, and also fascinated me, was what was going on in the clubhouse the afternoon Jack took me there. There was a young boy, probably about the same age as the others, maybe fourteen or fifteen—it was hard to tell because he was very effeminate—performing oral sex on all the boys in the group, one at a time, for fifty cents each. The boys waited their turn patiently, watching the action. Although I had seen graffiti on the walls in the men's room, I somehow hadn't realized that people did things like that to one another, and especially that they did it in groups, but the boys were very casual about it, as if it were a fairly common thing, which it probably was. They seemed to consider it a form of communal masturbation.

Thinking back on it while I was sitting on the bench near the county office building, I was amazed that Jack permitted me to witness this, especially since he took such pains to hide the gang's other sexual activities from me. I remembered one drizzly night in midwinter when I sat under a tree at the edge of the cemetery with most of the rest of the gang while an elaborate charade for my benefit took place—a charade that fooled me entirely because I knew next to nothing about sex. Nobody but a couple of friends in school had told me much of anything, not even Jack.

That night, while we sat for such a long time under a tree in the cemetery, trying to keep dry, Jack told me that the boys were taking turns riding a beautiful white horse in a pasture just beyond the cemetery. He said the farmer didn't permit them to do it, but the horse was very wild and they loved to ride it. So they did it secretly at night. There was a farm off in that direction, and I bought the whole story. One by one, the boys got up and headed off toward the farm. After a while, each would come back, breathing hard and looking satisfied. It wasn't until years later that I figured out they weren't riding a white horse but a woman or girl, although I never knew if she was in the barn or one of the outbuildings of the farm or in the farmhouse.

It wasn't their sexual activity that made me fearful for Jack. The sexual stuff baffled and excited me, as if I were looking over a wall into an abyss, and of course I was, looking from one side of puberty to the other, but the rest of it scared me. A few days after I saw the eye-opening sexual activity in the clubhouse, one of the gang members showed me the gun they had acquired with money they made from the sale of cigarettes. I can't remember exactly what it was— probably a .45—but it was big and mean-looking. He asked me to hold some of the bullets while he loaded it. They were going to do some target practice that night, getting ready to make the transition from burglary to armed robbery. Jack was fourteen. I doubt that any of them were older than sixteen. The idea of telling our parents about this never occurred to me. Perhaps it was loyalty to Jack, or fear of him. It was also my conviction that Red and Hazel wouldn't be able to do anything about the situation if they were aware of it. Red would shout and cuss, and Hazel would plead and cry, and that would be the end of it. Jack would do whatever he wanted to do. When Red announced that we were leaving California, going back to Boise, I felt enormous relief. It was the only answer to the problem that was undermining our lives.

We had been in San Bernardino only seven months, but that was almost as long as we had lived in any one house in Boise, and San Bernardino had become home to me. I loved it, although I missed the ranch, but I didn't miss Boise. For the rest of my life, I would miss San Bernardino and the smell of eucalyptus after rain, the beauty of the citrus groves, the fog that made walking to school in the morning an adventure, the elaborate movie palaces where I spent many hours on weekends, the rain that flooded the streets coming down out of the mountains and washing everything clean, the house on Lucas Street with its wonderful little gas heaters making magical flames in every room like little fireplaces, and I had never lived in a house with a fireplace, the sound of rain on the tin roof, the warmth of December, going barefoot on Christmas Day, the palm trees, the cool, overgrown cemetery without monsters or ghosts. As I sat beside that ugly government office building, I realized that when you lose something you love at the age of nine, you never lose it entirely, even if it is totally gone when you try to find it again.

When we set out for Idaho, we still have the trailer and the pigeons, although Sandy and I hope that we can simply turn them loose and let them fly back to Idaho on their own steam. It seems ridiculous to be dragging *homing pigeons* back home. Sandy and I don't really expect our opinions to be considered. But there is something that will make this trip much more comfortable. Red has bought the Denkers' Chevy sedan. No more riding on the little ledge in the Dodge coupe. No more breaking down every hundred miles. And we will have somebody with us to make the trip fun. Betty and Monty. Monty has gotten a leave, and they are going back to Boise with us to visit family and friends. Monty's large family lives in Boise, although two of his brothers are away in the service. When his leave is over, he and Betty will return to California by bus.

So we are six, not counting Sandy, in the Chevy sedan, and it's much better than four in the little Dodge coupe. I am able to ride in the backseat next to Betty. I love it. Red still drives at forty miles an hour, but Monty drives part of the time while Red sleeps, and he picks up the pace considerably. Betty volunteers to drive, but everybody hoots with laughter.

Betty knows how to drive, more or less, and sometimes she drove in San Bernardino, but she is a nervous driver and gets easily rattled. Shifting gears is a challenge and parallel parking is simply beyond her. Years later, in Boise, she will entertain us with the story of how she started out from home one icy morning to take one of her daughters somewhere and wound up in the fish pond at Platt Gardens in front of the depot. The fish pond at Platt Gardens is far from any road and would be almost impossible to get to by car. In a tank, maybe. Betty managed it by confusing the brake and gas pedals and, in her panic, closing her eyes to avoid seeing what was coming at her. Since it was winter, the deep fish pond had no water in it, and Betty and her daughter, although badly jounced and battered, escaped drowning. Several of the cops who came to get her out marveled at the whole thing and felt it should be written up in *Ripley's Believe It or Not!*

We drive straight through the night, hitting snow and sleet in the mountains. Even though Sandy's cage in the trailer is covered with a tarp for this trip, we bring him into the car with us. He sleeps on the floor in the backseat. Betty and I take our shoes off and he keeps our feet warm. When we get to Pioche, Nevada, in the wee hours of the morning, it is very cold and spitting snow and sleet. Pioche, once a thriving mining community in the mountains, has become almost a ghost town. We had planned to get gas here, but the only gas station is closed and will not open for three hours. Gas is rationed and scarce. We are almost out of gas and cannot possibly make it to the next town across the great desert expanses of Nevada. We have to wait until the gas station opens.

It is very cold in the mountains. We cover ourselves with quilts and blankets and try to go to sleep. It is the first time our whole family has slept in such close quarters—Hazel, Red, and Jack in the front seat and Monty, Betty, and me in the backseat—bundled together against the cold, and I am totally happy. Betty is at my back, tickling my ribs and whispering secrets in pig Latin and reciting her mantra that has delighted me since I can remember: *Dicky bom bicky tialigo ticky. Teelegged, tielegged, bowlegged Dicky.* Sandy has crawled up on the seat and is in my arms, keeping me warm. We are a family and we are all together and nobody is drunk and we love one another. Jack is safe from the danger he was in. Frost covers the car windows, and we are closed in from the world, at peace, sleeping. We have one another for warmth.

Then Red says, as I somehow know he will, "Nobody better let a fart!"

I will always remember those three hours bundled in that 1939 Chevy as among the happiest hours of my childhood away from the ranch. And we are on our way back, inevitably, to the ranch. When we return to Idaho in early May 1943, we stay at the ranch for a month while Red and one of his Boise drinking buddies paint the outside of Charlotte and Sherman's house. According to Charlotte's journal, *Sherman and Jack did first irrigating of the season. Hazel washed woodwork in kitchen light frost.*

After he finishes painting the house, Red begins to travel in a car pool back and forth to Mountain Home, where he has found work painting the newly constructed Mountain Home Air Force Base. It is a long drive, and he spends most weeknights in Mountain Home. When he returns to the ranch, it is worth noting in Charlotte's journal: *Leonard came home.* I wonder if Charlotte sometimes feared that he wouldn't come back at all, that she would be stuck with us. She had raised her four children by doing other people's laundry and cooking other people's food. If Red should disappear, Hazel didn't seem to be equipped to do much of anything that would make a living. While Hazel was a good housekeeper and worked hard at home, the idea of working outside her home seemed an impossibility for her. She said she had never worked outside the home after she was married because Red would not permit it, that it would shame him. Actually, I think it was Hazel's notion of gentility that would have been offended.

PART V

HAZEL'S JOURNALS

Hazel wrote her journals in two spiral notebooks and a lined ledger. The first notebook covers 1942 to 1970. It has few entries. At the top of the first page is the notation, "Copied from Mothers Diary," although the entries are not exact copies of any entries in Charlotte's journals. Instead, Hazel has excerpted and rephrased some of the entries in Charlotte's journals that pertain to the Sheltons.

Hazel became a widow in 1969. After the entries for 1970 is a page devoted to what were important numbers for her: her Social Security number, the doctor's address and phone number, her checking account number, her savings account number, and the phone number for Don's Beauty Parlor. Near the end of the notebook is a series of notes from her reading of the Old Testament, including a list of Hebrew weights and measures.

In addition to being lined, the pages of the ledger book are numbered in the upper right-hand corner. Hazel's entries begin on page thirty-three. All the pages before that have been torn out. The first few pages are a hodgepodge, including a list of books she has read, a list of her surgeries and serious illnesses, two lists of financial transactions, and the information recorded on Red's death certificate. The entries proper begin in 1957 and cease in 1986, but they are sporadic. At the end of the ledger are several lists: dates of birth of older family members beginning with Hazel's and Red's parents, dates of deaths, marriages, births of grandchildren, names of great-grandchildren, and even high school graduations. There is an inexplicable entry on page thirty-seven: "a thirsty monkey on an Arizona Well Rope."

In the second spiral notebook, after an entry in the margin of the first page—"1939 Hazel had Typhoid Fever"—the entries begin in August 1942 and end on February 15, 1971, although the entries are so sporadic that they cover only eleven pages in the spiral notebook. Many of the entries are dated by month but not day, and during some years, there is only one entry. Clearly during this period, Hazel was trying to list the important events rather than keep a daily record.

MOSES LAKE AND
OTHER MISERIES

After Josie's terse but engaging journal and Charlotte's journals packed with sometimes cryptic information, Hazel's journals are disappointing as a daily record but rich in basic genealogy. Hazel isn't much of a journal keeper in the way her mother and grandmother were. Unlike them, she is not faithful to the journal. She does not make an entry every day. She often lets long periods pass between entries and then tries to catch up. Consequently, some of her dates cannot be trusted.

But she delights in making lists and keeping records, or perhaps, as her memory loss and her anxiety increase with age, she feels compelled to keep lists of things to reassure herself about the past. She had access to a family Bible that has since disappeared, and she copied from it lists of births, deaths, and marriages back to her great-grandparents' generation. I remember seeing that Bible. I hope it is in the hands of some younger members of the family who cherish it.

On the Shelton side of the family, she lists Red's parents and their children with dates of birth. I am surprised to see that Red's oldest sister, Lula, was the same age as his mother-in-law, Charlotte. When I was in my mid-teens, Lula seemed like a sweet but very old woman. Her hair was white, she wore old-fashioned black high-top shoes, and her voice was spidery but kindly. She was shrunken and had a fussy manner. Her face was deeply lined like an apple left over from last year.

Charlotte, at the same period, was a vibrant and active, somewhat raw-boned farm woman with black hair (that she kept dyed, but I didn't realize it), pale blue eyes, a gold tooth, and the look of a much younger woman. I also notice from Hazel's lists that several of Red's older brothers were only slightly younger than his mother-in-law.

Nowhere in Hazel's journal does it indicate that Charlotte preferred younger men, nor which of Red's older brothers she had preferred, nor for how long.

⁓

The Sheltons have one more wartime gypsy episode. Hazel's journal indicates that we leave in June 1943, for Moses Lake, Washington, where Red has been hired by a paint contractor to work on an air base under construction. According to Charlotte's journal, I am back at the ranch by September 29. Could it have been less than four months we spent in Moses Lake? It seems like four years, like some long sojourn in hell.

Moses Lake was a tiny hamlet with unpaved streets beside a mudhole called a lake and surrounded with acres and acres of khaki-colored government-issue trailers rounded at both ends like huge, surreal baby carriages in rows, all exactly alike. The trailers house the families of the men who are building the air base, and will later house the air force personnel stationed there, Lord help them. Beyond all this is sagebrush desert as far as one can see, and much farther. The dreadful heat is relieved only by high winds and sandstorms. The heat in the trailer is intense, and the little electric fan we have does almost no good, though we fight over who gets to sit in front of it.

There is no library or any form of entertainment for children in Moses Lake, and the lake itself is too foul-smelling to swim in. I spend a good deal of time fishing, but all I catch are turtles. The lake seems to be full of turtles. I take two of the more likely specimens home, name them Moses and Rebekah, and keep them in water in a large washtub under the trailer. They do not prove to be very exciting pets, and Sandy finds them offensive.

Toward the end of the summer, Hollywood finally comes to Moses Lake. Some enterprising soul arrives with a movie projector, a portable screen, a tent, and some relatively recent films. I am in line for the first matinee. The film is *The Hard Way*, a gritty melodrama starring Ida Lupino as the older sister who sacrifices everything to boost her younger sister out of poverty, only to be betrayed and destroyed. Perhaps she kills somebody—I can't remember.

The tent is an old army mess tent, the seats are boards on apple boxes, and the floor is dirt sprinkled with a hose between showings to keep the dust down. At one of the most tense moments in the film that afternoon, while Ida Lupino, all hard jaw and flashing eyes, is telling her sister what she must do to get ahead, and it isn't pretty, there is a loud crash and several screams directly behind me. One of the boards has slipped off the apple boxes and dumped its human cargo onto the dirt floor. The operator stops the movie. The patrons get up and dust themselves off. No one seems to be hurt. The operator replaces the board and the customers sit back down, somewhat gingerly, to watch the rest of the film. Nobody leaves—it's a long way to the next movie palace.

Red had gone ahead of us to Moses Lake to secure the job and work for several weeks before he returned to Boise in the faithful Chevy to get us. He traveled with a painter friend of his from Boise. His name was Don. He is a few years younger than Red, very good-looking, and he has a large family in Boise—a wife and five children. When we arrive in Moses Lake, we find Don living in the trailer next door to our trailer with a young woman named Billie. Hazel is outraged and will barely speak to Billie when they are introduced. I like Billie. She has blond hair that's almost silver, the same color as Cassy's, the rodeo star I fell in love with when I was six. Billie invites me over for iced tea, but Hazel says I am not to go to that trailer under any circumstances. She is tight-lipped whenever she looks in that direction, and turns her back to Don's trailer when she goes out to hang up the laundry.

Hazel knows no other woman in all those hundreds of trailers, in all that dreadful heat and dust and desert. No other woman to talk to over coffee in the middle of the morning, or to go to the dingy, fly-specked little market with. About the third weekend the men decide we should all go to a roadhouse on the Columbia River at Vantage, about forty miles to the east. For Hazel, it means spending all day and most of the night in the company of that silver-haired . . . well, she wouldn't use the word in front of the children . . . or staying home with only me for company in our sweatbox of a trailer. She goes, which means I go too. She also gets drunk and has a good time, but because she is drunk, she and Red fight all the way home. From then on, she is friendly with Billie, although she sets up a barrier between them like a pane of glass, and Billie seems to understand and accept the arrangement. Hazel impresses me with the fact that Billie is "a bad woman." I have a little trouble with that concept because Billie is so pretty, and she never drinks too much.

Going to the roadhouse at Vantage becomes a weekend ritual. We usually leave about midmorning on Saturday before it gets too hot. The roadhouse is Vantage and Vantage is the roadhouse. There is nothing else. It's on a wind-swept bluff above the Columbia River, dwarfed by a landscape of vistas that seem to go on forever, and an enormous, mind-boggling chasm at the bottom of which is the Columbia River.

While we are at the roadhouse, the adults sit at the bar, drink beer, and laugh all the time. There is nothing much for Jack and me to do but drink Cokes and play the jukebox. I always take a book, although Red doesn't like people to see me sitting around reading a book. I'm not sure why. Then, after it gets dark, if there's an empty booth, I can get in it and go to sleep. The trouble is the place usually gets busy later on Saturday nights, and I have to give up the booth. Then I go out and sleep in the car, but sometimes it gets wild and crazy in the parking lot. Hazel doesn't like for me to be out there alone. It's hard to find anywhere to *be*.

When they close the roadhouse at 1 a.m., we head for home. Hazel always tries to get Red to eat a sandwich or something before he drives us home, but usually he won't. He says, "Never spoil a twenty-dollar drunk with a two-bit meal."

I become ten years old while we are at Moses Lake and start the school year—fifth grade. It's a terrible school. Unlike the teachers and school board at Bayview, nobody at Moses Lake knows how to handle the huge influx of students that have come with the construction of the military base. There must be fifty students crammed into each classroom, and the heat is unbearable. Several students faint.

One day a sandstorm sweeps down on the school, and before we can get the windows closed, everything is covered with fine sand. The sand is in our hair, our mouths, our eyes, and other places we aren't allowed to mention in the classroom.

At the end of the second week of school, Red announces that we are heading back to Boise. Again I don't know why his work has ended so abruptly, but all of us have had enough of Moses Lake, and some of us have had too much. I take the turtles, Moses and Rebekah, back to the lake and turn them loose. They seem to accept freedom with the same composure they did captivity. I have never really been able to get very attached to them anyway, although I tried, and Sandy is heartily glad to get rid of them. Almost as glad as he was when Jack discovered he preferred girls and got rid of the pigeons.

When we return to Boise, we move into a tiny house that we have always called "the chicken coop." All of the many other houses we rented in Boise we later referred to by street names—"the house on 22nd Street, the house on 17th Street, the house on 13th Street, the house on Flume Street, the house on Holmes Street, the house on Broad Street"—but this little structure, although it was on Albion Street, was always to be referred to as "the chicken coop." It had begun as a chicken house and had that distinctive shape, but it had later been converted into a mother-in-law's house behind a larger farmhouse. When we rent it, it has one small bedroom, a tiny kitchen, and a living room, where Jack and I sleep on a heavy old-fashioned couch that opens up to make a bed of sorts.

As Jack, who is neither working nor going to school, spins more and more out of control, the relationship between us worsens. He comes home one night at about 2 a.m. and punches me to roll over and make more room. His breath smells of beer and cigarettes. Half asleep, I come up swinging. He pins my arms down and sits on my chest. Then he takes my feet, one at a time, in his hands and twists my little toes until they break. I am screaming with pain. Red, who has been asleep, comes out of the bedroom cursing.

"Goddammit, will you stop that racket? We're trying to sleep."

"He broke my toes."

"I'll break more than your toes if you don't stop that damned caterwauling. Shut up and go to sleep!"

I shut up, except for low sobs, but I don't go to sleep. The next morning my toes are so swollen I can't get my shoes on, and I stay home from school for a couple of days until the swelling goes down some. Both my little toes will be permanently deformed.

Knowing I can't overcome Jack physically, and as I become old enough to understand how wantonly cruel he can be, I am learning to depend on my wits and also beginning to illustrate the truth of what W.H. Auden said: "All schoolchildren learn, / Those to whom evil is done / Do evil in return." I develop a bitterness and slyness and am capable of doing very bad things to Jack. The following year, when we live in the little house on Hill Road, I hear Red say, "Back the truck out of the garage for me, Jack," and Jack goes to get into the panel truck. I see Jack's bicycle lying on the lawn near the driveway. A sudden impulse comes over me, and I don't hesitate. I run to the bike and, bending down so Jack won't see me in the rearview mirror, lay the bike down directly in the path of the oncoming truck. Jack runs over his own bicycle with a great crunching sound.

The beating Jack gives me for this, when he finally catches me, is severe but worth it. The worst is when he knocks me down and kicks me, but I have learned to weigh the pain I will get from his beatings against the damage I can do to him. I am becoming consumed by this equation. Sometimes Jack looks at me with surprise, almost shock, as he sees my former trust and adulation turning into snarling hatred. But he has discovered that girls like him, and he has other things on his mind.

⁓

The order of Jack's ensuing troubles, which continue for the next two years, has grown hazy in my mind, and I probably never knew many of the details. I'm sure, however, that the destruction of our prized Chevy is the first serious one, and it is devastating.

We are living in the chicken coop. Jack's closest friend is a boy named Kay, who is slightly older than Jack and much more experienced when it comes to seducing girls. While Red is working at Mountain Home, Jack and Kay take the Chevy, get a case of beer and some black-market gas, pick up two girls they have recently met, and head for Arrowrock Dam, about twenty-five miles away. On the unpaved mountain road around the reservoir behind the dam, Jack lets Kay drive so that he can make out with his girl in the backseat. Kay, drunk and driving too fast, misses a curve and the Chevy plunges down a steep embankment into the reservoir. All four of the teenagers manage to get out without drowning, but the girl Jack is with has had one ear nearly severed.

The Chevy is totaled, the best car Red has owned or will ever own, and the state will require that Red pay a large fee to have the wreck pulled out of the reservoir and towed back to a junkyard in Boise. The parents of the injured girl attempt to sue Red and Hazel, but when they learn that Red and Hazel own no property and have nothing, not even a car now, they drop the suit. They seem to be more upset about the sexual activity than their daughter's mutilation.

Later, after Red gets through his initial fury and the story has been told and reshaped into a more palatable version, and after the amnesia curtain has fallen, Jack will become a hero for rescuing his girlfriend from the submerged automobile. Kay will become the villain, and will remain the villain in all of Jack's later escapades. "Jack is so easily led" will become the family mantra. I know there is some truth to this, but in my bitterness at the age of ten, I tend to phrase it differently, although not out loud. *Jack is stupid and dangerous. I must be more careful not to make him angry. Someday, if I wait and stay alert, I may be able to kill him in such a way that nobody will know I did it.*

The desire to kill one's only brother, a desire that haunted me when I was between ten and thirteen years old, might not be unusual. I'm sure the onset of puberty has something to do with it, and the desire to be the only focus of the parents' attention. Also there were the beatings. On the other hand, it isn't *normal* to want to kill your older brother. I felt guilty, but beneath the guilt was the desire, and I was waiting for an opportunity. Beneath all that was some feeling for him I couldn't identify or admit. I must have loved him. I must have loved him still.

According to Charlotte's journal, Jack goes to the ranch after this debacle with the Chevy. It is evidently the result of some agreement with the juvenile court system that Charlotte does not spell out in her journal. Jack is banished to the ranch in order to separate him from Kay and his other friends in Boise. According to Charlotte's journal, Jack spends twelve days at the ranch in December painting the interior of the house. At that point his penance is evidently complete and he returns to Boise. What Charlotte does not record in her journal, and what I pray she never knew, was that during this stay at the ranch, Jack managed to seduce the young daughter of a neighboring farm family whose parents were two of Charlotte and Sherman's closest friends.

As soon as Jack leaves the ranch, I arrive, and I spend much time listening to the heartbroken daughter weeping because Jack had not attempted to contact her after he left. It was her first great love affair. For him, evidently, it was good sex while he was in exile.

⁓

We move from the chicken coop to a tiny house on the side of the hill on Hill Road. Hazel's journal says, *Gall Bladder Surgery. Lived on Hill Road.* From this point on, Hazel's journal will often focus on her health problems, but this period also marks the end of Hazel's drinking, and I think we all breathe a sigh of relief. The amnesia curtain comes down with a great clang—it was like one of those solid curtains that dropped from above the stage in vaudeville houses—and in later years Hazel will laugh at the preposterous suggestion that she had ever taken a drink.

Also about this time, Hazel begins to record ill health. Her neurasthenia gradually increases until, by the time we are living on Broad Street, she spends much of her time in bed and her attention is focused on her various illnesses, real and imagined. In spite of nearly dying of typhoid in her thirties, and later gall-bladder surgery, a hysterectomy, a broken hip, arthritis, and the fact that she was a heavy smoker until a few years before she died, she lived to be ninety-two. My wife, Lois, who entered the family in 1956, and who knew and loved Hazel for almost forty years, best expressed her situation: "Hazel enjoyed ill health."

I began to take care of Hazel and take over her household duties for weeks at a time when I was eleven and we lived in the house on Hill Road. There was nobody else to do it. Betty and her husband were living in California, Red was at work or in the bars, and Jack was . . . well, nobody knew exactly where Jack was most of the time, although he usually ate at home. During those periods Red did some of the cooking—he was always good for breakfast—and otherwise Hazel told me how to do it and I managed to produce enough food to keep us from going hungry. Years later, during my high school years, I became aware that Hazel was manipulating me by means of her bouts of illness. It had come to be understood that I would take care of her when she was ill. Several times, just as I was planning to go out of town with friends, she would become ill and I would have to cancel my plans. Finally, I figured it out and went anyway. After I was gone, she had a remarkable recovery. When I was sixteen, Betty said to me, "You know she isn't really sick, don't you?" I was angry at Betty and shocked to hear it put so bluntly, but I knew, deep down, that Betty was right.

BROAD STREET

Hazel's journals cover the years we rented the house on Broad Street, from 1944 to 1949—five years in the same house, a record for the Sheltons. During this period, Red was working as a painter for various paint contractors in Boise, especially the contractor Ralph Diamond.

Broad Street runs east and west one block south of the railroad tracks near downtown. Even in 1944 it was rapidly becoming an industrial area bordering the railroad tracks. Standing like a protective barrier between that cinder-strewn no-man's-land and the old residential area behind them were four tall, gaunt houses with steeply pointed roofs. They were all exactly alike, and each was about eight feet from the one beside it. Together they created something between a slum and a mini-ghetto.

When we first pull up in front of those houses in a truck Red has borrowed to move our furniture in, I am upset and disappointed, reflecting a snobbishness I have no right to feel. The houses have not been painted in many years, if they ever were, and their wooden siding is silvery gray. They are awkward, unattractive houses whose small front porches are almost on the sidewalk, with no yard to speak of in front and nothing but a narrow passageway in back. They look too much like extreme poverty. I am old enough to have begun to care about appearances, and Hazel has done her best to indoctrinate me into the necessity of keeping them up. While the last two Boise houses we lived in were far too small to accommodate the four of us, they had at least not looked so shabby. The house on Hill Road, although tiny, had been rather classy-looking, I thought. But this looming barn looks as if it might fall down soon except that it is so tightly crammed against its neighbors. These ugly buildings seem to lurch down the street, leaning on one another.

It would be hard for me to believe on the day we move into the third house from the east that I will come to feel as fiercely a part of the neighborhood as any ghetto dweller, and that I will come to love our house and its surroundings. The house had something we hadn't had in a long time—interior space. It came at exactly the right time since Betty would soon rejoin the family, bringing with her her infant daughter when her marriage to Monty Barnes fell apart. Not since we had lived in the house on 17th Street, long before the war and our journeys started, had we had so much interior space, although there was no room outside, no lawn, no garden. The house had a cellar and a sun porch across the back. There was a large kitchen with a pantry so big the sink was in the pantry. There was a dining room, living room, bathroom, and one bedroom downstairs, and two more bedrooms upstairs.

Red, with the help of two of his drinking buddies, Ed and Clyde, immediately began to transform the interior of this house. He couldn't do much about the exterior, but he could make the interior aesthetically pleasing, and he did. The painting went on for more than a week. The front bedroom became "dusty rose" and the kitchen, with its several tall windows, blossomed with a pale shade of blue Red had created himself. The most extraordinary thing he did in the entire house was probably in the pantry. While he painted the exterior of all the cabinets white, he painted their interiors a rich, earthy red. There was a window over the sink in the pantry facing south. Red must have studied the position of this window carefully in relation to the angle of the sun. During the entire winter and much of the spring and fall, if we left some of the cabinet doors open, the entire room became suffused with rosy light that spilled out into the kitchen like a bath of pink champagne.

He gave the living room and dining room an even more luxurious treatment. His drinking buddy Ed had helped with the painting, but his drinking buddy Clyde was a paperhanger and a good one, when he was sober enough to work. With Red and Ed assisting him, Clyde papered the living and dining rooms with a deep scarlet brocade paper with a striped pattern textured like velvet. Such wallpaper has become fairly commonplace in hotels and restaurants in more recent years, an attempt to create, I guess, the opulence of a nineteenth-century western brothel. The paper might have been something left over from some large commercial job, but I had never before seen anything like it, and I thought it was magnificent.

Thanks to the work of Red, Ed, and Clyde, the building that was ramshackle and ugly on the outside became beautiful, even elegant, on the inside. We got used to passing through a doorway from one condition to the other, but those who entered the house for the first time often stood in openmouthed amazement. I don't know whether Red felt we were going to remain in that house for several years, or if he was trying to provide work for Ed and Clyde, or if it was just his natural instinct to make his immediate surroundings beautiful. I think it was the latter.

Red had known Ed and Clyde for years, and they would become a tangential part of our lives for several more. They joined Red's closest circle of friends, his drunken admirers, his court. They followed him from bar to bar and often wound up sitting with him at our kitchen table late at night. While I had learned to ignore most of the smelly old drunks who hung around Red, there was a comic earnestness about these two that made it impossible to dislike them. I knew that Clyde had a wife and daughter and Ed had a wife and two sons slightly older than Jack and me. Both men were estranged from their families, and although I can't remember whether or not the two of them shared their quarters, they seemed to spend all their waking hours in one another's company. We always spoke their names in tandem, as one would say the names of a married couple. They were Ed-and-Clyde.

The Ed-and-Clyde episode I remember best happened a couple of years after we moved away from the house on Broad Street, when the two men were well past their prime. One night Clyde came to the door asking for Red. He was upset. Later, I heard the two of them at the kitchen table with a bottle between them. Clyde was beseeching Red for advice and help. Something terrible had happened and he didn't know what to do about it. There had, it seemed, been an accident.

Clyde owned an ancient panel truck in which he hauled his paperhanging tools from one job to another. Ed didn't know how to drive and had neither car nor license. That night they had both gotten very drunk. So drunk, in fact, that while Clyde was driving down a hill and around a curve, he fell out of the truck. He simply rolled off the side of the road into a ditch and lay there for a while, trying to figure out what had happened. Ed, still in the moving truck but nearly passed out himself, was not so lucky. The truck continued down the hill, sideswiping two parked cars along the way and finally colliding head on with a car coming up the hill. Fortunately, no one was hurt seriously. The cops arrived to find Ed in the wreckage of the panel truck and more or less behind the wheel. Since there was no one else in the vehicle, they could only assume that Ed was the driver, a driver in a sad state of intoxication and with no driver's license. They took him to jail, and because he had no money for bail or even to hire a lawyer, that's where he stayed.

As soon as he sobered up a little, Clyde got up and went in search of his truck and Ed. He never did find the truck—it had been towed to a junkyard, never to be heard of again—but he finally found Ed in the county jail with a long list of charges hanging over him, including drunken driving, reckless endangerment, driving without a license, and several more. Out of some sense of loyalty to his friend, Ed, who had sobered up considerably by this time, had not told the police that he had not been driving the truck when the accident happened, or that he had never driven a car of any kind and, in fact, didn't even know how to drive. Ed and Clyde had a furtive conversation in the visiting room of the county jail, during which Ed assumed the pose of the noble martyr and said he would "take the rap" and never "rat on a true friend." He said it would give him pleasure to know that Clyde was "walking the streets, a free man" because of Ed's ability to "hold the line and not squeal."

It was at this point that Clyde, distraught and unable to decide what to do, came to Red for advice and counsel. After a good laugh, Red advised him to go to the police immediately and straighten things out. Clyde couldn't be charged with drunken driving because enough time had passed that they couldn't prove he was drunk when the accident occurred. All he was guilty of was falling out of his own truck, which he could blame on a faulty door latch. I'm not sure how the police responded to Clyde's "confession." Probably with wild amusement and some embarrassment that they had arrested the wrong man. At any rate, both Ed and Clyde were back at our kitchen table within a week, although they arrived in a taxi.

Years later, when Lois and I were visiting in Boise, I asked Jack what had happened to Ed and Clyde. "Well," Jack said, "they had some kind of falling out and didn't speak to each other for a long time. Clyde died first. His liver went bad. After Clyde died, Ed just stayed on skid row and became a nuisance cadging drinks from everybody he could. Finally one night somebody stomped him to death in a gutter. They never pinned it on anybody."

"Stomped him to death? My God, how horrible."

"You remember his two sons? I used to go over and hang around with them when we lived on Flume Street. Well, the youngest one went to prison for a while, like everybody expected. But the oldest one was a real surprise. He became a lawyer and finally a judge. He's a judge now. And his old man was stomped to death on skid row."

~

The house on Broad Street was part of the most exotic neighborhood we had ever lived in. Boise had—and still has—a large Basque community, and we managed to wind up right in the middle of one of its enclaves. In addition to the Basque sheepherders who drifted into town between jobs and usually stayed at the DeLamar or one of the other Basque boardinghouses, there were two layers of Basque society: the respectable and the not so respectable. Many of the second and third generation Basques had inherited the property and nest eggs of their parents and grandparents and had taken their place in Boise society. Then there were the Odiagas.

The father of the Odiaga clan was Amado Odiaga, always referred to as "Old Man Odiaga," although I doubt he was much past fifty. He was short and stocky with a large belly hanging over his belt. He stumped when he walked, his feet placed far apart for balance, as if he were walking on very uneven ground or on the deck of a rolling ship.

He owned the row of four ugly houses on Broad Street, and he and his wife, Rosa, and their daughter Christina and her husband and child lived in the one on the corner. Amado and Rosa had come from their home in the Pyrenees and settled in Boise, where Amado owned and ran one of the most notorious bars on skid row, the White Horse. The White Horse had a large illegal gambling room in the back with an entrance from the back end of the bar and one from the alley for those who didn't want to be seen going into the bar. It was called simply "the back room" and provided slot machines, poker, black-jack, roulette, and the infamous panguingue, which we pronounced "pangingi," a card game so serious that one of Monty Barnes's brothers lost his house and his car in a few hours, and when he went home and told her, he lost his wife too.

Amado and Rosa's only daughter, Christina, ruled the back room with a pretty face, a quick laugh, a glad hand, and an iron fist. Christina could handle about anything that came along, including a 250-pound sex-starved drunk with mischief on his mind, and if things got out of hand, she had only to press a button and her brother, Ruffino, who tended bar up front, would be there with the blackjack he always kept in his pocket. The handsome Ruffino wasn't a particularly large man, but he was slender, agile, and quick. With his weapon in hand, he was a match for most anything that came along. As chance would have it, Ruffino was married to Edith, the non-Basque woman who had been Betty's best friend in high school. Ruffino, Edith, and their daughter lived in the house next door to the west. But it wasn't Betty who got us mixed up with the Odiagas. It was Red.

Red isn't much of a gambler, partly because he never has much to gamble with, and when it comes to a choice between spending what he has on gambling or on booze, it's no contest. So he usually stays clear of the back room and hangs out in the bar where he becomes friends with both Amado and Ruffino. For Amado, who speaks little English but generally understands it, life in America has become a serious business filled with work and responsibility, as he tries to provide for his family and invest in property. For years he has spent most of his time keeping books, paying bills, paying salaries, counting money, paying off the mortgage, paying off the cops. He misses the Old World, the irresponsibility of youth, the laughter over a bottle of wine on summer evenings.

Red, with his easygoing charm and funny stories, makes Amado laugh. Sometimes he laughs till he cries. Each time he sees Red, he gives him a big, rib-breaking hug, and finally offers to rent one of the four houses he owns on Broad Street to Red and his family at a figure so cheap that Red can't afford not to accept it. As we soon find out, we aren't just moving into a house, we are moving into an extended family where Rosa takes care of everybody's children all day, nobody knocks when they enter any of the four houses, and the odor of homemade Basque sausage floats in one door and out the next at any time of day.

At first I'm a little dubious about the Basque sausage when I watch Red and Amado prepare it by stuffing some unidentified animal's intestines with a mixture of ground meat, spices, and hot peppers, but once I taste it, all my squeamishness disappears. I find out that it goes down very well with the pickled pigs' feet and sauerkraut Red has put down in crocks in the basement, that part of his German heritage that he can't give up, although he denies the heritage.

The situation on Broad Street is difficult for Hazel, who has always kept her distance from her neighbors, and when Amado walks in our front door without knocking and finds her in her slip, she is furious. Red ignores her complaints. Gradually the Basques decide either to treat her with exaggerated courtesy or to ignore her entirely. They come to realize, as even I do, that while Red is constantly surrounded by cronies, Hazel has no friends. Only her family.

On Saturday nights Amado stays in the bar all night. After closing, he tallies the week's receipts and works on the books. Each Sunday morning he comes home in a taxi about nine. All the children from the four houses and probably several visiting cousins are lurking about in front of the houses, trying to guess where the taxi will stop. As he gets out and pays the driver, the children crowd around him. He looks at them, scowling, and says something gruff in Basque, as if they are a great nuisance to him. Then, with a big grin, he reaches deep into the pocket of his baggy, rumpled pants, pulls out a big handful of silver dollars, and throws them into the air while the children shriek and scramble for them. Then he goes into the house on the corner, where Rosa cooks him Basque sausage and eggs for breakfast before he goes to bed.

Rosa is tiny and wizened and probably not nearly as old as she looks. She takes care of her grandchildren so their mothers can work, as well as the children of any other family members—nieces, nephews, cousins—who might happen to need taking care of. Most of the time the children play kick the can in the street, or hide-and-go-seek in or around the four houses. It's not unusual to have a breathless child dash in the front door and say, "Hide me! Hide me quick."

About midmorning Rosa emerges from the house on the corner and starts out resolutely for the corner store, a tiny one-room market that gives credit and carries a tab for every family in the neighborhood. It is operated by two elderly sisters who know what brand of cigarettes every child's parents smoke and what kind of soda pop every child prefers. As Rosa emerges from the house on the corner and the screen door slams, children suddenly appear as if they have sprouted from the ground, and down the street she goes with her flock following her like a mother hen with her chicks running wildly along behind.

Rosa always has a reason for going to the store. A bottle of milk or maybe a dozen eggs or a can of peas. She would never admit what all the children know: it's time for a midmorning treat—popsicles or fudgsicles in the summer, sometimes candy bars or licorice sticks or red hots or candy corn, sometimes Nehi sodas.

On long summer evenings, just before twilight turns into dark, Rosa will appear on the front porch to call the children in. She will call a single word, *Mamoo*, in a hollow, ghostly tone. The children will drop whatever game they are playing and run as fast as they can for the safety of Rosa and the house on the corner. Years later I asked a Basque friend what *Mamoo* meant. He said it was a colloquial term for an *embouche*, a particularly awful hobgoblin who has had all its orifices sealed shut. It can't see, of course, but it bumbles through the dark in search of children who do not come home when they are called, and when it finds one, it turns that unfortunate child into an *embouche* like itself. These Basques don't fool around, I thought. I'd rather face the menaces that Little Orphan Annie spoke of, the "two big black things" or the "gobble-uns" that "will get you if you don't watch out."

When we first move into the house on Broad Street, the Odiagas occupy only two of the four houses. A middle-aged man and his two grown daughters in their early twenties rent the house next door to us to the east. One morning at about ten o'clock, the man slashes his throat with a butcher knife in the downstairs bedroom, about eight feet from our living-room window. The girls come home soon afterward and find him. It's too late for an ambulance, but one comes anyway. I remember how the two girls stand on the front porch while the medics and a doctor are in the house, awkward and somehow out of place on their own porch, as if they aren't sure whether they are going out or coming in. As soon as somebody takes them away, I slip through the narrow space that separates our houses and look in the window of their downstairs bedroom. There is a man in there mopping, and a little blood is still dripping from the ceiling.

After that, Amado's "nephew" Johnny and his family moved into the house next door, and we are the only non-Basque family in the four houses. Red says Johnny is really Amado's illegitimate son, and this is generally believed. It doesn't seem to matter whether Johnny's children are Amado's grandnieces and grandnephews or grandchildren. They join Rosa's brood and off they go to the store for treats each morning.

By this time there is an attractive young woman living in each of the four houses, starting with Christina on the corner, Johnny's wife next door, Betty in our house, and Ruffino's wife, Edith, on the other side of us, and we enter the period of the Window-Peeker Hysteria. It lasts several months. A man has been seen peeking in the windows of several of the four houses at night. One night, while we are all sitting in the kitchen at the end of supper, Betty, who is facing the sun porch, freezes and points, unable to speak. A man has been bold enough to enter the sun porch and peer into the kitchen through the window.

By the time Betty can find her voice and make us understand what she has seen, he is gone. We run down the narrow passageway behind the houses and down the alley, but we don't find him.

A few nights later, I am home alone, doing my homework at the dining room table. Suddenly the back door—the door to the sun porch—bursts open. I can hear it, but I can't see it from the dining room. I run into the kitchen, and there is Christina with a huge butcher knife in her hands. She looks like she means business.

"Where is he?" she demands, as if I'm hiding him somewhere. "He came this way. I'm going to cut off his balls. He's never going to look in my window again."

She stalks through the house with her butcher knife at the ready. She looks in Red and Hazel's bedroom, then the cellar. Nothing. She goes out the front door and heads for the next and last house of the four. The window peeker is disconcerting, but I think that I prefer him to Christina and her butcher knife. When I tell Red what happened, he grins and says, "If the guy looks in her window, he won't see anything but asses and elbows." I notice, however, that he never says it to Christina.

The men in the four houses never get to have the violent confrontation with the window peeker they say they want to, and Christina never gets to cut off his balls. Somebody notices an unfamiliar car parked a couple of blocks away, where Broad Street turns into a district of warehouses. One night, Jack and Ruffino decide to watch the car from a distance to see who it belongs to. The driver who returns to it is a sad old man, but he fits the description of the window peeker, and when confronted, he admits his guilt and cries. I don't know what Jack and Ruffino say to him, but he never returns to the neighborhood. On Broad Street you don't call the police when you have a problem. You take care of it yourself. The police come often enough anyway. Evidently the large sums Amado pays them not to raid the back room cover only the White Horse Bar and not his residence.

Central School

When we move into the house on Broad Street, it means I will go back to Central School, which I had attended in the third grade, and this time it will be without Jack in the same building. Central School, built in 1881, had been one of three huge and handsome Victorian buildings on "Capitol Square," including the state capitol building and the county courthouse, all surrounded by a gracious park-like area of trees, grass, and flowers. By the time I first went to school there, Central School was the only one of the three buildings that had survived. The square had been enlarged to the south to provide space for the new state capitol, and the area around Central School had been sold off and was by then a residential area made up of houses and apartment buildings.

Central School was a four-story brick and stone Gothic eminence, built to impress and last forever. It had a main-floor hallway so wide that it was used as an auditorium, and huge staircases with magnificent oak banisters, flat, smooth, and two feet wide—perfect for sliding down when no teacher was in sight. Each classroom had its own cloakroom and many tall windows on one wall. The high-ceilinged rooms were spacious and airy, flooded with light in which the dust motes danced. It was a wonderful place to be a child, with plenty of space and surrounded by the beauty and dignity of the past.

I loved Central School in spite of my fear of the basement. Down those stairs the really hard cases were led to where the janitor, the only male employee in the building, waited with a rubber hose. When I was in the third grade at Central School and Jack was in the sixth, before our wartime travels began, I had seen Jack taken down those stairs by the stern-faced lady principal, and I had seen him when he came back up, pale and trembling.

The third grade had been my best year in school because I got to stay in the same school all year, even though we moved once, and because I adored my teacher, a tall, boyish woman with a big mouth-ful of teeth who wore Girl Scout oxfords and was given to bursts of enthusiasm. She gave me the starring role in the Christmas play, al-though my part consisted mostly of sleeping on stage while the other students acted out my dreams.

The only thing I had really hated about the third grade at Central School was the visits by the dentist and his assistant. Twice a year the dental assistant would show up in the morning and check everyone's teeth. My teeth were a disaster. I never passed the test. The assistant would note which teeth needed to be pulled, and in the afternoon the dentist would arrive, set up shop in the hall, and start pulling teeth. I was willing to go to any lengths to avoid having the dentist pull my teeth.

Jack and I both went home for lunch, and it was my one oppor-tunity between the time the assistant identified which teeth were to be pulled and the actual pulling by the dentist. We had to work fast, and Hazel assisted in any way she could, but she wasn't much help. At first we tried the old method of tying one end of a string around the tooth and the other end to the doorknob, then slamming the door. No success, and we were simply wasting precious time. So Jack got the pliers out of the garage and went after it in earnest. Sometimes he would pull several of my teeth at a time, and when I returned to school after lunch, the dentist would be amazed that there was no need for his services. Somehow I could face Jack with the pliers much more readily than I could face the dentist.

When I return to Central School in the sixth grade, I am placed in Miss Herme's class. Miss Herme is short and stout, probably in her sixties, and has a reputation among the students for being fierce. She dresses very conservatively in solid black or navy blue—no prints—and her only extravagance of self-expression is reserved for her hats, which range from grotesque to ridiculous. Her taste doesn't run to-ward artificial fruit, it gallops. She has a particular fondness for cher-ries. One hat seems to have the product of an entire tree piled on it. Nor is she satisfied with a few feathers when she can get the whole bird on her head, which she does with one hat.

Every few months she provides her sixth-grade class with a fashion show. She brings in seven or eight of her hats in boxes and places them in the cloakroom at the rear of the classroom. She comes out of the cloakroom wearing one of her hats and strolls down the aisle between desks as if it were a ramp and she were a fashion model. At the front of the room she spins around and strolls back down the ramp to the cloakroom, only to reemerge in a different hat. While the girls handle this fairly well, the shows are a sore trial for most of the boys, especially me. The lengths to which we go to keep from laughing include stuffing handkerchiefs in our mouths, clenching our teeth until they ache, and pinching ourselves to cause severe pain. As a last resort, one or two of us can raise our hands and ask to go to the bathroom, but this is considered the coward's way out. We all know that if anybody breaks ranks and starts laughing out loud, the rest of us won't be able to control ourselves, and we'll never get out of the sixth grade.

The first morning of class Miss Herme calls the roll, and when she gets to my name, she seems agitated. "I once had a student in this very class," she says, "named *Jack* Shelton. Are you by any chance related to that student?"

I know, at that moment, I should lie. It's my only chance. I can tell by the expression on the teacher's face that my only hope is to lie and say I have never heard of *Jack* Shelton, but I can't. Somehow, it seems a dreadful thing to deny your own brother, even to save your own skin. "He's my brother," I say so faintly I hope she won't hear.

There is a long pause. Miss Herme's face turns red, even under her rouge, and she grinds her teeth audibly. Her agitation increases as the big clock on the wall ticks, and my fear increases with it.

"First it was *Jack* Shelton," she says. "Now it's *Dick* Shelton. Why have I been singled out by the gods for this honor? I want you to know whom you are dealing with, Mr. *Dick* Shelton, as your brother learned to his sorrow. I will be watching your every move. I don't expect you to learn anything, but at the slightest sign of misbehavior, you will go down to the basement to visit the janitor, and that's a promise."

During this unexpected tirade the other students hold their breath. They look at me in awe. I must be a real ripper, some kind of twelve-year-old mass murderer with a long prison record. As it turns out, I will disappoint them badly. I don't kill anybody all year, but I can read and write better than any other member of the class. Miss Herme's suspicion fades, and in a few weeks I glance up from my book to see her beaming at me with genuine fondness. *Oh, shit!* I think. *Out of the frying pan, into the fire.*

Miss Herme is a moralist who illustrates her lessons with stories. She tells us we must never hesitate to ask to be excused from the classroom if we need to and tells the story of her friend's fatal accident. Her friend was riding a city bus with a full bladder. When the bus stopped and she stepped down to get off the bus, her bladder burst and she died. After that story there is a regular stampede of girls toward the bathroom.

Miss Herme's room is on the second floor and has a bank of large windows across the west wall. Each morning in the middle of the first period class, which is geography, most of the students start to glance surreptitiously out the windows on our left as we face Miss Herme in the front of the classroom. Geography consists mostly of filling in the names of countries on a blank map and listening to Miss Herme tell stories of her travels in Europe. When Miss Herme tells these stories, particularly about her trip to Italy, which took place many years earlier when she was many years younger, she becomes so moved that she is oblivious to everything else.

So it is usually during her stories of her travels in Italy that we begin to look out the windows to our left, where, directly across the street on the second floor of a vintage redbrick apartment building, a dark, hairy-chested, and purely naked young man stumbles out of bed and comes to the window, stretches hugely, scratches his balls, and looks out on the weather, unaware that he has an audience of sixth-graders across the street. He not only displays the tumescence common to young men first thing in the morning, but he is enormously endowed.

Most of the students in Miss Herme's class pretend that they aren't seeing what they are seeing, although several of the boys have difficulty controlling their laughter, and I'm afraid I'm one of them. Most of the girls avert their eyes, but some look back several times. Miss Herme natters on with an account of her adventures in Italy that we have already heard. Eventually the young man stumbles away from the window, probably in search of a cup of coffee.

Our morning entertainment goes on for several weeks before it stops abruptly and the window across the street is covered with blinds. We boys never know if Miss Herme has aroused herself enough from her reveries about traveling through Italy to notice the show across the street or whether one of the girls in the class has squealed. We try to imagine the principal, a gaunt spinster who wears navy blue serge dresses with detachable white collars and cuffs, striding across the street to confront the naked young man, but we can't. Finally, we decide that she must have sent the janitor.

For years, whenever I think of Miss Herme's travels in Italy, I will picture her wandering hand in hand with a naked, hairy-chested Italian who is hung like the proverbial horse. I'm sure all the boys in the class hoped someday to measure up to the model set before us, but I suspect we were all disappointed.

On the last day of class Miss Herme makes a little speech to the students. First, she apologizes to me for her harsh words the first day of class. I am petrified with embarrassment and shame. Why can't she just leave it alone? Then she says she has been guilty of exactly what she tries to teach her students to avoid: she had judged someone on the basis of no real knowledge of that person. I am so embarrassed and upset that during the summer, when I am not at the ranch, I spend most of the time hiding in the stacks of the Carnegie Library to avoid meeting any of my classmates. It's the last free summer I will have. By the following summer, I have a job.

⁓

When I returned to Boise in search of ghosts in the 1990s, I bicycled over to have a look at the old Central School and found a parking lot used by employees in the nearby government buildings. A parking lot! Surely it couldn't be. I checked and double-checked the location, but there was no mistake. The good citizens of Boise had turned the most magnificent example of public Victorian architecture they had into a parking lot. Central School was opened the year Charlotte was born. Like her, it not only represented the best of its time, but it continued to be useful and beautiful throughout most of the next century.

FILMS

Shortly after we move into the house on Broad Street, before I turn twelve, Jack disappears. The first night he doesn't come home, nobody seems to be too worried. The second night, Hazel becomes alarmed. The following morning I get a phone call from a girl I have never met. She says she is a friend of Jack's friend Kay, and that I must not tell my parents she has called. She says that if I swear not to tell my parents or anyone else, she will tell me where Jack is. I swear.

"Jack and Kay are in the jail on the top floor of the county courthouse. Jack doesn't want your folks to know where he is. He wants you to bring him some things without anybody knowing."

"What kind of things?"

"A carton of cigarettes and some doughnuts and lots of candy bars. He says there's some money in the top drawer of the bureau in your bedroom. Can you get him that stuff?"

"I guess so."

"He says to bring it up to the top floor of the county courthouse but don't use his name. Ask to see Jack Leonards. You mustn't let them know what his real name is. He says he's depending on you."

"OK, I'll do it."

I know where Jack keeps money in our bedroom, and it's no problem to buy the cigarettes. I buy cigarettes for Red and Hazel at the corner store all the time. Jack may not like the brand they smoke, but that's tough. If I try to buy a different brand, the two sisters who own the store will be suspicious. When I've got everything, I put it in a paper grocery bag, put the bag in the basket of my bicycle, and pedal to the county courthouse. Jack's in the juvenile section at the very top of the building. I can see bars on the windows from outside.

I go in, take the elevator to the top floor, and tell the clerk that I want to visit Jack Leonards. I'm afraid they won't let me in without a parent, but they do. After they search the bag I'm carrying, they send me into a visiting area where there are tables and chairs. Soon Jack comes in. I give him the stuff I brought and ask him how come nobody has called Hazel and Red? He says because he gave the cops a false name and threw away his wallet and all his ID before he was arrested.

"What were you arrested for?"

"Just crazy stuff. It doesn't matter."

"I'm going to tell Red and Hazel where you are. They can get you out."

"If you do, I'll break your neck when I get out."

"What am I going to tell them? They'll worry a lot."

"I'm going to have somebody call them and say I'm out of town."

"They won't believe it. They'll say, 'Why doesn't he call himself?'"

"I'll think of something. You just keep your mouth shut and bring me some more candy bars tomorrow. And bring me the rest of the money in that drawer. Remember, my name is Jack Leonards."

"Where's Kay?"

"They've got him locked up somewhere else. He's being treated as an adult."

I don't stay long. While riding home I worry about trying to keep from showing I know where Jack is. I can't stand to see my mother so upset. I don't think they will call missing persons or the police for a long time because they probably realize he's in some kind of trouble, but I don't know how long I can keep lying to them and watching Hazel fall apart.

It turns out to be easier than I expected. Red and Hazel don't ask me anything because they assume I don't know anything. The next morning Hazel calls Kay's stepmother and finds out Kay is in the county jail. She puts it all together and calls the jail. They don't have any inmate by the name of Jack Shelton, but they have one they suspect is using an alias, and he fits the description Hazel gives them, and as Red would say, "That's all she wrote."

I never found out the details of what Jack and Kay did that caused them to land in jail. It involved stolen tires and gasoline and the black market. Years later Jack told me a wild story about him and Kay going to the Idanha Hotel and stealing hundreds of rolls of toilet paper. Later, when the cops were chasing them, they threw the toilet paper rolls out the window at the pursuing police car. During the chase, Jack drove onto someone's prize tulip bed and skidded in a big circle, destroying the entire bed. I have no idea whose car Jack was driving nor why he would want to steal toilet paper out of the Idanha Hotel, or if any of this happened at all. If it did happen, it might have been in conjunction with the more serious crimes for which he was arrested.

Jack had a juvenile record going back to the time he was eleven and we lived on Flume Street. He and his friends, the same group whose clubhouse was in a privy turned on its side, had found an abandoned but historically important sawmill on the river. By sawing away a section of the floor, which took them weeks, they were able to watch the huge main saw drop into the river. Because he was so young, he was not sent to the reform school.

Even earlier he had had problems. When he was in the first grade, which he flunked, he and a friend activated a fire alarm on a telephone pole and ran away. Unfortunately, Jack left one of his schoolbooks with his name in it beside the alarm box. This was the pattern for what was to follow. Purely gratuitous acts of mayhem, and extremely clumsy, downright dumb, attempts to avoid the consequences. He flunked the fourth grade, but only after an escapade so daring it made him a hero to the other students.

One of the most hated teachers was a fairly young man who was not only autocratic and pompous, but also sarcastic. One day in class Jack lost his temper and threw a glass inkwell at the teacher. The teacher ducked, the inkwell hit the blackboard, and ink and glass splattered all over that section of the room. Jack ran out the classroom door and down the hall, with the teacher in pursuit. The classroom was on the third floor. At the end of the hall was a stairwell, and down the middle of it hung a rope connected to the bell on the roof. Instead of taking the stairs, Jack leaped for the rope, grabbed it, and went down it hand over hand like a monkey, gaining time on the pursuing teacher and, of course, causing the bell to ring wildly. The students and other teachers, hearing the bell ringing, assumed it was a fire drill and poured out of the classrooms, further impeding the teacher trying to catch Jack. Jack got away for the moment, but he had to go home sooner or later, and when he did, a school administrator was waiting for him. He never seemed to be able to make a connection in his mind between the crime and the resulting punishment, probably because he was so seldom, if ever, punished at home, no matter what he did.

When Red and Hazel found him in the county jail, he was lucky again, although I don't trust the official family story about how that luck came about. That story says that when Jack was arraigned in the juvenile court, the judge told him that since it was wartime, if he could manage to get into some branch of the service (and out of town), the charges would be dropped. Jack was sixteen. I find it hard to believe that a judge would advise Jack to lie about his age in order to get into some branch of the military service.

Another possibility, and a more likely one, is that Red hired a lawyer who advised Jack, while he was out of jail awaiting trial, to try to get into some branch of the military service and disappear. At any rate, Jack managed, at barely sixteen, to be accepted into the Merchant Marines. It happened very fast. He was gone before I realized that both our lives had changed profoundly. For at least two years I would be free, and even when he came back, much changed for the better; he would soon marry and be occupied with his own family. He would never again be the major figure in my life, the one I feared, hated, loved, admired, and lied for. The one who alternately tortured me and protected me and whom I either adored or wanted to destroy. The one who convinced me I was a useless, clumsy tool.

How do I assess the damage after so many years, and he is dead, and I am left to try to figure it out? I can't, of course. I can only remember scenes, knowing they are contradictory and conflicting, just as my feelings for Jack were contradictory and conflicting and will always be. I remember them like short films, mini-documentaries, that play over and over in my head:

We are living on 17th Street and I am six. Jack got a BB gun for his birth-day. He needs to practice on a moving target, he tells me. He puts an old leather jacket on me and tells me to run toward the garage and not look back. I run and he starts shooting. I can feel the BBs hitting my back and they sting. A couple hit my leg and go in. Jack will work them out later. I won't play the game anymore, and I hide in the cherry tree. The following week a neighbor comes over threatening to call the police and sue Red. Jack has shot a neighbor boy with his BB gun and barely missed his eye. Red curses the neighbor but reluctantly takes the gun away from Jack.

We are living on 13th Street. I am out back feeding the rabbits in their cages. I see Jack coming down the alley. He is more than two blocks away. He is walking funny, hobbling. Something is wrong. I run to meet him and see that he is dragging a long board attached to his foot, leaving a trail of blood behind him. He has stepped on a nail in a board and the nail has gone through the thin sole of his tennis shoe and lodged between the bones in his foot. He can't get it out, so he is dragging the board home where he knows there are tools. He is pale but not crying. I am crying as I walk along with him, feeling the pain of every step. I run ahead to get Red. Red cuts off the head of the nail and pulls the board free. Then, with the pliers, he pulls the nail out of Jack's foot. Jack never makes a sound during the operation, but he's sweating heavily. I'm wiping his face with a wet cloth.

We are living on Hill Road where Jack and I share a room in the basement. I am in bed when Jack and his friend Kay come in. They have stopped by for Jack to change his clothes and get something he needs. I wake up when they come in, but I pretend to be asleep. Kay is giving Jack a lesson in sex education. I am all ears.

"So I bent her over the table and did it doggie style. You should try it. It's great. That's why they call them bitches."

We are living on Broad Street. I am in the sixth grade. I have become one of a group of neighborhood boys who play touch football in nearby Julia Davis Park every afternoon during the summer. It's a casual bunch. We choose up sides and sometimes we don't have enough players to make up two full teams, but we play anyway. I really enjoy it, although I'm not one of the best players. I usually play center because I'm lighter than most of the others, but I'm fast and I can hold the line at center. If I ever get hold of the ball, I can run like crazy. We always have a good time.

One afternoon Jack joins us. He is older than any of the players and they defer to him. He takes over the team I'm on and starts calling plays. I immediately fumble a catch and he tells everybody what a useless turd I am. On the next play I get the signal wrong and we are destroyed before we can make a single yard. Jack becomes angry and lays into me. Why in the hell do they allow such a klutz to play on the team? Get rid of him! Jack is older and more experienced. And he's my older brother. They think he ought to know. I leave the field and walk home, fighting back tears. I won't be able to play football again, ever. I never do.

HANDS

About the time Jack leaves for the Merchant Marines, my childhood ends, and I go to work. From then on, there is little time for anything but school and work. My time at the ranch is stolen from school, but as long as I can keep up, it doesn't seem to matter. Before this I have been mowing lawns, trimming hedges, raking leaves, or setting pins in the Boise bowling alley, but I hadn't had a real job. Now I learn about working set hours under the eyes of a boss.

That boss is Mr. Pepper of Pepper's Drug Store on Main Street, where I am hired as janitor, delivery boy, and general flunky. As soon as school is out in the afternoon, I ride my bicycle to the drugstore, make prescription deliveries, sweep the store out, wash the beakers and bottles in the back sink, scrub shelves, wash windows, chip ice for the fountain, and do the dishes. I work until nine at night when the store closes. On Saturdays I work from seven to five. When summer arrives I work nine hours a day and my duties are expanded to include being the soda jerk at the fountain and, at certain hours, cashier.

I shudder to think about some of the duties I performed as general flunky. I filled little sacks with DDT powder from a large drum. Nobody suggested that I wear a mask. I poured carbolic acid from a huge glass container I could barely lift into quart bottles. Breathing it was bad, but once a great dollop splashed into my eye. I held my head under the faucet at the sink until I got it all washed out, but it was painful.

Mr. Pepper, who owned the store and was its chief pharmacist, was a strange little man, bad-tempered and totally bald. He looked like an irascible leprechaun with malevolent eyes. He treated most of his employees with withering contempt, but in spite of that, I believe he liked me. While Mr. Pepper blew hot and cold, vacillating from temper tantrums to unexpected acts of kindness, the steady power in the store was Ila, the beautiful silver-haired and gorgeously groomed manager, who was almost a head taller than Mr. Pepper and was thought to be his mistress, although he was married and had a son away in prep school. It was Ila who often stood between me and Mr. Pepper's rages, and it was Ila who pushed to expand my duties to include soda jerk and even cashier when she wasn't available.

Red said everybody on skid row knew that Old Man Pepper sold "goofballs," some kind of narcotic he had concocted. I doubted it was true, although some of the customers who insisted on seeing him were certainly strange. As a pharmacist he was very quick and secretive about some of his transactions, but I figured he was simply protecting the privacy of his customers in a community where buying a package of condoms was a highly suspect and furtive transaction.

As a pharmacist he performed many of the functions of a doctor, as I'm sure most other pharmacists of that time did. One small, windowless room in the back was filled with nothing but hundreds of trusses, where Mr. Pepper would take customers with hernias and fit them with whatever kind of truss they needed. Most evenings I had to wash several small glass containers with little nipples at one end and a plunger at the other, like syringes without needles. At first I had no idea what these were for, but eventually I found out they were used to inject some kind of liquid into a man's penis to alleviate the symptoms of gonorrhea. A man would come in and have a quick consultation with Mr. Pepper, who would then take him into the room with all the trusses and close the door. Later, one of the little syringe-like gadgets would appear in the sink for me to wash. I washed these and the bottles and beakers the best I could in the primitive sink, but we had no facilities to sterilize anything, and sometimes we even ran out of hot water. One minute I was washing these gruesome little gonorrhea tubes, and a few minutes later I was making sandwiches at the fountain.

If I was squeamish about any of this, I got over it quickly, since I needed the job and enjoyed aspects of it, like delivering prescriptions on my bicycle and working as a soda jerk. I'm sure Ila realized it made me feel important, at the age of thirteen, to operate the huge and complex brass cash register. Everybody else in the store seemed to take my somewhat odd combination of duties as a matter of course, so I did too. Except for one awful day the second summer I worked at the drugstore, and that wasn't the fault of anybody at the store.

It had to do with Boise's Grove Street, the most fashionable and beautiful residential street in Boise for more than a decade after the late 1870s. In order to water the lawns, trees, and gardens of the mansions on Grove Street, a sizeable ditch was built along its north side, with tall paddle wheels at intervals to scoop the water out of the ditch and direct it to sluices leading to the various properties. Eventually the neighborhood decayed and the mansions were torn down, although I remember two of them that were still standing when I was a delivery boy at Pepper's. I delivered prescriptions to one of them, every boy's version of a haunted house, and waited for what seemed like hours while an ancient person shuffled from somewhere deep inside to answer the door.

By then most of Grove Street had been given over to used-car lots and warehouses. The ditch remained, although it had been covered over for many blocks all the way through the downtown area. Most people didn't know it was there. The paddle wheels were gone, as well as the lush greenery the ditch had made possible. At East 5th Street the ditch had been left uncovered, and there was a wooden grating to stop debris just before it disappeared under the street.

It is summertime, early morning, and I am pedaling my bike as fast as I can go, heading for the drugstore where it is my responsibility to open up for the early morning coffee drinkers and be in charge until Mr. Pepper arrives about eight. I turn off Broad Street onto 5th and go over the slight hump in the road where the ditch runs under the street. As I go over the hump, I glance to the right and see a human arm and hand sticking out of the water against the grate. I nearly have a spill, but I get control of my bike and stop. I look frantically for help. There is no one in sight this early in the morning. I'm terrified, but maybe the person is still alive. I've got to get whoever it is out of there. I have a moment's hesitation before I touch that ghastly hand, and then I do it. The hand is stiff and cold but also slimy, and it seems to grasp my hand as I begin to tug against the current rushing through the grate and holding the body there. The hand vibrates as the body shudders in the current. For a moment I don't know if I'm pulling the body out of the water or the body is pulling me in. It's an old man, and finally I get him onto the bank beside the ditch, lying on his back with one stiff arm pointing skyward, and at the end of it the hand with curled fingers I have just had difficulty extricating my own hand from. I would swear that he took hold of me rather than the other way around.

Just as I get him out, a car stops, and I ask the driver to go down to the 5th Street Market on the corner, where there's a phone, and call the police. It's much too late for an ambulance. As I wait for the police, I'm shaking visibly. It's chilly this early in the morning, but not that cold. I keep wiping my hands on my pants and finally turn back to the ditch and try to wash my hands. I'm doing that when the cops arrive. I tell them how I found the body, and they take my address and phone number and tell me I can go on to work. In spite of the delay and a couple of grouchy customers waiting in front for their morning coffee, I still make it to the store before Mr. Pepper does, so he won't know how late I am. I bring the bundle of newspapers in and wash my hands before I make the coffee. I have to chip ice for the fountain. Everybody has coffee and I'm chipping ice when Mr. Pepper comes in. I've already washed my hands three times.

"You sick?" he asks, looking at me closely. I know that under his gruff manner, impatience, and often brutally sarcastic tongue, he is really fond of me, or at least he feels sorry for me because I obviously do not have the advantages of his son, who is home for the summer from an eastern prep school.

"No, I'm OK. I had a little trouble on the way to work. Nothing much. I'm OK." I can't bring myself to tell him about it. What a big baby he'll think I am. Can't bear to touch a dead man's hand.

At midmorning I have to make the sandwich spreads for the lunch crowd. I start with egg salad. Something about the texture of the cold hard-boiled eggs gets to me as I chop them. I almost gag, and I stop to wash my hands again. I have washed my hands eight times, and it isn't noon yet. Mr. Pepper watches me closely but says nothing.

The next day he says, "I saw a small article in the paper about an old man who drowned himself in the little ditch that runs along Grove Street. The article said he was despondent and had been living in his car parked by the ditch for several days. Said some teenage boy going to work on his bicycle pulled him out. At 5th and Grove. I wonder who that could have been."

"How should I know?" I answer, and head to the back of the store for another block of ice.

～

Mr. Pepper tries to show me that in spite of his abrasive ways, he values me and the fact that I work hard. Perhaps he sees some contrast between me, the poor boy, and his overprivileged son—some contrast that bothers him. At any rate, he throws us together, and the result is not, I think, what he intended. Young Mr. Pepper is three years older than I am, old enough to drive, and he has obviously been told to treat his father's least employee well, but he feels the need to impress me while at the same time being condescending. I'm used to it. You don't grow up the son of a drunken house painter in Boise, Idaho, without getting used to it. Years later, when I am a professor at a major university and someone with more impressive academic credentials lords it over me, I will be known to say, "Don't worry about it, my friend. I've been patronized by experts, most of whom were far better at it than you."

Anyway, I am invited to spend the weekend at Mr. Pepper's luxurious place on Payette Lake near McCall, about a hundred miles north of Boise, the same McCall where Charlotte had worked and Red had arrived under a freight train. Many wealthy Boiseans have "cabins" at "the lakes." Mr. Pepper's son picks me up at the store and drives me to McCall. He drives recklessly and too fast. I'm sure he has driven this tricky Highway 95 many times, but I am aware of how dangerous his driving is, and I'm not impressed.

That afternoon, at the Pepper's luxurious lakeside home, the son wants to take a ride in his father's new boat, a magnificent, sleek cabin cruiser, worth a fortune by my standards. The boy wants to impress me. Mr. Pepper hesitates, but finally says OK for a short ride. The son shows off his ability to handle the boat at high speeds, and his ability isn't all that great. After almost an hour, we see Mr. Pepper pacing on the dock, waiting for us. His son brings the boat around and heads for the dock at too high a speed. I keep thinking he will be able to slow it down, but he can't. We ram the dock head on, with Mr. Pepper standing on it, or rather doing a dance of rage on it, like an imp from hell, until he is knocked down by the impact. The son and I scramble out of the boat and onto the floating and now wildly heaving dock, and as I watch that magnificent boat slowly sink—blub, blub . . . blub—and go to the bottom of the lake, I realize that I am a survivor. But I have no idea I will survive so many years, looking back, chasing ghosts.

PART VI

BEAUTIFUL

FATHER AND SONS

Red died before any of us. He died long before Charlotte, and Hazel outlived him by twenty years. He died before Betty died, or Jack. I was with him in his long dying. We should have known that he would show us how to do it, that he would go ahead of us and show us the style, the flair for it, and that he would throw in that one last flourish at the end, sheer bravado, the sign of genius. We should have known he would go out as a showman, though years earlier he had stopped living in the bars, where he had always been a showman. Perhaps the others knew what to expect, but I didn't; and from the moment I arrived to take care of him, I was astonished. And I think, before we got through with it, he was a little astonished at me too. During the last three months of his life, we lived in a state of mutual wonder, never knowing what would happen from one day to the next. Often then, even as he was dying, he made me laugh. And since we were on stage together, since his illness had dragged me onto the stage with him, his performance made it possible for me to do things I never would have believed I could do. When it was over, I was proud of both of us. I think that's what he intended.

I didn't read the early signals well. Perhaps none of us did, but they are apparent in Hazel's journal. I'm not sure even she recognized the significance of what she was writing.

> *August, 1968 Dad not well and getting worse—Went to Dr. Peterson and St. Lukes for test and exRays—He has Diabetes. On diet & medication—no improvement.*

Hazel's journal records that the Shelton brothers, all older than Red, are beginning to die. The beloved Minnis Richard, father of legion and a very good friend of Red's, dies in October 1967. When Red's parents had moved their family from Illinois to a ranch near

Carbondale, Colorado, in about 1907, it was because Minnis had gone there first and got a job as a cowboy on a large Colorado ranch. When Red told me, just before he died, that his family members had been horse thieves and the less I knew about them, the better off I would be, this, it seemed to me later, was the only period he could have been referring to because my ghost chasing had accounted for all the others. It does seem that the Sheltons left Colorado rather precipitously. But to think of my uncle Minnis, with his bandy legs, spectacles, pot belly, and ultra-respectable wife, as a horse thief, even in his younger days, boggles my mind. I'll never know. It's possible that Red used the expression figuratively, meaning something like "they didn't amount to much."

Then Everett Charles, known always as "Hap," dies in late August 1968. Hap, who had lived in California after he married, had left his family when he was in his fifties and joined the circus. Once, when I was about nine and Hazel was taking me to the circus in Boise— Hazel loved the circus above all other forms of entertainment and was bitterly disappointed when she no longer had a child at home to furnish an excuse for going—I met Hap, possibly for the first time.

Hazel and I stood in line near the entrance to the circus to get tickets. When we got to the little kiosk where a man was selling them, she put down the money and the old man in the kiosk said, "My God, Hazel, is that you? Don't you know me? It's Hap."

He emerged from the back of the kiosk and came around to talk to us. I could tell that Hazel was embarrassed. He was scrawny and unshaven and he smelled bad. He had left his wife, Jesse, and several mostly grown children. The only one whose name I can remember was Bobo. How could you forget a name like that, especially since Bobo's father ran away and joined the circus? I could tell Hazel was not at all happy about this unplanned encounter with her husband's older brother, although she was cordial to him. He was severely damaging her image. We got away as soon as possible and went on into the circus tent with the tickets he had given us free.

Years later, before he died, he came back to Boise and lived with his widowed sister, Leola, for a while. Just before that, when Lois and

I arranged to see him in Boise on one of our visits, he was living in a room upstairs over a bar on skid row. We took him on an outing to Lucky Peak Dam. Lois's father had been one of the major contractors who built it. Hap shyly gave us a sack full of candy bars. His name suited him. He was devil-may-care and jolly. Besides Red, he was the only other one of the siblings who had that ebullience, that ability to make others laugh. I don't think he ever got to be a clown in the circus, but they should have let him try it. With his self-deprecating grin, his sad, rolling puppy-dog eyes, and his comic gait, he would have been sensational.

Although Hazel does not record it in her journal, in the fall of 1967 Red came to Arizona to visit us and see his only grandson—all of Betty's and Jack's nine children were girls. He came on the bus and alone. We were greatly surprised at this. He was thin and quiet. Most amazing of all, he wasn't drinking.

He had come to Arizona to see us several times before, but always with Hazel, and he had always driven. In 1961, after a particularly nasty fight with Jack and Lillian, he had packed up a two-wheel trailer and he and Hazel announced that they were moving to Arizona. They showed up in Tucson without any real plans and very little money. It was my first full year as a faculty member at the university. Lois was teaching music in a junior high school. With our three-year-old son, we were living in a two-bedroom apartment near campus while our house was being built in the foothills. It was a tight squeeze after Red and Hazel arrived, but we managed.

Red was bitter at Jack. The problem had arisen after Jack, who had developed a thriving business as a paint contractor, hired Red to work for him. Jack's dramatic conversion to the Mormon Church had paid off for him in terms of many big jobs whose contracts were controlled by Mormons in southern Idaho, where Mormons had always formed a powerful political and economic consortium. Jack's company painted state buildings, county buildings (including the county courthouse in which Jack had once been incarcerated, although that was all forgotten by this time), Mormon churches, and even the elaborate new Mormon temple. *Jack Shelton, Painting Contractor,* with

Lillian handling the books (and, it was believed by the family, telling Jack what to do), had become a big success. They worked hard, they made money, and they lived well, with a two-story A-frame at Payette Lake for the summer, a sleek boat, a motor home, and all the trimmings. Once Hazel told me on the phone, in disbelief, how much Jack had spent for a new car.

"What kind of car was it?" I asked.

"Well, it was one of them foreign cars with a strange name. I think he said it was a Mr. Sadie's Bends. Do you know what kind of car that is?"

When it came to hiring his father, who was somewhat down but not completely out, anyone, even from a great distance, could have seen that it was a doomed proposition, and I did, but I was out of the loop and there was nothing I could do about it. Jack was a staunch party-line Mormon, and Red was a confirmed and practicing alcoholic. It was madness. I never knew what Jack's motives were when he hired Red, but they were probably mixed. On the one hand, Red was no longer young and could not always find work. There was probably a certain amount of altruism in Jack's offering Red a job. On the other hand, Red was a highly experienced master painter who had taught Jack most of what he knew. Red could paint anything with a three-inch brush, and when he was able to work, he pulled more than his share of the load. Generally, when he was working locally, he could work all the time. When he tried to live somewhere else because there was a job there, he often drank so much that he missed work and was let go.

In 1961, when Red and Hazel suddenly showed up in Tucson, Jack had ridden Red in front of the other men on the crew and treated him in ways Red's pride couldn't tolerate. Getting the story from Red, it was obvious that Jack had lost his temper, which was not exactly news to me. Evidently his conversion to Mormonism hadn't changed him in some ways.

Red and Hazel stayed with us three months that winter, long enough to help us move into our new house. Hazel said it was the first time she had seen anybody move who didn't pack first. Red did some exterior brickwork for us, a little brick house to cover the gas meter and some steps up to the front terrace. He built bookcases in two rooms and helped me start a stone wall that would occupy me for the next five years. On a later visit he would paint the entire interior of the house. Years after his death I found that he had signed his work when he painted our kitchen. On top of one of the kitchen cabinets, where it could be seen only from the ceiling, he had signed his name with a flourish, a gesture of such fierce pride and painful irony that I broke down when I found it. "I'm a damned good house painter," it said. "I can paint anything with a three-inch brush."

Ultimately the worst differences with Jack were ironed out somehow. Red and Hazel returned to Boise and settled back into the little house on Randall Street they had bought in 1951, the year I graduated from high school and went away to college. It wasn't much, but Red had painted it barn red with white shutters, planted trees, shrubs, flowers, and a vegetable garden, and turned it into a delightful doll's house. It was a miniature beauty in a lousy neighborhood on the wrong side of the tracks and much too close to them.

Less than a year later, Hazel calls. She is crying. "They had a terrible fight. Jack fired him. Dad is real bad upset. His pride is hurt. He won't stop drinking. I don't know what to do. You know how mean Jack can be, and Lillian is cold as ice. She hates Dad. She's always been jealous of anybody Jack cared about. Can you come home and talk to Jack? Betty won't have anything to do with him. He'll listen to you. Can you come talk to him, please?"

Somehow it is too difficult for me to explain to my mother that talking to Jack about his treatment of our father is not high on my list of priorities. In fact, talking to Jack at all is not high on my list of priorities. But I get on an airplane, rent a car in Boise, and prepare myself to "talk to" Jack.

I find Jack and Lillian living in a mansion in the lovely section of Boise called the "North End." I am flabbergasted by the house and grounds. Either Jack and Lillian are terribly rich, I think, or they are living far above their means. Hazel, Red, and Betty have been complaining for years about them "putting on the dog," but I had no idea it was such an impressive dog. It looks to me like a Saint Bernard, at least, or maybe an Irish wolfhound. Years later, I will be told conflicting stories about the mansion. Lillian will tell me they bought the mansion in order to resell it at a profit. Jack will tell me they bought it to live in because they got a very good deal on it, but they couldn't afford it and lost their shirts.

My interview with Jack and Lillian in their mansion is not satisfactory. The sight of the mansion has made me hostile. I hate this kind of ostentation. Jack and Lillian tell me they can no longer carry Red. He is not only not pulling his weight in terms of the work, but he is corrupting the other painters on the crew. His thermos is full of whiskey and there are many days when he is needed and he can't make it to work. I don't dispute any of this.

"You knew all of this when you hired him," I say. "You hired him as he is and you should accept him as he is. Did you hire him only to humiliate him?"

"We can't afford to carry him," Lillian says. "The business hasn't been as good lately as it was. He's undependable and a bad influence on the other men."

"Well," I say, getting a little heated now, and that's always a mistake for me, "I guess none of us knew before you hired him that he was a bad influence. We all know that he was the best influence in the world on his children. Especially on Jack. I remember when Jack was sixteen years old and Red would get into fights in bars. He would call Jack up and tell him to come down to the bar and beat the hell out of Red's adversary, and Jack would do it. Surely Jack knew what kind of influence his father was. And as far as your business reverses go, I can see you are suffering from dire poverty and are practically at the door of the poorhouse."

Then I left, having made no impression on Jack or Lillian at all and hating myself for giving in to sarcasm when what I needed was negotiating skills. It was a very "Red" thing to do. No day passed that I didn't realize how much like my father I was, although he would not have believed it. My visit to Jack and Lillian had been a lost cause from the beginning, and I knew it.

Red didn't go back to work for Jack. He took other work as he could get it, often dreadful work. On one visit, in the middle of the summer's heat, we found him painting white stripes on the new asphalt parking lot of a huge mall near Caldwell. He painted roofs. He took whatever jobs he could get. Some of his old friends found him work when they could. His son was the most successful paint contractor in the state and everyone knew the name of his company, but it gave Red little satisfaction and brought him no employment. He was effectively blackballed by most contractors because everyone knew that his own son had fired him for drinking on the job. He would have been better off if he had never worked for Jack.

As he turns sixty-five, Red and Hazel struggle to get him Social Security benefits. The paper work is daunting because he has no birth certificate. He was born at home, and there was no attending physician. "To hell with them," Red would say in frustration while trying to fill out yet another form. "How do they think I got here if I wasn't born?" Finally he obtains a birth certificate and, in time, small monthly payments. His benefits are small because he has been paying into the Social Security system for a relatively short time. I think when Red came alone to visit us in the fall of 1967, he sensed that something was terribly wrong. Lois and our son and I went to Boise for Christmas that year. Red is subdued. The following Christmas Hazel's entry in her journal describes Red as "failing." Her entry for May 13, 1969, is *Dad not doing at all well—Losing weight fast. Still trying to work. Went to St. Lukes Hosp. For tests & exrays—Has ulsers now.* Three days later he is *very weak and thin—On insulin shots—Bed fast most of the time.*

Hazel's entry for June 28 through July 1 records the blow she had been dreading and the beginning of my three-and-a-half-month stay in the little red house on Randall Street near the railroad tracks. *Dr. Peterson sent Dad to Dr. Molloy. He sent him right to Hosp. for surgery. Sad news—termanel cancer of the Pancreas with only three months to live—Jack & Betty & I at Hosp.—Dick came by plane.*

When I arrived at the hospital, Red was heavily drugged on Demerol. I stood at the foot of his bed and watched him go through the motions of reaching into his shirt pocket, getting a cigarette out of a pack, lighting it, and smoking it with satisfaction while sound asleep, perfectly miming the action I had seen him perform a thousand times. His surgery had been, ostensibly, to remove his gall bladder. It was also exploratory and extensive, and when the surgeon saw his pancreas, he simply sewed him up again.

Hazel insisted that Red not be told the truth. Jack and Betty agreed. Jack said that if he knew what he was facing, he would commit suicide. That seemed odd to me, and I wondered if Jack really knew his father very well, although he had spent much more time with Red than I had. I went along with Hazel's wishes because I figured Red could not have gone through all he had without getting some idea of his condition. In fact, I thought he must have known he had cancer before he ever submitted to the surgery. I wasn't sure how I would respond if faced with a direct question from Red. As it turned out, he was playing the game too. Since he could tell they didn't want him to know, he pretended he didn't know. He maintained this fiction to the end, even when it became obvious he had only hours to live.

Our immediate problem is what to do with him during the next three months or however much time he has. He hates the hospital. "I want to go home," he says as soon as he is fully conscious. "Dick, take me home. I hate it here. Jack won't take me. You take me home, or I'll get up and go home on my own."

"Yes," I say. "As soon as the doctor releases you, I'm taking you home."

Hazel looks horrified. When the four of us huddle in the hall, she says, "I can't do it. I can't take care of him. I don't know how. I can't even keep my own medicines straight, and I can't lift him even though he's lost so much weight. The last month has been terrible."

"I know, Mamma, but you won't have to do it," I say. "I'm staying. I'm on leave from the university this year, so I can stay as long as . . . as long as necessary. I'll talk to the doctor and find out what I need to know. Jack can get us the equipment we need. I'm a good nurse. I was taking care of you when you were sick before I was twelve. I can do it." All three of them look relieved.

Betty has been chewing her lower lip nervously, as she does when she's under stress. "You have to promise not to tell him. He mustn't know."

"OK, I promise." And I accept my role in the game of deception we will all play. None of us realize yet that Red can play it much better than any of us.

HANDS II

Although he grew weaker day by day and continued to lose weight, the worst problem arose during the first week he was home, and it wasn't cancer. It was constipation. Just before his surgery, he had been given upper and lower gastrointestinal tests that involved drinking barium and having a barium enema. Somehow, much of the barium was still in his digestive tract when he was operated on, and from then on, he was taking heavy doses of constipating pain-killers and getting no exercise. The result was a large mass of barium like moist but solid plaster of Paris lodged in his lower intestine and blocking all elimination.

I tried enemas. No luck. I tried soapsuds enemas. Nothing. Somewhere I had heard of the efficacy of molasses enemas, so I sent Jack out to get me some molasses. The result was molasses all over the room, the bed, the bedding, the floor, Red, and me. We even had it in our hair. I scrubbed for hours to get rid of the sticky mess. The barium remained firmly lodged where it had been. Red was miserably uncomfortable, even with the Percodan I doled out to him.

Finally, I call Red's doctor's office and tell them I am coming in for advice. The doctor has told me to come in if I have trouble, and they will work me into the schedule. I borrow Jack's pickup and drive to the doctor's office. When I tell the doctor the problem, he looks grim.

"This happens rarely," he says, "but it's very serious. Sometimes it's necessary to intervene surgically. That might prove fatal to your dad and would make the time he has left more painful and uncomfortable. Any subsequent bowel movements he had would be very painful. It sounds like enemas aren't going to do it."

I notice he is staring at my hands. He seems ill at ease, almost embarrassed. Strange, I think. I've never known a doctor to be embarrassed. It's the patient who is supposed to be embarrassed.

"Would you consider . . ." He trails off, and there is a long pause. "You have fairly slender hands," he says. Another pause. "Would you consider . . . using your fingers . . . possibly your entire hand? The mass of barium has probably lodged just behind the anal sphincter. That sphincter can be expanded if you work with it slowly. It would be very painful for him, but you could give him a heavy dose of pain-killer and just . . . and just . . . go in with your fingers and hand and dig it out."

My God! I think. Does this man know what he is asking me to do to my own father? He'll hate me as long as he lives. Then I remember that won't be very long at best, and if something isn't done about his bowels, it will be shorter still. I didn't sign on for this kind of duty. Torture was never my thing.

"How long will he live if I don't?" I can't believe I'm asking this.

"I can't be sure. Probably a matter of days."

"I guess . . . I guess I could try."

He launches into instructions. Trim fingernails, surgical glove, the lubricant, getting the sphincter to relax, and on and on. And he adds, "If I know your dad, he's not going to take it quietly. Be prepared for some stormy weather. And, uh, if I were you, I'd do it right away . . . for his sake and . . . uh . . . before you have too much time to think about it."

On the way home, my mind is running double time. *I already have the gloves and lubricant. I'd better do it this afternoon while Jack is at work. I don't want him blundering in in the middle of this nightmare. What about Hazel? The house is so small. She'll hear him screaming. Get her out. How can I get her out? Maybe Betty. She usually has some time in the middle of the afternoon if she has enough help to run the nursery school. Maybe she could take Hazel over to visit Grandma Charlotte. Call Betty. What will I tell her? Can't tell her the truth. She won't stand for it. Tell her Hazel is in bad shape and needs to get away for a while. What if I kill him? He's going to die if I don't do it. But what if I kill him? What if I kill him?*

Betty comes over almost at once after I call her. She's not fooled. She knows something is going on and that I want Hazel out of the house. She doesn't want to know what it is. I call Lillian and tell her Red is going to be sleeping the rest of the afternoon and to tell Jack not to come by. Less than one week as a nurse, and I'm already an accomplished liar.

Then I have to tell Red. There's no lying to him. I give him a Percodan. "Dad," I say, looking him right in the eyes, "you know your lower bowel is blocked with that damned barium they gave you before your surgery. If we don't get it out, it will kill you. We've tried enemas with no success. I've been to see your doctor. Now we have to take more drastic action."

While I'm talking, I'm getting the lubricant out and beginning to put on the glove, watching his eyes to see when the drug kicks in. He notices the lubricant and that I have only one glove. He questions me wildly with his eyes.

"I have to dig it out. You're going to hate me, but I can't help it. I've sent Mamma away with Betty. Make all the noise you want. Call me every name you can think of, but don't fight me. It will only cause you more pain if you do. I have to do this, and I'll be as gentle as I possibly can."

He knows now. His pale blue eyes blaze for a moment and then he closes them and moans softly. As he rolls over onto his stomach he says, "Did you hear the one about the old fart who was having trouble hearing, and he went to the doctor and the doctor dug around in his ear and found a suppository . . ."

And so we begin. He does scream and he does call me every name in his extensive vocabulary. I stop from time to time to let him rest, and he says, "I don't mean it. You know I don't mean it."

There is more barium than I expected, and some of it is almost like concrete. Fill him up with concrete, then cut him open and give him drugs that make it impossible for him to get rid of the concrete. I think of the *embouche* that used to frighten the Basque children on Broad Street.

"Do you remember Old Man Odiaga's wife, Rosa?" I ask while we are resting for a minute between struggles, breathing hard.

"Yeah," he grunts.

"Do you remember what she used to call when she came out at night to get all the kids in?"

"*Mam-ooo,*" he says.

"You know what a *Mamoo* is?"

He shakes his head.

"It's a creature that has had all the openings in its body plugged up. It must be terrible. You've got only one of them plugged up and look how bad it is. Of course a *Mamoo* can't communicate with anybody, and you can certainly communicate. Are you ready to start again?"

"Do I have any choice?"

"No, but you could think up some new cuss words. I'm getting tired of the same old stuff."

"You educated bastards are a bunch of smart ass . . . Ohh, ohh. Stop! Please! You goddamned . . . Did you hear the one about the nun . . . ohh, you're killing me . . . came into the liquor store . . . oh, Jesus Christ . . . said she needed a bottle of whiskey . . . dammit, you're killing me . . . for Mother Superior's constipation . . . No! No! Son of a bitch . . . later saw her drunk as a lord . . . Oh, stop! I hate you! . . . and I thought that whiskey was for Mother Superior's . . . Damn you! . . . constipation . . . Damn you to hell, damn you . . . it was, she said . . . no more please no more, son of a bitch . . . when she sees me, she'll shit all right . . ."

When it's over, I help him to the bathroom and give him an enema. He has a massive bowel movement, waits a few minutes, and has another one. When I help him back to bed, his hair is stuck to his head with sweat, but he's smiling. I put him in bed and wipe his face with a cool, wet cloth.

"I don't know what we'd do without you," he says.

I have never heard him say anything like that to me before. I turn away so he won't see how moved I am, and he says, "Did you hear the one about the sheepherder who always . . ." but before I can tell him I've heard it ten times, he's asleep.

Nobody Rich
or Famous

Hazel is right about her inability to cope, and she proves it. Had it been almost any other patient, I think she would have done better, but with Red, she is psychologically unequipped to do what is necessary. She becomes frozen with fear, afraid she will do the wrong thing. The one time I give her a chance to prove she can do it, the result is a near disaster.

After about three weeks, I begin to feel the need for a car. Red's old car isn't running and isn't worth putting any money into. Jack and Betty bring us whatever we ask for, but I would like to go to the grocery store and pick out things for myself, since I'm doing most of the cooking. Also I miss my family. So I decide to fly home to Tucson, spend two days with my family, and then drive my little blue Triumph nonstop back to Boise. I write out careful instructions for Hazel about Red's diet and medications. I organize Jack and Betty to bring her whatever she might need. Jack lives less than a mile away and will stop by every day. Although overweight, he is very strong and can lift Red easily. When Betty drives me to the airport, Hazel seems to be on top of everything and assured. When I return five days later, she is trembling and pale with fear that I will yell at her for what she has done. Red is starving and dehydrated.

Shortly after I left, she tried to feed him something prepared according to the instructions I left. His system wouldn't tolerate it, and he threw it up. She was too filled with anxiety to try anything else. She simply didn't try to feed him anything, awaiting my return. She gave him water, but not enough. Since he was taking pain medication and getting no exercise, he wasn't hungry and didn't ask for anything but water and juice.

I didn't yell at her, but I was shocked at her high anxiety level. How can this woman, I thought, have raised three children? But that was a very long time ago, and she was a different woman then, although it was only seventeen years ago that she had the guts to walk into a bar with a loaded gun and shoot hell out of the place. What a dramatic change. I don't think any of us recognized it that early—she was only sixty-seven—but she was beginning to suffer from hardening of the arteries, which years later would bring on complete senility. As she grew senile, her anxiety level increased to the point where she was afraid to do anything but sit at one end of her couch clutching her checkbook, her security blanket, in her hands. First she quit reading, then she quit watching television, and then she quit watching the neighbors. Watching the neighbors had been her passion, and years earlier, I had given her a pair of binoculars for Christmas. In hindsight, I can see that her decline started much earlier than we realized.

Upon my return from Tucson, I quickly got Red eating and drinking again, and I could tell that he, too, had been anxious while I was gone—anxious about Hazel. "Do you think she's a dingbat?" he asked as I handed him his second fruit milk shake of the day, now his favorite food.

"Has a cat got an ass?" I answered. "Is the Pope Catholic? But we love her. How could she have put up with you if she wasn't a dingbat?"

It's good to hear him laugh.

The house has four small rooms and a tiny bath. Hazel sleeps in one of the two bedrooms. The other one has a single bed, and it's been set up as Red's sickroom. It was my bedroom when I returned from college after my freshman year and had to lay out a semester to make enough money to go back, and after Hazel had done her "Frankie and Johnny" routine in a downtown bar. Red and Hazel had just made a down payment on this house and moved in. Red built bookshelves on two walls of this little room and painted it chocolate brown because that was the color I wanted. It was like being inside a small chocolate bar.

Since then he has painted the room a more civilized off-white with pale blue inside the bookshelves. One of Red's talents as a painter has always been his ability to mix colors in precise shades no one else can seem to come up with. Family folklore, which may or may not have any basis in fact, says that he developed two new colors, both pastels, for some major paint company like Dutch Boy or Sherwin-Williams, but because the company patented them, he received no credit. I suppose most families have that kind of folklore, where somebody invented something or developed something but was cheated out of their rightful recognition and reward by a major company or corporation. It seems to be an integral part of the American Dream.

None of the doors in the house will accommodate a wheelchair, and the bathroom is much too small to get one into, so there's no sense in fooling with that. At first I can get Red into the bathroom and sometimes into the living room to watch TV by supporting him around the waist and walking him. Then, as he continues to lose weight, I simply carry him in my arms. Toward the end, it will be like carrying a child.

The couch in the living room makes into a bed, but it's too uncomfortable to sleep on, so I make a pallet for myself on the living room floor, and set up a card table there with my portable typewriter. I can work and sleep close enough to Red that I can hear him if he needs anything. From mid-July to September, it's hot, and I struggle to keep Red as cool as possible. There's a small, noisy window air-conditioning unit at the far end of the living room, but none of that air makes it into Red's bedroom. The little bedroom has two large windows on two different walls that I can open at night and get the cool air. Otherwise I depend on several strategically placed fans, one of them huge, to keep him comfortable.

The yard and gardens, where Hazel waters and putters in the mornings and evenings and I mow the lawn from time to time, are glorious. Often I move my card table and typewriter outside in the shade of a catalpa tree near Red's window where I can hear him if he needs me. I am writing poetry every spare minute, trying to take advantage of my year free from teaching three classes a semester. Looking back at my first full-length book, published the following year, I find a series of poems that take me back to those long afternoons while Red slept and I sat just outside his window with my typewriter on a card table, pounding away at it.

AUGUST

All summer
surrounded by unconditioned air
my father has been dying.

Anybody coming by here
at night
could see me looking out the open window
and wonder what I am waiting for:

the stars to move perhaps,
the big dipper on its delicate
hinges to tilt,
the earth to cool.

Today smelled like burning rope
and tonight the moon is cut in half.
Promises are unimportant to us now.
The past is sufficient.

I choose his memories with care
and hold them
before vague eyes
as if they were charms on a string.

Life drops
from his white hand,
a scarab falling into thick grass,
and the look on the face of silence
is surprise.

At night I work in the living room after Hazel goes to bed. I become concerned that the sound of my typewriter is keeping Red awake, disturbing him.

"Red," I ask him sometime in July, "is the noise of my typewriter keeping you awake or bothering you?"

"Oh, no! I like it. I wake up sometimes in the night and hear you typing away and it sounds like money."

I am greatly amused at his notion of making large sums of money writing poetry. "I'll never make any money writing poetry," I tell him.

"Or taking care of me," he says, almost under his breath.

"That's enough of that! You know I wasn't working this year anyway. I'm letting my hardworking wife support me. The trick is knowing who to marry."

"You did all right in that department." He adores Lois. She is the first educated, professional woman he has ever gotten to know, and she's a locally famous singer as well. During his visits in Tucson he would go everywhere with her, as if she radiated some kind of magic and he wanted to soak up as much of it as he could.

But there is another very real disturbance that does keep him awake—him and everybody else. The neighbors. Next door and about fifteen feet from Red's window is a tar-paper shack built on logs without a foundation and surrounded with debris, odds and ends of lumber, and dead cars. In it live an elderly man with one leg who gets around with amazing agility on crutches, his elderly wife, and their huge fat daughter, who is probably in her forties. They all drink heavily, and their fights are epic. One night the old man throws his daughter and all her clothes out in the road. The next night the daughter throws the old man and all his clothes out in the road. They stand outside in what would be the yard if they had a yard and scream obscenities at one another. They throw anything that isn't nailed down and attack one another with sticks, bottles, or anything they can get their hands on. The old lady seems to be the only thing that prevents the father and daughter from killing each other, and sometimes she and the daughter both knock the old man around.

My first Saturday night in Boise, the war breaks out about one thirty in the morning when the neighbor family comes home from the bars in a taxi. They are screaming at each other even before they can get in the house, and soon a major battle is going on outside. The old man hits his daughter with his crutch, and she knocks him down. She begins to stomp on him, but the old lady stops her. The women go in the house, and the old man sits up and looks around. They have taken his crutches inside with them.

I come into Red's room and see, by the light from the hall, that he is sitting up in bed, staring out the window and listening intently.

"OK, Dad," I say. "I've had it. You are sick and you need your rest, and they are keeping you from sleeping. They're disturbing the peace, and I'm calling the police. Right now."

"No, no! Don't do that. I enjoy it. It's better than anything on TV. I can sleep later. I wouldn't miss their fights. I've paid good money to go to wrestling matches that weren't nearly as good as this. I'm so lucky to have a ringside seat."

So I don't call the police. When a drunken fight breaks out, as it does several nights a week, I sit beside Red in his bedroom with the lights out, as if we were in a theater, watching and commenting in whispers on the action. We have discussed the possibility of betting on which one will win on a given night, but there seldom seems to be a clear-cut winner, and just when it appears that one or the other of them has won for the night, hostilities break out again, so we give up on the idea of betting on winners. Considering that the participants are an old woman, an old one-legged man, and their grossly fat daughter, the primary contenders have enormous staying power. At one point during the summer, the police come and take the daughter away. Things are boringly quiet for a couple of nights, but by the weekend she is back. Red and I are much encouraged to see the show resume.

⁓

Red is the ideal patient—never complaining, never demanding, and above all, never whining. He knows his time is short, and he wants to make things as pleasant for all of us as he can. *Never let them see you sweat* was always his motto, and he lives up to it now. If he feels any guilt about the past, he never shows it; and if he has deep thoughts or fears about the eternity he is facing, he wrestles with them alone, late at night when Hazel and I are asleep. He doesn't embrace his death, but he doesn't fight it either. He seems to lean into it, relaxed and trusting. All the tension that has ever been between us dissolves as if it had never existed. We become co-conspirators in an enormous practical joke—his death at the age of sixty-eight.

In a way, Hazel seems to feel that he is already gone. It must be the way she prepares herself. Her journal records other things rather than Red's slow descent. It seldom mentions him. She makes an exception for his birthday, August 7, but even then the entry is mostly about me and sounds as if I am there to care for her rather than Red. *Dad's birthday, all the children here. Dad bed fast all the time. Dick is with me. How thankful I am for him.*

The next two entries, the only ones for September and October, suggest the depth of her self-absorption while her husband is dying:

> *Sept. Had bad tooth ache—Dick took me to the Dentist. Had 3 absessed teeth pulled. Have to have them all pulled real soon.*
> *Oct. Dick gave reading at College of Idaho. Write up in paper. Dick takes me riding and out to eat. He works on his writing at night and nurses Dad so I can rest.*

I also manage to get Red into the car twice and take him for drives, but Hazel doesn't mention that. At the end of our second outing, I realize it will be his last. He simply doesn't have the strength left to go through the ordeal of being carried into and out of the car and to sit up and watch the scenery during the drive. He attempts to be animated, but the world of his bed and his room is all he needs now. Somehow I think of it as our world, and it seems to me that he does too. When he hears Jack's heavy footsteps coming through the kitchen, he often says, "Tell him I'm asleep." When I tell him that his brother Lester, his only surviving brother, has come to see him, he says, "Tell him I'm asleep."

When visitors do get in to see him, he is always pleasant and makes an effort to talk to them. If they stay only a few moments, before his energy flags, they leave thinking he is not nearly as far gone as they had been led to believe. Jack and Betty come almost every day. The granddaughters come from time to time, but they usually give him a quick kiss or hand-squeeze and spend their time with Hazel. Everyone seems to be embarrassed by the entire situation. Everyone but Red. He is getting younger, I think. As he loses weight, his face becomes more youthful—the cheekbones, the cleft chin, the wonderful brow. His complexion, normally bright red, has become a youthful pink. Sometimes he winks at me when visitors aren't looking, as if I am the only one who shares the secret of his impending death. I know that's not right. They have all accepted his death, but he and I seem to be the only ones who have accepted his dying. We live it every day, we touch it, we talk to it, we make it feel at home.

BEAUTIFUL

Autumn comes on inexorably, and it is glorious. In all my years growing up in Boise I don't remember an autumn to match the autumn of 1969. Boise, city of trees, could not ever have been more heartbreakingly beautiful. The maples go into paroxysms of gold and scarlet, the walnuts, oak, and dogwood go crazy in brilliant shades of yellow, pink, and shocking red. Silver-dollar birches drop golden dollars all over the lawn. The weather is perfect—clear, cool, and sunny. It's glorious Indian summer.

On the first of September, during the afternoon while Red is asleep, I slip out to take Grandma Charlotte for a drive. It's her eighty-eighth birthday. She is living with Jim, her oldest son, and his wife. Jim's wife works long hours in a nursing home, and Charlotte keeps house and does the cooking. In her spare time she gardens and makes quilts. Jim is retired on disability from World War I, and nobody knows exactly what he does. I think he plays cards with his cronies much of the time. Charlotte lives only a couple of miles from Red and Hazel's house on Randall Street.

When I arrive, I find Charlotte at the top of a tall ladder in an apple tree, picking apples for me to take home. I know I should be frightened and upset, but somehow I'm not. This is Charlotte. If she wants to die by falling out of an apple tree at the age of eighty-eight, that's her business. Fortunately she doesn't. She comes down with a bucket of apples, not even breathing hard, and gives me a big smack on the cheek. "The best ones are always at the top," she says. "Give these to your folks. Maybe Hazel will make an apple cobbler." She has stopped dying her hair since my last visit to Boise, and it's a mass of silver curls. Everybody says Hazel is still a good-looking woman in her late sixties, but her mother is simply beautiful. Once I have taken the bucket of apples, she gives me a strong hug and says, "So here's my little Dick. I'm right pleased to see you, Dickerino. Tell me how your dad's doing and how Hazel's holding up."

We get in my little Triumph and off we go with the top down, along Highway 44 through the valley and then up into the foothills above the veterans' hospital, which reminds her of when her son Jim was there, so sick, after being gassed in World War I. Then back through town where I think we should stop and have a milk shake at the drugstore next to the Pinney Theater on Jefferson Street.

"But I just have on my house slippers," she says while I'm parking the car.

"Oh, Grandma, come on. You sound like Hazel."

She laughs and her gold tooth sparkles in the autumn sun.

"Let's go," she says. "I haven't had a milk shake in a long time."

After we've had our milk shake and are crossing the street to get into the car, a fire engine with siren blaring nearly runs us down, then another. The engines stop on Jefferson Street in the next block. We can see smoke coming out of a building on the north side of the street.

I look at Charlotte and she looks at me. "Let's see what's on fire," I say. We begin to run down the street toward the fire. Suddenly I realize that I am running down the street, chasing a fire engine hand in hand with my eighty-eight-year-old grandmother in her house slippers, and we are alive and having a good time, and for the moment, nothing else matters. We watch the fire for a while until the firemen set up a line and herd all the spectators across the street. Then we return to my little car that she always has trouble getting her feet in, and head for home.

"About your father," she says, with no introduction or question from me. "He wasn't always the way you remember him as a child. When he was younger, he was different. I don't know how to describe it. He was a good man who made a lot of bad decisions. I didn't want Hazel to marry him, I won't deny that, but I saw his good points and I never criticized him. He was weak in spite of all his bluster, and I guess he couldn't help it. You suffered the most because you came along last, when he was in the worst shape. But everybody suffered, and some of us suffered just watching it. I'm glad you've come back to take care of him. I expected you would."

"I love him, Grandma. In spite of everything, I love him. And I think he has come to love me a little bit now, near the end. It's enough. It's more than I expected."

Grandma blows her nose, a loud honk, into her tiny embroidered handkerchief that smells of lavender. When I help her out of the car in front of Jim's house, I try to make her promise not to climb that ladder anymore.

"I always take it slow going up and coming down," she says. "It's a sturdy ladder. You like my applesauce, as I recall, and you can't make applesauce without apples."

I tell her I'll come over the next day and pick apples for her and take her to see Red and Hazel. She likes that idea.

"Then I'll make you some real applesauce," she says.

⁓

Late in October, Red's kidneys begin to fail. He is having more and more trouble urinating. The doctor had warned me about this possibility. When I call the doctor, he says, "You'll have to bring him in to the hospital for catheterization."

"Can he come back home?"

"Yes, as soon as I'm sure he'll tolerate the catheter, I'll send him home. How much does he weigh now?"

"I quit weighing him a couple of weeks ago. He couldn't stand on the scale and I figured it was better if we didn't know. I'd guess he's down to about eighty pounds."

Red doesn't want to go back to the hospital, but he's getting very uncomfortable. I explain to him that he will be there only one night, long enough to make sure the catheter is working, and I'll stay with him all night. Then I'll bring him home. Jack arranges for the ambulance and rides with him. I drive Hazel, and we follow the ambulance in order to be with him when they get him out. *It's like a funeral procession*, I think, *before he's dead.*

We go to Saint Alphonsus, the old Gothic pile of bricks painted a pale cream and with tall windows and turrets like a medieval castle. It's the Catholic hospital where I had my tonsils removed when I was about fourteen. It's set well back from the street and surrounded with a lawn and maples, birches, elms, and walnut trees. The entire neighborhood is old and park-like, and all the streets are lined with huge trees in the last throes of autumn color.

They get Red into a private room on the ground floor quickly. He is so small now, he hardly takes up any room in the bed. A young, attractive nurse holds his hand and talks to him about the catheterization process. She had taken care of him when he'd had surgery, more than three months earlier, and she remembers him. If she is shocked to see him now, seventy pounds lighter, she doesn't show it, but she is obviously fond of him from their earlier acquaintance.

Red says he needs to have a bowel movement before he gets in bed. He doesn't want to use the bedpan. I pick him up and carry him into the bathroom. When he's finished, I carry him back into his room. The nurse is bent over the bed, pulling the sheet down. As we pass her, Red reaches out and pats her on the fanny. It happens so fast no one knows how to react. I try to apologize to her, but she says, "No, it's all right." She holds Red's hand for a minute. As she turns to go, I can see she has tears in her eyes. Suddenly I realize he'll never get out of this place alive.

After the catheter is put in, Red dozes. Betty has to go back to the nursery school. I tell Jack I want him to take Hazel home. She has been wandering around the room aimlessly in great distress. At one point she blunders into a stack of stainless-steel, kidney-shaped containers on a shelf and they fall to the floor with a great clatter, waking Red and bringing medical personnel running from all directions. The plan is for me to stay with Red through the night, and in the morning, Jack will return with Hazel and we'll take him home. We behave as if we believe it's possible. I don't think any of us do.

During the night, while I sleep in a chair beside him, Red slips into a coma. When I wake before dawn, he is breathing so quietly I can barely detect it, and he has been spitting up some ghastly substance full of small black flecks. I ring for the nurse and wipe his mouth. Later, the doctor comes in and says very little except that I should go home. Red is unconscious, he says, as if I can't tell, and doesn't know I'm there. I refuse to leave, but I call Jack and Betty and tell them that Red has lost consciousness and may not regain it. There is no hope of our taking him back home now. I tell Jack to go over to Randall Street and tell Hazel what the situation is. Then, if she wants to come, bring her to the hospital.

Before the doctor leaves the hospital, he stops in to tell me that he doesn't believe Red will regain consciousness. Somehow I believe he will. It's just a hunch, maybe wishful thinking.

I have come to realize something about this man—he's a trickster. Just when you think you know what he's going to do, he does something else.

Hazel, Jack, and Betty arrive about 10 a.m. There has been no change that I can see except that the foul black substance has been coming out of his mouth more frequently. I keep wiping it away and rubbing his hands and talking to him to let him know I'm there, hoping he can hear me, and sometimes I think he can. Hazel is in terrible shape. Her eyes are wild and she is somewhere near panic. The doctor has prescribed a sedative for her, and I think she should go home and take it.

About noon I take Betty and Jack into the hall and say, "Look, there's nothing we can do here. I will stay, at least until midnight or so. What I'm concerned about is Hazel. I'm counting on you both to take care of her. She can't take much more of this. Take her home and get one of your girls to stay with her. I promise to call if there's any change."

When we go back into the room, Hazel has put her head down on Red's arm, and she is sobbing. *Good*, I think. *She's said good-bye. Crying will be good for her. She hasn't cried through any of this.* Jack tells her he is going to take her home. As Jack and Betty lead her out, she looks back over her shoulder with a look of longing so great it tears me up. She still loves him as much as she did when he was a young man with bright red hair and a cigarette behind his ear. The knowledge somehow shocks me. I have been selling her short. All these years she has loved a man who, after their first few years together, did nearly everything he could, at one time or another, to show her how little he cared for her.

That kind of rejection can twist a person. I guess I know something about it, but she is the one who has remained absolutely loyal in spite of everything. Jack and I have reversed our roles. Jack, who was Red's boy, has become estranged from his father and attentive to his mother. I, who was clearly Hazel's boy, have drawn so close to Red in the last three months that I will not leave him if there is any hope of one more word from him, one more look.

After everyone goes, I sit beside him through a golden afternoon. A little wind has come up and the trees are dropping their leaves as if they are frantic to embrace winter naked. Outside the tall Gothic windows of the old hospital, there is a rain of falling golden maple leaves. I want to write a few lines of a poem but have nothing to write on. I take one of the small paper napkins with a border of flowers from his bedside table and begin.

> *my father went in search of death*
> *like a mole*
> *blind and beautiful*
>
> *his life was an unmade bed*
> *nobody rich or famous ever slept there*
>
> *old Father it was harder than hell*
> *to love you*
> *and impossible not to*

The ink bleeds into the soft tissue of the napkin and is hard to read. Suddenly I am aware of something else, some movement. Quickly I look at Red. His eyes are open, that startling blue, and his right hand is moving slowly, slowly upward.

"Yes, Red, I'm here."

The hand is gesturing toward the window and the rain of golden leaves.

"Beautiful," he says softly. Then his hand is lowered, his eyes close, and his breathing becomes more labored. I talk to him, but there is no response. Then I look down at the paper napkin on which I had written *blind and beautiful* a few minutes before he said the word. I can't recall him ever using that word before, nor could he have seen what I had written. I have my blessing.

~

It's getting dark outside and the wind is increasing. A front is moving in, I think. The end of Indian summer. The nurse whose fanny Red patted yesterday—could it have been only yesterday?—comes in with a tray of food for me. She says I ought to go out and walk around, get some fresh air before it starts raining. I eat what she has brought me. It's tasteless, but I have been living on coffee since yesterday morning. I decide to take her advice, at least once around the block. My brain is going numb.

When I get outside, the wind has kicked up and the temperature has dropped. Tempests of bright leaves are blowing down the streets, and the birches are lashing their branches as if to extricate themselves from their pelage. I walk, hands in my pockets and head down against the cold wind. Suddenly something flits across the street in front of me, then something else. They are ghosts, white ghosts. For a second I think I'm hallucinating. Too much coffee and too little sleep. Then I realize they are children dressed in white sheets running across the street, their sheets whipped by the wind. Trick-or-treaters. It's Halloween. I've lost all track of the date.

Tomorrow will be All Saints' Day, when the graves are supposed to open and give up the spirits of the dead. My father will be dead before morning. Will he pass the spirits as they move in the opposite direction? He would like that, since most of his life he moved against the grain. It's getting colder. I feel the first drops of rain on my head and face and make a dash for the hospital entrance just as the heavy rain begins. Indian summer is over.

ABOUT THE AUTHOR

RICHARD SHELTON is a poet, author, and Regents' Professor Emeritus at the University of Arizona. He is the recipient of many awards, including a Lannan Foundation grant and the inaugural Arizona Literary Treasure Award. His 1992 memoir, *Going Back to Bisbee*, won the Western States Book Award and was a *New York Times* Notable Book. His memoir *Crossing the Yard* was a 2007 Southwest Book of the Year and was featured on *The News Hour with Jim Lehrer*.